Remapping the
Foreign Language
Curriculum

Teaching Languages, Literatures, and Cultures
MODERN LANGUAGE ASSOCIATION OF AMERICA

Learning Foreign and Second Languages: Perspectives in Research and Scholarship. Ed. Heidi Byrnes. 1998.

Cultural Studies in the Curriculum: Teaching Latin America. Ed. Danny J. Anderson and Jill S. Kuhnheim. 2003.

Modern French Literary Studies in the Classroom: Pedagogical Strategies. Ed. Charles J. Stivale. 2004.

Remapping the Foreign Language Curriculum: An Approach through Multiple Literacies. By Janet Swaffar and Katherine Arens. 2005.

Remapping the Foreign Language Curriculum

An Approach through Multiple Literacies

Janet Swaffar
and
Katherine Arens

THE MODERN LANGUAGE ASSOCIATION OF AMERICA
New York 2005

For information about obtaining permission to reprint material from MLA
book publications, send your request by mail (see address below), e-mail
(permissions@mla.org), or fax (646 458-0030).

Library of Congress Cataloging-in-Publication Data

Swaffar, Janet K.
   Remapping the foreign language curriculum : an approach through multiple
literacies / Janet Swaffar and Katherine Arens.
       p. cm. — (Teaching languages, literatures, and cultures)
   Includes bibliographical references and index.
   ISBN 0-87352-806-9 (cloth : alk. paper) — ISBN 0-87352-807-7 (pbk. : alk. paper)
   1. Language and languages—Study and teaching (Higher)—United States. I. Arens,
Katherine, 1953– II. Title. III. Series.
   P57.U5S93 2005
   418'.0071'1073—dc22   2005015953
ISSN 1092-3225
ISBN-13: 978-0-87352-806-1 (cloth : alk. paper)
ISBN-13: 978-0-87352-807-8 (pbk. : alk. paper)

Printed on recycled paper

Published by The Modern Language Association of America
26 Broadway, New York, New York 10004-1789
www.mla.org

In memoriam

Lucille Wenner Kaufman and
Mary Sylvia SSND, née Mary Irene Tembreull

CONTENTS

PREFACE TO THE SERIES   ix

PREFACE TO THE VOLUME   xi

ACKNOWLEDGMENTS   xv

Introduction: The Case for Remapping the Curriculum   1

Chapter 1: Scholars, Teachers, and Program Development   11

Chapter 2: Linking Meaning and Language: Remapping the Discipline   28

Chapter 3: The Holistic Curriculum: Anchoring Acquisition in Reading   57

Chapter 4: A Template for Beginning and Intermediate Learner Tasks: The Text Matrix for Staging Genre Reading   78

Chapter 5: A Template for Advanced-Learner Tasks: Staging Genre Reading and Cultural Literacy through the Précis   98

Chapter 6: From Reading to Reading Literature: A Language Teaching Perspective   139

Chapter 7: From Multiple Literacies to Cultural Studies: Constructing a Framework for Learning Culture   161

Coda: Professional Responsibility and the Identity of Foreign Languages in Higher Education   189

WORKS CITED   195

NAME INDEX   203

SUBJECT INDEX   207

PREFACE TO
THE SERIES

The Teaching Languages, Literatures, and Cultures series was created in response to recent transformative changes in these three areas. By curricular necessity or personal choice, many teachers work in more than one area of specialization. Current theories and methodologies encourage them to incorporate multiple perspectives in their courses. This series aims to help teachers meet new challenges by examining how teaching different languages, literatures, and cultures intersects in theory, research, curriculum and program design, and pedagogical practices. The series is intended to reach specialists and nonspecialists and to create cross-specialty dialogue among members of the profession engaged in what were previously separate efforts.

Series Editors

PREFACE TO THE VOLUME

Remapping the Foreign Language Curriculum was written to encourage a new type of engagement with adult learners in junior colleges, colleges, and universities. Since World War II, interest in language learning and in research on teaching and learning foreign language has gradually assumed academic status in postsecondary schools. That research has, however, remained predominantly the provenance of specialists and those faculty members, administrators, and graduate students in language departments who design and teach courses for beginning language learners in their institutions. Language faculty members as a whole have not had much exposure to perspectives that have emerged in research on language learning and the teaching of foreign languages, particularly with regard to more advanced learners or to considerations of their program as a holistic enterprise from start to finish. Given the historical bias for scholarship in literature and linguistics in most institutions, broader professional discussions about what it is that postsecondary language learners can and should learn at all levels in a particular language program rarely occur. When such discussions do take place, the focus is generally only on policies and procedures for beginning and intermediate language acquisition, often the "required courses" in a college curriculum. Seldom do departments discuss their programs in their entirety, that is, consider the ways in which their courses may or may not build toward consistent and realized achievement for majors and nonmajors alike and prepare their students to use language effectively in the real world.

This volume suggests avenues faculty members and graduate students in all types of postsecondary institutions can follow to engage in such deliberations. It does so by illustrating how, regardless of the institution or the particular emphases in a given foreign language program, the program can contribute fundamentally to the kinds of critical literacy and multicultural literacy that so many publics and administrators value today. It makes the case, therefore, that the professional face of teaching literature, culture, and language needs to be rethought as the teaching of multiple literacies: the ability to engage with culture, with its forms of knowledge and communication, and with its various publics. *Remapping the Foreign Language Curriculum* is thus aimed at those wanting an overview and introduction to what might be done to improve whatever curricular situation they work in.

This is not to say that the authors propose that a "right" curriculum exists for all institutions, faculties, or student bodies. In particular, many of the ideas presented in this volume with regard to the reading and writing of western European languages do not apply as well to Eastern and Middle Eastern languages with their independent, non-Western rhetorical traditions, writing systems, and phonologies. We do propose, however, that a number of established, well-researched assumptions about what is teachable and learnable now exist and that these assumptions have relevance to teaching practices at all levels, with caveats and further modifications implied for non-Western languages. This volume exemplifies these assumptions as they might be applied in various contexts in postsecondary FL departments, not as theoretical principles but rather as a set of interlocking considerations for people who design courses in a given program—faculty members and graduate students alike.

Thus no model curricula as such are offered here. Instead, we propose approaches to developing curricula appropriate to particular settings, student bodies, and faculty strengths. These proposals are made in two stages. First, we identify what we see as newer principles that research has supported as useful in teaching and learning foreign languages in a range of institutions. Then we present templates that language faculties might wish to consider in their reflections about how their program might serve as a portal to various cultural literacies across disciplines in their institution.

Considering the intended audiences and the aims of this volume, the authors felt that an extensive bibliography to support claims regarding the research and pedagogy related to foreign language instruction was counterproductive on several counts. First, the bulk of that research is about English language acquisition, addressing the differences between the learning of English as a second language (where, how, and why it is learned) and the learning of foreign languages in most postsecondary institutions in North America (e.g., Norris and Ortega). Second, the citation practice in the field of second language acquisition tends to give multiple sources without closely exploring the distinctions in setting, research design, and materials that may vitiate generalizations about similarities across studies. Results may seem similar, but the studies conducted do not always use similar parameters. Third, while unanimity cannot be claimed, many of the assertions about language learning made in this volume represent shared knowledge and accepted thinking in the field accompanied by nuanced disagreements. A comprehensive study of accepted thinking and research about foreign language instruction has yet to be undertaken.

Consequently, we have elected in many instances to rely on the validity of our experience and long professional engagement with the topic of foreign language instruction at the college and university level as the basis for selective citation. Where references to language research are made, they are made because a work supports the line of thinking presented in the book or seems to indicate a research or teaching need. Where possible, we have attempted to privilege more recent commentary, theory, and research. In references to literary and cultural studies, we apply these same criteria.

ACKNOWLEDGMENTS

The authors acknowledge the support of the University of Texas, whose faculty research program afforded leave time to work on this book. In addition, the university provided ongoing support for travel and research.

Thanks are also due:

to Sharon Forester, Delia Montesinos, and Laura Sager for their help in working with the Spanish-language texts used in chapters 4 and 5;

to Judy Liskin-Gasparro for inviting one author to the ACTFL session and for the brainstorming there about how to present the Anderson Imbert fables in our context; and

to two anonymous MLA reviewers, who contributed significantly to the rewriting of an earlier draft of the manuscript, and the editorial board, whose comments helped shape the final version. Michael Kandel proved to be an editor par excellence, whose sharp eye caught anomalies in content as well as style. Our indexer, Bob Swaffar, put method to our madness.

To Heidi Byrnes, however, must go a special category of accolade. Her input, trenchant critique, suggestions, and editorial contributions reflected her unflagging concern for the writing of this volume and, on a much broader scale, her commitment to making foreign language pedagogy an integral component of the profession's intellectual work.

The Case for Remapping the Curriculum

Introduction

This volume looks at foreign language programs for adult learners, positing a critical need to rethink the constellation of programs and pedagogies that now characterize the presentation of foreign languages in United States tertiary education, in junior colleges, colleges, and universities. Rethinking such a diverse enterprise precludes offering one-size-fits-all solutions. In consequence, we start this project by considering the pivotal issues facing all institutions that teach foreign languages to adult learners, whether beginning, intermediate, upper-division, or graduate students.

Any approach to teaching foreign language encompasses, tacitly or overtly, an intellectual identity that frames and motivates how that discipline is taught and learned. Consequently, we begin by reflecting about what foreign language programs offer their learners as a distinct disciplinary entity located within the humanities. What do they offer that other programs do not? What do they hold in common with departments of English, history, religion, the social sciences, and the arts? Can students be taught means of expression that enable them to become social agents capable of joining knowledge-producing communities or founding distinctly new communities? Why should such teaching be done in a foreign language and not merely in the students' native language? In other words, what is the core mission of the humanities, broadly conceived, and of foreign language programs within them?

The answer is, we believe, aptly summed up in a single word: literacy. Literacy describes what empowers individuals to enter societies; to derive, generate, communicate, and validate knowledge and experience; to exercise expressive capacities to engage others in shared cognitive, social, and moral projects; and to exercise such agency with an identity that is recognized by others in the community.

THE CHANGING ROLES OF DISCIPLINES IN HIGHER EDUCATION

Such concerns are by no means limited to the study of foreign languages. Increasingly, for instance, the social sciences are rethinking for themselves the implications of social contexts for their various disciplines. Along with psychologies that examine human perception and behavior in terms of measurable or hypothesized internal and external stimuli, a social psychology component has established itself as a significant player; hence quantitative approaches to sociology now are more often accompanied by qualitative analysis. Anthropology has also been reexamining its relation to its subject matter and its moral responsibilities to the social groups it studies.

Closer to home, the humanities in general are also rethinking their disciplines in terms of social contexts. Thus the study of English-language literatures in the United States has increasingly turned to literature as documentation of various identity politics: as records of individual engagement with the power structures, values, and history of the culture in which one lives. In the service of a variety of other disciplines, English rhetoric and composition studies focuses on personal expression and communication in student writing, as modeled in popular literature, in the classical traditions, or in the high culture of students' heritages. History turns experiences and facts from the past into narratives that convey a perspective on how those facts cohere—as national, institutional, or individual histories, as memorable records of ways of being, of cultural identity, and of group problem solving. Art history explores the visual and acoustic means cultures use to translate cultural experiences into narratives of line, color, shape, and sound. Philosophy looks at the origins and rationales for moral and ethical behavior.

Literary theory has complemented trends in sociolinguistics that look at the influence of communities on language use and emphasize the permutations of broad societal contexts. For example, Michel Foucault illustrates how all artifacts of a culture, including its institutions and individuals' traditional practices within them, reflect a culture's definitions of what it means to be human, definitions that the literate reader of that culture can recapture by looking at the meaning systems implied by dominant social practices (*Archaeology*). Reception theory stresses the text-extrinsic factors that influence what and how a text says, is produced, and is accessed by its public. Jacques Derrida ("Différance") and Mikhail Bakhtin (*"Speech Genres"*) explore written language as inevitably echoing or revealing traces of earlier or other voices, the presence or absence of historical precursors in any text. Reader-response theory looks at how those textual voices are transacted by a reader within the limits of that reader's own perspectives and background. In these ways, allied disciplines in the humanities and social sciences have contributed to the picture of what textuality and older forms of canonicity imply for scholars and students of culture alike.

The question remains, then: What is the special domain of foreign languages within these larger intellectual changes? The roots of foreign language study run deep into philology (the study of older forms of today's languages), into the study of the language itself (for personal use and in various frameworks borrowed from linguistics), and into the study of monuments of world literature. In recent decades, however, foreign language departments have moved increasingly to claim an intellectual commitment anchored in the teaching of textuality and genre in cultural context. Foreign language programs now assert an identity in cultural studies in a much broader sense than was understood heretofore—one that includes not only the social sciences but all sciences.

Indeed, what was formerly the study of languages and aesthetic genres has now become a self-conscious cultural studies mirroring intellectual directions first taken in the 1970s and early 1980s and now dominant in higher education research and theory, at least since postmodernism called into question the preferred status of high culture. As a result, FL programs have opened the door for expanded choices of what texts to read and for revised notions about what students can expect to learn from those texts. The palette of course offerings today now incorporates movies, Web sites, and popular writing along with the high-culture literary works that predominated in courses until the 1970s.

Such changes reflect an understanding of literacy as socially bounded and contextual, no longer accessible solely through command of language as traditionally presented in many FL classrooms. Research sensitive not only to cultural norms but also to the power differentials, identity politics, and interests of various groups and individuals within those cultures has forced scholarly attention in the humanities squarely onto what Pierre Bourdieu calls the "field of cultural production" (*Field*). That field encompasses not only the structures of linguistic cultural artifacts (texts, artworks, films, conversations, group-identity formation strategies) but also how they are transacted or negotiated with, used, managed, circulated, and originated in various cultural settings.

Within more narrowly defined versions of FL teaching, this new focus on cultural production has led teachers to less dogmatic insistence on linguistic correctness and linguistic equivalencies. While the profession's intellectual identity has shifted, program development and commensurate teaching identity have lagged behind that theoretical vanguard. To be sure, such transitions between theoretical paradigms and disciplinary practice (as Thomas Kuhn would define it) always pose difficulties. In the present situation, the broader spectrum of cultural artifacts with which to work and of the perspectives of understanding that need to be accommodated has prompted many FL departments to rethink their role within the humanities. Would historical documents perhaps be better served if taught by historians and sociologists, movies by experts in film studies, or paintings and music by specialists in the fine arts? Current debates about "studies" programs (French studies, Italian studies), for example, quite logically ask what, beyond conveying the grammatical rudiments of a foreign language, the legitimate purview of a foreign language program can be. After all, cultural history has long been included in many history departments, and English departments often teach world literature in translation. Why have a foreign language department at all?

Discussions about the role and identity of a language department seldom arrive at consensus about what makes FL departments unique. Rarely do colleagues discuss what competencies FL teachers possess and need to teach so that learners understand texts as documents of a culture written in that culture's language. Yet the answer to the question of competencies becomes crucial to remapping what FL departments do, for literacy comprises more than the language forms, canonical works, and the everyday life experienced in that language's world.

In this volume we argue that, if culturally identifiable and valorized forms of language use are inseparable from the contexts in which they occur, it follows that the FL departments by definition instantiate a unique cross-cultural literacy, since their documents reach from the students' source culture into the target culture (or from cultural sphere into cultural sphere). In other words, a foreign language program can define its identity as teaching students the social and linguistic frameworks of texts and genres for spoken and written communication—across time periods, across cultures, and in multicultural frameworks.

In this vision, FL departments represent the only segment in the humanities that empowers students to become readers, listeners, or viewers who are able to identify how cultural production in a foreign language is transacted and managed and how foreign language speakers contact and influence one another in cultural and multicultural frameworks. FL departments teach students to transact such differences across cultures, as producers of discourses, texts, and other artifacts (practices, gestures, and the like) that bridge their own identities into other cultures. In other words, they teach students to become agents of culture across hegemonic lines.

In claiming such an identity, foreign language departments assume a bridge function that is an essential component not only in the humanities but in the social sciences and the arts as well. Their faculty members serve as theoretical experts with practical experience in characterizing knowledge between cultural frameworks across cultures and across groups within a single culture. Their expertise lies in the ability to interpret language in context, to identify linguistic equivalences and mismatches, to read foreign sign systems and interpolate them. Those interpolations range from identifying the ramifications of master narratives of nations (France the culture of Paris, cooking, and painting; the United States the culture of wealth, freedom, and enterprise) to assessing the dynamics of counterhegemonic narratives among groups and individuals within those nations.

Recognizing significant moments in foreign countries and cultures involves first knowing how to read texts to identify that culture's expectations at any given time or place in its history (the dominant practices and speech acts of the day) and to assess how those expectations have been challenged or renegotiated by alternative discourses. The intellectual charge of a foreign language program, regardless of its specific content focus, is to teach students how a language other than their native tongue produces and distributes knowledge within communicative frameworks.

THE VISION OF THIS VOLUME

With such a span, the scope of this book goes well beyond those found in texts written for teachers of elementary and intermediate foreign languages. Indeed, our focus is not on the planning and teaching of these, often the required, courses in a college curriculum. Instead, we explore how to articulate a sense of the profession as a whole and as a practical matter of planning for an entire undergraduate language program. The learning stages that we propose address the range of courses from the college students' initial exposure to a foreign language to graduation.

To introduce and support such discussions, this volume speaks to all faculty members of foreign language departments teaching at all levels of instruction. Its goal is to spur and support dialogues among them and within college and university language departments that will result in substantive changes in program and course planning. If such planning is to work, it is essential that it be based on faculty members' shared vision of the department and its institutional needs, regardless of their individual academic specialties or teaching focus.

Such dialogues must decide whether or not cultural literacy, in this exposition, will emerge as meaning not only the mastery of a mass of facts about a culture but also, and more important, a complex understanding of the communication, knowledge, and authority frameworks of a culture, the frameworks that generate, empower, or disempower and that stage the way the available facts are negotiated.

Dialogues of that scope are long overdue. The study of foreign languages is in a period of transition. Within a relatively short period of time, new courses and new demands have sprung up with overarching precepts about goals for learners. Such changes, in and of themselves, call for major rethinking of disciplinary expectations about teaching foreign languages, literatures, and cultures. Unfortunately, these dialogues must take place at a time when FL departments find themselves in transition externally as well as internally. Under budgetary constraints, institutions increasingly hold departments accountable to pragmatic standards measured in student performance and seats occupied. FL scholars find themselves under siege by new demands, often without the support of faculty development, funding, or new materials that could facilitate the implementation of their scholarly values into classroom practice.

At the same time, FL departments are now situated to address a world characterized on the one hand by the effects of positivist science, global media, and increasing political and economic institutionalization and on the other hand by volatile political and military instabilities. These changes have impinged on societal language functions and needs in dramatic ways. More than any other single factor, the relation between English as a global lingua franca and other languages informs such functions. That relation has also refocused the mission of English and foreign language departments by according to languages, to their study and their use, a new role and status.

In the age of information, rapid and inexpensive private exchanges now occur between individuals and communities around the world; at the same time, official and popular messages increase their dominance through global cartelization of mass media. The capacity to engage in context those ways of knowing that are anchored in awareness of how different languages express different negotiating styles and forms of meaning making has become an urgent necessity for any nation interested in preserving humanist thinking and encouraging a thinking populace. Without the capacity to identify the way different language use creates different meanings, citizens lack the linguistic and cognitive dimensions to compare messages and their ideologies, the essential first step in making discerning choices that lead to responsible social action. In tangible ways, then, foreign language departments have a vital role to play in the twenty-first century.

THE FOCUS OF INDIVIDUAL CHAPTERS

To explore how program building can strengthen that role for foreign languages in the postsecondary institution, we begin in chapter 1 by examining the culture of social sciences and humanist disciplines. Our goal is to identify the increasingly important interdisciplinary trend in many fields toward rethinking the role of context and communities in cultural production and transmission. We turn next to foreign language departments today and to the significance of rethinking context in terms of interest in interdisciplinary research and curriculum development. We focus particularly on the separation of form and meaning in many postsecondary FL programs and suggest why that separation is being rethought by members of FL departments as it becomes increasingly apparent that understanding any language means understanding it in context and that acquiring such understanding to high levels of ability necessitates curricular development.

Chapter 2 proposes a remapping of the FL curriculum as a holistic project that eschews the traditional distinction between lower and upper division in favor of coherent program building. Teaching language in contexts, as proposed in chapter 1, necessitates teaching the textual conventions of the language. Chapter 2 thus illustrates how, through work with a variety of written and spoken genres, students learn to read about and construct acts of communication that occur in private and public settings.

In chapter 3 we present a design for a holistic curriculum that uses the genres of texts as the basis for all facets of language learning. Commencing with criteria for selecting texts for readability at various levels, we illustrate sequencing of learner tasks from beginning classes to advanced students, from comprehension of textual messages to spoken and written expression that appropriates and varies the language of those messages. Consequently, the stages described represent a literacy sequence as well as a language-learning sequence, one that leads to multiliteracies appropriate for advanced knowledge.

Chapter 4 illustrates how beginning and intermediate classes, using a short work of literature, move from reading to an increased command of language in holistic ways. We show how learners with relatively little language knowledge can use a guided information matrix to read for the content and implications of a Spanish-language text. We also propose ways to apply literary theories in a variety of related tasks to elicit oral and written responses that reflect different program goals.

Expanding on the holistic tasks presented in chapter 4, we turn in chapter 5 to their application when advanced students work with multiple genres and their divergent discourse practices. Illustrating how to develop guided précis as interlocking assignments designed to help learners engage with a novel, a film, a book review, and an author interview, this chapter shows how teachers' tasks can direct learners to cultural as well as aesthetic insights and enable them to assume increasing responsibility as strong readers.

Chapter 6 reconsiders literary genres beyond their aesthetic and formal constructs as high-culture forms and expands the scope of what is generally understood by the term *genre* to encompass the palette of socially constructed discourse practices within any given culture. We propose a design for sequencing learning that is keyed to learner stages by distinguishing different learning aims for different program levels. We suggest that students learn the patterns of literary texts in their contexts initially in order to move ultimately to formal descriptions of genres. In contrast with the foreign language emphases in chapters 4 and 5, the proposals here also apply to humanist and interdisciplinary courses taught in English.

Expanding on the genre literacies introduced in the previous chapter, chapter 7 proposes three curricular levels that use the genres of different texts, those of both dominant and marginalized groups, to teach a FL culture. It describes the shifts in learning focus that must occur if learners are to progress from identifying the culturally familiar to identifying the unfamiliar in a variety of genres and media and to undertake a systematic accounting for the habits of context and evaluation that characterize a given communication community within a foreign culture.

The eighth section of the volumne, the coda, returns to our overriding theme: the curriculum as a framework for accountability, for a vision of how various cultural contents can be made relevant to students' literacies, which are gauged as their ability to engage in professional and personal lives within and outside higher education.

Scholars, Teachers, and
Chapter 1 Program Development

In our introduction, we argued for an intellectual identity for foreign language studies that anchors its teaching in multiple textualities and genres in a variety of cultural contexts. Our case was motivated by theories that humanist disciplines have taken as central in the past twenty-five years, at least since the arrival of poststructuralism from France. That foreign language faculty members have applied these theories to stake out new directions not only in research but also in course development has been documented in a variety of books, periodicals, and departmental Web pages. To take into consideration cultural politics, identity politics, and other new options in analyzing cultural production and transmission, faculty members in foreign languages have been responding with courses and programs that reflect their revised perception of the field's disciplinary mission. This chapter looks at current thinking about the role of language departments in colleges and universities and identifies how the altered sense of the field can lead to further change in FL programs, courses, and their classroom implementation.

We begin by acknowledging that many existing initiatives at program building and new course development inform our project. Many new content courses have been put in place over the last two decades; many initiatives have been supported through funding agencies, notably the National Endowment for the Humanities and the Spencer Foundation, and disseminated through professional organizations, notably the Modern Language

Association (MLA), the AATs (American Associations of Teachers of French, German, Spanish, and others), and their affiliated groups. Actively engaged in providing forums for innovative FL programs, the Association of Departments of Foreign Languages (ADFL) has, for over a decade, foregrounded deliberations about issues in education and the role of foreign languages in colleges and universities. Sections devoted to the teaching of language and literatures, as opposed to those reporting on research, are increasingly visible components in national conferences at seminars and workshops. Similarly, the decision of the MLA that its *International Bibliography*, the major resource for research in the discipline, now includes references that deal with English and FL teaching acknowledges the importance of translating into teaching practice the intellectual developments that we have outlined (Arens). The introduction of the series in which this volume appears gives a similar signal: aligning FL teaching and scholarship constitutes a major concern for the profession's primary professional organization (see Byrnes, *Learning* vii–viii).

At the same time, these forums bear witness to deep concerns about the present state of foreign languages in postsecondary institutions and a felt need to rethink current departmental programs and teaching practices. The extensive discussions following Dorothy James's query in the *ADFL Bulletin* about "who is minding the store" reflect concerns about our teaching missions ("Response"). These concerns arise in departments with MA and PhD programs, as we recognize the clear disconnects between what we value as scholars and what is taught in individual courses and across entire curricula.

FL departments need to address two practices if they wish to make a case for their intellectual credibility as humanists and re-create a teaching mission commensurate with their scholarship in a fiscal environment that is loathe to fund the humanities because the humanities are viewed merely as an enrichment to a postsecondary curriculum. The first is a tendency to use teaching practices that separate form from meaning, with pedagogies that run counter to the field's own scholarly insights, which point to form, content, and context as inextricably linked whenever people engage in meaningful communication. The second practice is a tendency to treat courses as separately owned property, independent of a larger curricular context. This practice becomes a substantive educational issue when administrative policy, following it, threatens the adoption of innovative courses and sets roadblocks to program coherency.

Both practices inhibit the development of FL programs with viable responses to the needs of the students and the institution. Both should be interrogated sharply in advance of our presentation of a new approach to curriculum.

FORM AND MEANING IN FL PROGRAMS: CHANGING INSTITUTIONAL PRACTICES

The traditional hierarchical relations among subfields within the larger purview of foreign language learning have in no small measure helped isolate "language" courses from "content" courses in the average post-secondary curriculum. That isolation appears first and most strikingly in the break between the initial years of language instruction and advanced (usually upper-division) work in literature, cultural studies, or linguistics. Language study, even at advanced levels, is rarely considered in relation to studies of cultural meaning (transmitted in literature, film, or other kinds of writing or performance). Attitudes divide meaning and language on an administrative level as well, because they often lead to a policy of separating "language teachers" and "specialists in their fields." Potentially, such a policy builds barriers to communication within departments when it encourages teachers at different curricular levels to assume that they have little to say to one another. Tacitly, it suggests that students can study text meaning only after they understand a text's language, not as a concomitant, interrelated activity in which language and ideas are mutually constructing.

As a practical matter, the distinction between language teachers and specialists exists primarily in research institutions and at public and private comprehensive universities. By contrast, most sites for foreign language instruction that lack graduate programs—liberal arts colleges, technical schools, hybrids of vocational and liberal arts schools, and community colleges—have the same faculty teaching beginning languages and whatever upper-division courses exist in the FLs. In consequence, the disparity between teachers of language and specialists originates mainly in institutions that educate future professors, not in the FL departments where most teaching of undergraduates takes place nationwide.

Yet precisely because more research-oriented schools educate future teachers of foreign languages, they are charged with rethinking their assumptions about program building and intellectual mission lest they isolate their scholarly work from the interests of their current and future students as well as from the professional marketplace.

A common case in point is that lower-division course work frequently concentrates class time and homework on texts with relatively restricted language form; the assumption is that beginners cannot deal with intellectually challenging materials early in their learning. Consequently, courses for advanced students or majors can quite literally scare students away, because their design often signals a shift from the basic vocabulary and everyday speech emphasized in the lower division to more demanding texts and specialized communicative situations. Compounding the problem, departmental offerings past lower-division requirements rarely ease students' transition from lower-division work with tasks and tests tailored to meet their learning level. The infamous break between lower and upper divisions in language programs is thus created by our program practices, and it is a given for students as they progress to advanced forms of literacy.

The origins of these practices lie in shared assumptions about language education in English as well as FL. Both fields have viewed language mastery as a prerequisite to doing advanced work in interpreting literature and now in reading culture too. Students who could not write well or did not master the fundamentals of English or foreign language prose took classes to remediate their deficiency. Such classes were explicitly cast as prerequisites to advanced (i.e., truly college-level) work. As a result, programs evolved that were openly designated or tacitly considered as remedial, with distinct practices regarding what to teach and how to teach it and what not to teach. Formal accuracy per se became their domain, not students' ability to learn and express challenging content in terms of contextually appropriate forms. Foreign and native language composition classes for beginners and intermediate students were considered preparatory, and most FL students remained outside the real scholarly concerns of the profession.

That this lower-division pedagogy was held apart from upper-division content meant also that it developed its own pedagogical culture, a trend that exacerbates today's divide between lower- and upper-division course sequences. Before the 1970s, classroom teachers with different approaches to pedagogy or methodology attempted to separate learning tasks into categories of isolated skills. In English, the focus was on the mechanics of sentence and paragraph formation and on the construction of arguments (as basic rhetoric). In foreign languages, the surge of interest in speaking a language helped divide the acquisition process into speaking, listening, reading, and writing. Early instruction used dialogues for modeling speech and short texts for reading comprehension. Written work centered mainly on grammar exercises; on the sentence level, students filled in blanks or built sentences from key words, the so-called dehydrated sentence exercise. Generally, these sentences in exercise series were unrelated to one another and had little direct connection to any dialogues or short texts assigned for mastery of reading, speaking, or listening comprehension. Sentences were considered as related to grammar and lexical choice; oral work was evaluated for fluency and pronunciation.

Twenty years later, linguistic research in teaching has called these assumptions into question. Current findings in instructed learning and discourse analysis strongly suggest that students benefit from a much more integrative use of language in language learning. The evidence points to the value of supersentential writing; of the use of longer texts; and of exercises that mix modalities, have practical applications, and allow multiple solutions. Indeed, evidence in both first- and second-language learning indicates that thinking in terms of skills is a flawed model for language acquisition, because students' cognitive processing of new information becomes more effective and the language material included becomes more memorable when new information can be introduced through multiple modalities. Learners' recall of spoken language is reinforced when it is viewed in writing or spoken in a particular context to communicate an idea that is stimulating or interesting to the learners.

Influenced by these findings, many FL professionals have become concerned with creating teaching practices that integrate the field's intellectual content with language instruction. They no longer view the instructed learning of foreign languages as a process of teaching separate modalities or skills that somehow promise to add up to language mastery. Indeed, FL researchers and practitioners now generally avoid the word *skills*, since it conveys a now-dated separation of verbal and mental capabilities. To be sure, skills (defined here as automatic or unthinking recognition of vocabulary and morphosyntax) remain acknowledged facets of language use (with possible diagnostic value, such as when a student's oral skills can be described as weak), but only as components in a richer picture of factors considered essential for students' language acquisition. Skills are not components of language use that can be taught.

The result of leaving the concept of skills behind is a new pedagogical focus in FL instruction on meaning, defined here as the systematic integration of language form with content and context. Related to meaning is a different concept of our learners, who are now seen as literate adult learners rather than as form-deficient students. Long viewed as disadvantaged when compared with a child learner, the adult is now seen by FL researchers as possessing cognitive capabilities that enable more sophisticated language acquisition than that experienced by a child under similar time constraints. Grown-ups may not achieve the degree of automaticity child learners acquire (their pronunciations, for example, may never seem native), but their comprehension and even their expressive capabilities can be acquired more rapidly and with at least equal if not greater facility. The most important distinction seems to be that adults are not learning concepts at the same time that they learn vocabulary. Instead, they are linking their established cognitive pathways and known sociolinguistic information to the unknown language. In this important respect, adults engage in FL acquisition differently than do children and adolescents, a distinction critical to rethinking instructed learning for adults (Birdsong and Molis).

When confronted with ideationally familiar texts whose language use exceeds their active command of that language, adults (unlike children or adolescents) can use their cognitive knowledge, both factual and strategic, to recover meanings and integrate information and language from FL texts into their own cognitive frameworks, long before they may be considered fluent in linguistic terms. Unlike FL teachers of children, FL teachers of adults can thus also link correction of form to meaning with some confidence that such explicit linking between the two reinforces both (Norris and Ortega). Adults can learn the rules of language use while they are learning content, cultural or language-based, because they already know how their native language works.

To work toward a curriculum that joins form and meaning, therefore, requires the adherence to three firm guideposts: that teaching practices need to foster overriding goals of the curriculum rather than privileging individual preferences; that multiple literacies need to be built into each task so that the students' learning is integrated, not fragmented; and that language use in communicative frameworks (rather than abstract language competence) becomes the benchmark for evaluation.

MATCHING GOALS WITH TEACHING PRACTICES

What is now known about the relation between adult capabilities and effective language acquisition cannot translate into new programs that bridge language use, content, and context without considerable readjustment of faculty thinking about what to teach and how, at all levels of instruction. Yet such adjustment is essential to setting new departmental goals. Faculty members need to make decisions about goals—about how a college program can best serve their adult learners and introduce them to the intellectual imperatives of the disciplines they work in. That task is not insurmountable, but it is one that necessitates working together to explore possibilities in building courses and programs based on existing strengths within a department.

Faculty members can, for example, explore together how to correlate their research interests with course and program development. They can visit one another's classes to identify and build bridges between classroom and assessment practices. Often their philosophical positions about what is teachable emerge more clearly from classroom practices that reflect their assumptions of what it means to learn a language than from their out-of-class observations about what they teach and what they believe students are learning as a result (Morgan).

Classroom practices will generally reflect a tendency toward one of two faculty positions. At one end of this spectrum, language dominates. Instructors teach language in a normative fashion, as a corpus of data to be learned "correctly." That assumed standard for communication relies on tasks such as reading texts for information alone, memorizing individual words in lists, and writing sentences outside a particular communicative context. Related classroom practices generally place teachers in an authority role; the learner is evaluated against correctness rather than on originality or content control. The underlying assumption of such a position is that language forms must be acquired before students can use the language to engage in intellectually challenging activities, such as reading its literature or investigating ideas in periodicals or on the Web, at a cognitive level commensurate with work in other college courses. Students are not presumed to be able to think about issues that they cannot yet speak or write about.

At the other end of the spectrum, instructors who believe that acquisition of specific content is important will teach in an individuated approach to language use, one that is also more responsive to student needs and motivations. They could, for example, decide to teach a corpus of texts whose information and messages reflect multiple cultural realities and multiple literacies. Since the form and content of a particular text will vary with the sender and the real or implied receiver, they realize that students must identify not only language elements but content and context as well. These teachers devise tasks that enable students to pinpoint systems of meaning in a given text rather than, as with a more normative approach to language competence, to find textual information in order to respond to questions about isolated facts. In such situations, the teachers create tasks, but the students create their own learning. Teaching methods—theoretical positions and their implementations as teaching methodologies—do not necessarily correlate with learning tasks and aims for language acquisition, and so it is critical for teachers to set goals to guide themselves in constructing tasks.

Thus the teacher's role in a pedagogy that integrates language and content issues is to fashion a learning environment in which students individuate their learning to meet requirements of communication—in the sense of Wolfgang Iser (*Implied Reader*), to respond as a reader and user of a variety of texts written for, viewed by, or spoken to native speakers of that language (so-called authentic texts). That individuated response, in turn, has to be substantiated (and possibly modulated) by recourse to information out of the students' own experience and out of the texts learned. Thus cultural literacy and communication can be joined in a sliding scale of competency and applied as a measuring stick to learners' performance instead of as a fixed norm against which mastery is measured. Authentic materials lead learners not only to new language but also to new textual messages and new ideas expressed in language unfamiliar to them; these texts also expose them to new discourse situations that need to be controlled—to language learning in the context of a culture's ideas, values, and practices, as all teachable within the context of language acquisition.

Stressing a learner's competence in negotiating meaningful contents in contexts, across all levels of the curriculum, means moving away from a teacher-imposed norm for correctness and building up instead predictable series of expectations, in both tasks and outcomes. Having students learn word lists does not necessarily translate into success on tests of communicative or interactive competence. In other words, the goals set for classes and sequences of classes determine definitions of successful language acquisition, and these in turn determine what constitutes success as established through assessment. Where the traditional lower-division and remedial curricula define competency as mastery of vocabulary and grammar rules (the "basic 2,000 words," "standard grammar forms"), an individuated, user-oriented curriculum that sets broad, flexible goals for learning will define students' ability to function effectively in real-world contexts, within particular social and occupational settings. An upper-division program that builds on those abilities will ease the transition between levels.

Naturally, that shift in objectives changes curricular practices in the language program as a whole. The normative grammar test, for example, no longer acts as a sufficient indicator of competence in expression. Effective presentation of messages and significance of content become as important as language form. Similarly, when speech performance is evaluated, formal correctness weighs in terms of situational appropriateness, and so does the learner's increasing ability to edit and self-correct language-based performance.

The user-oriented curriculum integrates speaking, listening, reading, and writing, because research on motivation suggests that adult students retain more (e.g., more vocabulary), that they have greater interest in learning the language, and that integrated tasks foster greater achievement. Reading the text of a video in conjunction with viewing it improves retention of information (Hanley, Herron, and Cole). Given appropriate tasks to facilitate comprehension of authentic texts, many students find complex, rhetorically sophisticated materials more informative than edited texts, because such materials provide redundant clues to meaning.

Adult beginners, even those with nascent language skills, are ideal candidates for programs that individuate instruction with tasks that foster "learning to learn" and that define entry-level courses as early steps toward content learning rather than as remediation. Not only can adults learn the French words to identify the rooms in one's home (a typical textbook task for beginners), but that learning can also be almost automatically incorporated into a more intellectually challenging lesson about French culture, with the addition of a French magazine article about interior design of houses or apartments or the addition of the description of a domestic interior from a realist novel.

To integrate speaking with reading at a cognitively challenging level, teachers might have students start by noting whatever they understand (it

will not be everything, to be sure) about the size, shape, and proximities of
rooms; about the style of furniture; or about the types of appliances used.
The students already know that home furnishings describe their owners in
many ways; any single text can be taken as exemplifying a French approach
to domesticity. Students might, for example, be led to consider architectural
features in terms of ethnographic or climatic factors, marketing, or parallels
as well as contrasts with their own cultural experiences. Language is thereby
linked to exploration of broader cultural issues. Studies confirm that adults
acquire new language forms most effectively when correctness is linked to
meaning in contextual use. When adults see that verb endings signal the
difference between present and past events, whether in a description of a
room, in a story, or in a how-to manual, the significance of that distinction
enhances the learning of a particular form in their memory. They also have
begun thinking about how a culture organizes its own forms of memory
and experiences into several aspects of its literacy, along with its characteristic practices and ideologies (Byrnes and Kord; Kern, "Reconciling").

THE NEED TO RETHINK CURRENT PRACTICES

Foreign language departments that want to overcome the gap in their programs between upper and lower division, between majors and nonmajors,
must set themselves the intellectual goal of enabling students to encode the
multiple literacies (language, culture, and other contents) that they encounter in a foreign language context and its texts—to deal with culture
and its communicative forms as mutually informing systems. That is, from
the outset of instruction, students must learn to consider who speaks or
writes to what audience, in what ways, from what perspective, and with
what demand. Language must be considered as a set of culture-based performances, situated in various public, private, and disciplinary contexts.

Teaching practices and program-building initiatives must go hand in
hand with this perspective that language is a performance engaged with
various sites and identities within a culture. Fulfilling that objective involves some genuine rethinking of traditional practices that run counter to
such intellectual challenges. For example, when presenting language that
describes homes, eating practices, or shopping, virtually all textbooks for FL
beginners offer language in isolated forms; excluded are all but minimal opportunities to access texts, here defined broadly as cultural artifacts in any

media. As noted above, however, words designating rooms and furniture that often occur as early as the fifth week of a beginners' course can be connected to social practices. Yet textbooks tend to isolate the furniture names instead of introducing them through authentic texts: FL movies, book excerpts, or magazine articles that illustrate various types of home or apartment interiors in the foreign culture, all of which would help students see the contexts within which the vocabulary resides.

Nor does the adult learner at advanced levels fare much better with regard to issues of intellectual challenge, through exposure to a pedagogy that joins form, content, and context. The very fact that the typical department has different sequences or tracks for language, literature, and culture suggests that these integrally related facets of language acquisition are separate. Instructors tacitly assume that knowing the furniture names will enable learners to understand scenes in realist novels. Yet they do little to bridge the gap between the names and the scenes, since they have not had those learners look at other representations of French rooms or compare descriptions of fictional rooms with real rooms from similar periods and locales. More advanced students, those who had done so, would be prepared to compare, for example, descriptions of art deco rooms with rooms in realist novels as representatives of different cultural ideologies.

In many curricula, FL departments inadvertently render habitual a division between language and language meaning. Graduate programs with special emphases (culture, applied linguistics, linguistics, literature) inculcate a mind-set that holds language and interpretive entities separate. All too often, courses at both the upper-division and graduate level focus on information conveyed in the foreign language to the virtual exclusion of the ways in which text language and context frame and mediate such information. Such programs inadvertently deny their students the intellectual challenge of analyzing these relations actively, to discover differences in literary and cultural ideologies.

Across college and university curricula, separatist practices work in various combinations. Frequently, upper-division courses in advanced grammar or conversation separate (marginalize, or even exclude) cultural context from language, even while they seem to stress performance. Such courses rarely propose, for example, that students assess grammar as a system of discourse tools used by native speakers or writers to engage in acts of meaning. Nor do such courses require students to identify, emulate, and transform situations as practice in how those tools are used. Learners speak and write; they don't necessarily learn how they might strategize to enter various speaking and writing positions within a culture.

Echoing these practices, advanced- and even graduate-level courses in literary studies rarely engage in interpretation of literature or cultural artifacts from the standpoint of discourse analysis or lexical semantics—or even as traditional rhetorical forms. Consequently, advanced students rarely receive instruction about links among dominant theories in literary, cultural, and linguistic studies as competing value-and-analysis systems within the *disciplinary* culture of literary studies. Rather, they experience courses in one or another theory or a set of theories applied to a limited subject matter. It is difficult to imagine how such instruction prepares these students for the interdisciplinarity and multiculturalism that are so highly prized in the field.

COURSES WITHOUT CURRICULAR CONTEXT: DEPARTMENT DILEMMAS

Precisely because no recommendation about how teaching practices should treat course content, linguistic form, and cultural context at all stages of FL instruction can apply to every institution, departments need to discuss this issue in the framework of a comprehensive review of their programs. Regardless of size and scope of program, that discussion will look for links between levels rather than review a particular learning level. Taking stock of course sequences necessarily involves having all faculty members work together to identify how best to serve their particular students (major, minor, and general) from the standpoint of developmental continuity and a specific program's goals.

Such discussions often ask departments to rethink the administrative as well as the policy problems that exist when curricula separate language form, disciplinary content, and cultural context. While a discipline's intellectual values may or may not correlate with pedagogical practices, administrative policies inevitably influence how programs and curricula are built.

One such policy stems from the time-honored notion of academic freedom. Traditional management of upper-division and graduate course offerings has supported a system in which courses are created by individual faculty members. They select topics, subject matter, and assigned readings; they compose course descriptions, including appropriate goals and forms of assessment. The result comes to express a tacit consensus about program offerings. Yet a list of topics offered by a particular program does not necessarily define a learning sequence or a teaching philosophy, no matter how easy it is to assume that such courses and their loose sequencing constitute a rational progression of language and content learning. At the same time, colleagues rarely challenge the assumption that everyone in the department shares comparable performance expectations, as embodied in tests, quizzes, assignments, and the grading of spoken or written work.

When a program neglects to monitor such expectations, an administration may be tempted to manage those expectations on behalf of the faculty involved: to entrench and hence nominally professionalize divisions by establishing language centers. One dean describes the centers as the management solution for the "vaguely schizophrenic" department, with scholarly life on the one side "and the lower-division language teaching life of the department on the other." This dean recognizes the importance of good language instruction and good professional content for the language component of a college or university education. Nonetheless, since, in his view, departments fail to appreciate this part of their own mission, he concludes that

> some mechanism must be in place at every university so that applied linguists, the teachers genuinely and creatively concerned with lower-division language instruction, will be provided with an administrative "space" where they can all come together so that their research, their concerns, their innovations, and their solutions can be shared and properly valued. (Lariviere 246)

Such an assertion says a great deal about current policies in or for foreign language departments and about the status granted lower divisions. It assumes as necessary to the health of a lower-division program the very arrangement that we have identified as flawed, because this solution works against integrated expectations for language performance across levels. It separates the staffing and planning of language programs into discontinuous chunks. At the same time, this mechanism implies a professional distinction between instructors at the various "learning levels." Unfortunately, when programs isolate teachers of language from the major, often using lecturers or senior lecturers to "maintain" the lower division, administrators are free to introduce a variety of administrative entities (e.g., language centers) that will welcome these faculty members but also isolate them even further from the university's broader intellectual purposes. As a result, language teaching can still seem remedial to the rest of the campus, not part of cultural literacy or critical-thinking initiatives for students.

What does such a proposal by the dean of a major research institution imply about language departments as a whole or those in prestigious institutions such as Berkeley, Brown, Columbia, Rice, Stanford, or Yale, all of which have a type of language center designed to augment departmental programs or to teach language to beginning students of major languages?[1] Simply this: foreign language departments are contributing to the emergence of new institutional structures that build on their own passé assumptions—structures born out of weakness rather than strength. Given today's tight budgets, administrators will divorce from one another what appear to be inefficient and incompatible units or will take whatever other measures they deem warranted to reduce the impact of that inefficiency on the larger academic community. Language teaching will be relegated to centers when administrators view departments as unable to integrate it with other forms of humanistic learning about cultures.

We are not arguing that foreign language centers are necessarily bad institutional practice. They serve a variety of valued roles in different institutions. But we want our readers to consider why centers have come into existence and the fact that they often reify, or at least exacerbate, the language/content schizophrenia that language-acquisition research has found to be undesirable. Managerially, they render virtually untouchable a more serious split in program development and coherent planning, placing students, faculty members, and materials under purviews separate from the departments and programs that teach about foreign cultures in various coherent disciplinary contexts. Unquestionably, centers may introduce students to other languages and the fuller contexts of their cultural meaning (gesture, material conditions, social practices). But departments capable of integrating language learning in context and content learning across various levels of their programs do not need such centers. Where centers exist, FL departments should address these same integrative tasks across two separate administrative entities.

RESPONSES TO INSTITUTIONAL PRESSURES:
SOME CONCLUSIONS TOWARD FL PROGRAM BUILDING

Concomitantly with the creation of language centers, a number of wake-up calls have occurred and FL faculty members in a variety of institutions have responded with innovative program building. When, for example, administrators merged English and foreign language departments at Mansfield University, the faculty sat down with consultants to find viable ways to continue programs (Porter and Sanders). Many such newly minted multilingual departments report on ways to respond effectively to administrative and budgetary pressures and serve their various language constituencies, not just burgeoning Spanish enrollments (Nichols). Yet another type of pressure was confronted when the change of requirements in general education at the State University of New York, Binghamton, created new conditions allowing its German program to survive by implementing a sequence emphasizing how language relates to cultural actions and perceptions: a first-year German requirement built around the relation between language and thought, followed by a content-based sequence integrating language and cultural knowledge (Morewedge). Other German programs in the SUNY system were eliminated when they failed to rethink their roles within a general education context.

Survival is not the only indicator of productive responses to institutional pressure. Programs in language across the curriculum (LAC) have, for instance, been particularly successful in establishing institutional presences across the country (Kecht and Hammerstein). Nonetheless, although LAC programs address the language/content divide from an interdisciplinary perspective and often develop interesting course content, they have not contributed to a general rethinking of instructional practices fostering more general kinds of cultural learning. We argue instead that programs must establish their identities as part of the humanities to recast language teaching as part of a curriculum's commitment to multiple cultural literacies, not just to language learning.

This volume attempts to recast curricular reform for FL language teaching within a larger context of curricular reform, driven both by the pragmatics of our profession and by our best scholarship on learning and cultural analysis. We sketch some templates representing how the intellectual premises of the humanities can find practical realization in curricula and courses. Our goal is to exemplify how FL faculty members might achieve accountable programs that construe language learning as seminal to learning as a whole within postsecondary institutions. At the same time, we affirm how curricular planning can link the acquisition of language and knowledge.

Redefining language teaching as the teaching of multiple cultural literacies also requires us to move away from the kind of curriculum planning and normative assessments that tend to favor high-culture usage as defined by the dominant or elite strata of culture. The use- and literacy-oriented curriculum and assessment criteria we advocate here require that nondominant groups and their common culture be considered, as they exist in dialogue with the practices of dominant communities within the FL culture, as well as the as yet unrealized aspirations of subgroups and minorities to express their own identities and ideologies of culture.

Such a rethinking is timely. Language programs have of late been subject to public as well as administrative scrutiny, and attempts have been made to remedy their perceived deficiencies. It would seem to be high time for foreign language faculty members to recast the image of their discipline, to engage in responsible rethinking of curricular practices so that foreign languages emerge as a substantive contribution to humanist studies across North American campuses—as accountable to the institution and to the adult learners in it alike.

We propose here that FL departments need to develop programs that can maximize learning: by presenting cultural content in an intellectually challenging way commensurate with institutional offerings as a whole; by capitalizing on the mature students' interests and academic background knowledge; and by making the study of humanities into the teaching and learning of critical cultural literacies, defined with respect to learner and institutional goals rather than as arbitrary documents of culture wars. We have argued the necessity of a program-planning framework that remains aware of short- and long-term goals at all stages of the curriculum, from beginners through graduate courses.

Chapter 2 turns to a set of principles that can act as a scaffold for faculty members who wish to implement such a framework.

NOTE

1. The wide variety of centers renders this designation misleading as an umbrella term. Centers such as those at Yale serve undergraduate students as technological resources. In contrast, the University of Pennsylvania's center serves beginners in less commonly taught languages. For a comprehensive overview, see Garrett.

Linking Meaning and Language: Remapping the Discipline

Chapter 2

The perspective on course and curricular development introduced in chapter 1 calls for a new way of thinking about levels of difficulty in the average course sequence. It has been proposed that, within a framework that integrates the learning of vocabulary and language forms with content, language "fundamentals" (grammar, syntax, phonology, semantics) must be taught as social and linguistic negotiations within and across cultures. This chapter considers more directly how to build tasks for such a language curriculum by thinking in terms of activities that promote learning to learn.

To be sure, each FL department must decide for itself what outcomes it finds feasible, what capabilities its students, faculty members, and institution desire and can afford to sponsor. If program planners want to link meaning and language learning, then those links must be fostered from beginning instruction into subsequent levels of the curriculum, albeit in expanded form and using increasingly sophisticated materials. FL departments can make such decisions, because today's students in postsecondary education typically have different learning capabilities and desires from those in high school, especially in terms of cognitive development, which the traditional lower division of postsecondary language instruction has in many ways failed to factor into its curriculum building.

Yet cognitive development does indeed play an important role in the order and ease with which students of different ages acquire language. Even among young adults, different age groups (first-year students, seniors, graduate students) have different learning propensities, which college programs in foreign languages can capitalize from the outset of instruction, especially if they hope to encourage those learners to continue course work beyond elementary or required levels. Language learning taken as literacy, for example, will be associated with other forms of humanistic learning if departments in colleges and universities with language requirements build their programs holistically, starting from the larger mandated audience of beginning or lower-division language and moving toward advanced classes, uniting levels with appropriate choices of tasks and materials.

We emphasize that lessening the isolation of the lower-division courses by designing a curriculum to serve students at all program levels is crucial, using tasks built on group agreement about what kinds of language competency, texts, and topics students value and about who the students are. That lower division will need to be reconstructed away from its present grammar-driven forms to meet the learning and acquisition needs of new audiences from widely varying backgrounds who, in consequence, have varying language abilities. When that reconstruction happens, as we argue in this chapter, the upper-division curriculum will assume a different shape as well.

Consequently, planning of larger scope, across all parts of a curriculum and based on a holistic, consensus framework about learning, is necessary to ensure coherent sequencing of instruction (Stenhouse). Accounting for our students and our shared values and paying consistent attention to tasks and texts that build on one another are vital to the continued survival of FL instruction.

MULTIPLE LITERACIES AS THE BASIS FOR
HOLISTIC PROGRAM BUILDING

Holistic programs at the college level take varying forms within different institutions, but each holistic curriculum design follows certain rules of thumb, framework principles that help place language learning in specific contexts with a given department and its institution. Several of these principles exert distinct pressure on the curriculum. If, for example, a holistic curriculum wants to capitalize on what language acquisition research tells us is optimally teachable and learnable, then syllabuses will have to attend to linguistic, conceptual, and communicative frameworks in tandem (see, e.g., Byrnes, "Role" 317–18). Moreover, courses in that curriculum will have to provide students with individualized feedback addressing discrete processes of language acquisition, including feedback about the specific literacies represented in interdisciplinary frameworks, in language, literature, and culture courses alike. Finally, such a curriculum will have to judge student command of language's formal features as a function of successful comprehension and communication of learning, not as forms in isolation, in order to create a learner-responsive syllabus that, from the first phases of language instruction on, addresses the different needs of student populations in different institutions.

For example, a teacher in a traditional program's introductory course might ask learners to produce the first-person singular form of the verb *to read* in the context of a paradigm review or a variation in a dialogue about a third person. In contrast, teachers in a holistic program might ask that students read publishers' descriptions of influential periodicals published in the country or countries where the foreign language is spoken; then, pretending to be Germans or Spaniards, the students might talk about which one they read and suggest why by describing its qualities (Kord). In both instances, the task requires learners to know and produce the first-person singular form of the verb *to read* successfully ("I read *Time*; it is interesting"). However, by introducing context, content, and a point of view or intent into the task, the teacher in the holistic program places the focus on correct use instead of on grammar terminology.

The learning context must join language production and content in other ways, creating sequences in which: students have a model for correct usage in the text; they are stimulated to engage in natural communication (storytelling) as the first stage of language production, reproduction; they are asked to produce language on the basis of their own synthesis of the text's messages (a content criterion); they therefore must use more than one sentence at a time; and they share and evaluate information as well as language. Tasks that structure such sequences foster holistic learning, since students will focus on how to manage a context, content, and tasks that enable them to practice multiple dimensions of language use. Even if their production is very simple, they are integrating language, which will prepare them for more advanced uses ("I read *Spiegel*, a news magazine. It appears every week. The feature articles are often ten pages long—they are much longer than articles in *Time* or *Newsweek*").

Such integrated language learning will quite naturally require error correction, since structurally rich input does not lead automatically to accurate output. However, each act of communication needs to be judged and assessed not only for correct language forms but also from several other dimensions. In this way, students are allowed flexibility in accomplishing these tasks. They can enter into language space from several perspectives, combining listening and reading with speaking and writing in more naturalistic settings. This flexibility and focus on success in communication alongside accuracy will be particularly important in an era when the majority of secondary school students have not been taught the terminology of formal grammar. Moreover, to judge learners on formal grammar in isolation is to ignore the multiple factors that contribute to their making choices among forms in line with the literate—that is, the textual—conventions of the language, not just its sentence-level forms. A holistic, literacy-based program thus focuses on teaching students how to make choices. Initial efforts at using textual information to express student intent need to be rewarded alongside the actual language produced—communicative intent is part of a pattern of social literacy.

A multiple-literacy-based program is appealing at the college level because beginning programs serve students whose learning styles are in the process of shifting toward a more adult, integrative mode. High school students who respond to encouragement to be uninhibited about speaking are at the age when they can express opinions fluently. By age eighteen or nineteen, however, learners are generally ready to be more concerned with correctness and effectiveness, and they will be less likely to function in situations where their speech is spontaneous rather than deliberate or even planned. Thus the first difference between a holistic course and traditional practice speaks to what kind of "grammar textbook" and other syllabus materials will be appropriate to the first year, a decision that can exacerbate any preexisting placement problems or, conversely, help students receive credit for the kinds of learning they have done already and will need to do as adults. The overriding interests highlighted in such an introductory course, and how they contrast with traditional tasks and materials, can be summarized in figure 2.1. While the holistic pedagogical framework summarized in the right-hand column uses terminology and techniques in common with different methodologies (e.g., communicative approaches,

Figure 2.1. Beginning Language Instruction in a
Traditional and a Holistic Curriculum

Traditional Rule-Driven Syllabi, Textbooks	Holistic Syllabi Tasks, Texts
Culturally neutral dialogues, edited texts, separate skill practice	Personalized language Culturally situated texts and multiple genres as the basis for oral, written work as well as reading
Sentence drill (fill in the blanks) Grammar rules linked to rules in formal accuracy	Integrative language use: grammar linked to its meaning function in texts at the levels of paragraphs, discourse, and sentences
Grammar rules taught in class (30% or more of class hour) Rules are cued by translation or grammatical terminology	Class time devoted to contextual practice cued by situational variables that encourage focus on forms Grammar rules learned by students as an independent activity outside class
Vocabulary lists to be memorized for active use—largely cued by translation	Distinction between words actively used and words comprehended—vocabulary learning focuses on words essential to messages of text, understood and cued in L2 context

the four-skills approach, the natural approach), it should not be confused with methodological pluralism or eclecticism.

Quite different from an "anything goes" approach, a holistic framework identifies appropriate pedagogical responses to learner sequences in language acquisition. From the onset of instruction, it structures encounters with intellectually challenging materials and the tasks for using those materials to reframe even the first steps in learning a language as entry points into various cultural literacies.

READING AND WRITING: RECURSIVE TASKS FOR ADULT LEARNERS TO LINK GRAMMAR AND CONTENT

The holistic curriculum building toward a learner's literacy in aspects of language and culture favors the abilities of adult learners, whose known cognitive processes underlie both comprehension and language production. Speaking and listening occur within real-world constraints different from those of reading and writing. Since oral responses offer little time for reflection, speaking involves simultaneous use of macro- and micromemory (the knowledge both of general frameworks and of immediate sequences in interaction). Hence speaking and listening are, cognitively speaking, immediacy tasks that restrict the learner's ability to use prior knowledge and cognitive processes. Speakers must forge ahead or lose their platform for communication, so that any self-correction may cost that speaker whatever attention the listener is paying to the message. The listener, in turn, expects an interaction proceeding from the general frame to the particular.

Readers and writers, in contrast, can reread, check data, and reconsider. Cognitively, then, these are recursive tasks that allow attention to language detail, requiring readers and writers to chunk, realign, or recombine ideas. Once readers and writers grasp the overall subject matter, they can focus on the micro or bottom-up processing in the context of the whole message. In consequence, from the standpoint of cognitive processing it is a mismatch to equate receptive skills (listening and reading) with productive ones (speaking and writing). Reading correlated with writing fosters learners' focal attention and cognitive interest on a text or situation as an accessible, reviewable language source. Thus even the very earliest writing tasks can be based on readings, with the focus on cognitive rather than linguistic demands. Equally important for departments who set speaking skills as a major goal for their students, writing practice based on FL texts can ease the transition to speaking, which requires a firmer, more automatic sense of shared frameworks than might be necessary in writing.

To illustrate: beginners working with authentic materials (i.e., texts written by native speakers for audiences in the FL culture) could be asked to reduce complex ideas from a reading text, listening passage, or video and restate them into more controlled, fundamental linguistic units. Cognitively and linguistically, this task affords them practice in managing their literacy skills and negotiating between reading/writing and speaking. Imagine the following sentences read out loud:

> A recent research report indicates that forests throughout the world are being subjected to a variety of ecological changes brought about by pollution problems. Apparently, all kinds of trees are vulnerable to this destructive trend.

Recapitulating these sentences directly—moving from listening into speaking—would be difficult even for native speakers. Yet combining reading (in class) and writing exercises (as homework) in this way, the learners need to produce only redundant propositions—to restate what has already been comprehended, in a variety of simpler ways:

> "Trees are dying all over the world"
> "Ecological problems kill trees"
> "Pollution kills all kinds of trees."[1]

Such restatements simplify a text's complex surface structures while using its vocabulary to formulate simpler topic-and-comment sentences. In a subsequent class, learners can compare their versions of the same idea, to pool their comprehension and acknowledge their differences—a speaking task based on reading comprehension confirmed by written simplification, all focused on message and accurate usage alike. Such comparisons practice short-term memory.

The assignment written outside class, in contrast, brings long-term memory into play. Classrooms with access to media programs such as *Blackboard* or *WebCT* (or any classroom-management software) can add an intermediate step between the initial oral use of the FL and the final writing monitored for form, content, and social factors (audience, register).

A classroom oriented toward communication will join these perspectives from the very first, so that surface language is learned as part of message systems. Remembering and reworking familiar messages ease the cognitive load of adult FL learners as they use ideas from their L1 culture to bridge lapses or weaknesses in their L2 language abilities, enhancing their automatic processing of text ideas. Such assignments can also help personalize a student's thinking about the text.

If, for example, a reader knows something about a former surgeon general's views on smoking, even a fairly sophisticated text discussing them can be used to practice reading or listening on the topic. A reader who understands the words "By the year 2000 the former surgeon general wants Americans . . ." can generally complete the thought "to quit smoking," "to stop using cigarettes," or "to give up their addiction to nicotine." When used in conjunction with recursive tasks (i.e., repeated viewing, recognition, and restatement of textual language), films and video can serve similar functions, bringing a content knowledge into the FL context. In such cases, learners can integrate subject matter and the language knowledge they have from various sources; they can then integrate micro- and macrolevels of knowledge, short- and long-term memory demands.

Adults not only have cognitive advantages but also possess sophistication and background about genres and the contexts of their reading. Most are aware, for example, that .edu or .org represents a Web site for an institutional rather than a commercial entity. Consequently, they more readily learn parallel labels or alternative conventions when accessing sites in France, Spain, or Germany. When students read to learn about new information and ideas from a foreign culture, they will do so in the light of their knowledge of those ideas in their own experience. Relatively skilled in recording information and expressing a point of view in English, these learners' capacity for recognizing speaker or writer intents is also well established. On a cognitive level, the practice of learning foreign languages initially by reading for information and writing to record that information dovetails with a broader, holistic educational practice, particularly at the college level. Comprehension is a fundamental anchor for production, and adult knowledge facilitates comprehension.

Linking content and language production can also improve a learner's grammar. Traditionally, teachers argued that writing accurate sentences was the first step toward writing accurate paragraphs, an assertion that seems to contradict the procedure just described that stresses learner focus on content. In ESL analyses, however, written performance in a controlled situation (prescribed usage with specified variables) and free writing do not always reveal corresponding performance advances. Emphasis on correct grammar use, in and of itself, seems to have at best an indirect relation to the ability to write grammatically. Intersentential writing, such as in compositions, seems to be of most benefit in fostering writing, since in such tasks language form and meaning are mutually informing of what a whole unit of discourse is intended to do. Choices are determined by discourse intent. Moreover, although students, particularly those studying a foreign language, often claim to need and use the thorough corrections many teachers conscientiously note, less may be more. Studies comparing correction styles conclude that "detailed feedback may be not worth the instructors' time and effort" (Robb, Ross, and Shortreed 91).

Learners, however, do need cognitively challenging reading and related writing tasks in order to link language and content. In many beginning textbooks, such reading texts and assignments are peripheral to the focus of the language lesson. Even worse, beginning textbooks often pose single point questions about texts (e.g., "What is the storyteller's age?") rather than ask students to look for and decide about language choices ("Which expressions indicate the age of the storyteller?"). When longer writing assignments are included, they remain closely bound to structural rules and sentence-level practice and thus isolate that writing from student engagement with complex ideas. Just as frequently, texts (oral, written, or viewed) are read for facts per se, not as the basis for learning about grammar choices as different modes of expression in different contexts. Worse still, reading passages rarely exceed five hundred words in first-year textbooks, even when they are authentic. Students have no practice in breaking down or chunking larger patterns into manageable units and are encouraged instead to read word for word.

Such limits probably inhibit activation of learners' metacognitive strategies in foreign language reading, since short texts are processed differently than texts of over five hundred words (Kintsch and van Dijk). Researchers point out that long-term memory functions are activated when the reader must synthesize larger quantities of information. Short texts prompt a different reading style and apparently influence language retention in a way quite different from the way a text of more than a thousand words influences retention. Shorter texts can also be more difficult to read, since they lack redundant features and clear breaks in structure, such as elaborations or shifts in topic focus.

To return to an earlier example, learners reading about the surgeon general's views on smoking will be more likely to understand and recall at least some of the text if that text discusses five opinions in relative depth in a longer passage than if one opinion is summarized in a brief paragraph or two. When the subject matter of such texts is accessible to students and the tasks related to these materials are constructed so that language choice (including correctness) is seen as integral to the texts' cultural messages, beginning students begin to acquire multiple literacies.

REMAPPING ARTICULATION BETWEEN
DIFFERENT FL LEARNING LEVELS

Not only must multiple literacies be taught and assessed across program levels, the goal of those literacies must also correlate with institutional missions, with group expectations about learner achievement, and with rewards.

Consider a typical first-year learner's task: learning the words for clothing and the pronoun patterns appropriate for designating who owns or wears those clothes. Irrespective of the language, many clothing items will simply be replicated across cultures (e.g., shoes and shirts as generic categories), and some items, such as blue jeans or T-shirts, will even be named by cognates. Yet early on, culture-specific patterns begin to emerge. Huaraches are not sandals; loafers are not dress shoes or wing tips. The differences exist not only in content but also in the syntactic context in which such words occur. In Spanish, pronoun usage will change not only according to gender and number, as in English (his, hers, theirs), but also with respect to formal or informal speech. In German, the same principles apply, with the additional complication of three gender categories (masculine, feminine, and neuter) and four case categories. Knowing that vocabulary thus includes certain kinds of grammatical and cultural knowledge, even in the first-year classroom.

By the intermediate level, often the second year of college instruction, many such general language categories are roughly in place, even if not completely automatic or grasped with complete accuracy by the learner. Learners can now focus on integrating cultural information conveyed in more complex language with existing communicative resources, and they can do so in a variety of contexts (social, grammatical, content). That complexity is necessary, because a language proficiency leading to literacy requires learners to manage cultural contexts as well as forms. Social situations and content areas often emerge as more central to correct usage than grammar norms alone. Students begin to recognize that language choices reflect social differences when, for example, someone is described at a formal event wearing pants (generic), chinos, or jeans (or the equivalents). Such distinctions are, in addition, important differences in content, since various disciplines within the foreign culture will refer to many items from different, fairly predictable perspectives: the salesperson's reference to pants will differ from that of the restaurant maître d'hôtel who is maintaining a dress code—one will praise the pants to persuade a buyer, the other will criticize the pants as inappropriate to the occasion. Again, language textbooks for beginning and intermediate levels rarely, if ever, work systematically toward this kind of sophistication; they neither add cognitive complexity nor reintroduce older materials and topics for increasing degrees of linguistic or cultural complexity.

Since foreign language learners in the United States do not have the kind of intensive exposure to the language in its cultural context, they cannot reasonably be expected to attain full control of the language after only a few years of high school and postsecondary study. Hence departments must establish standards for outcomes that reflect not mastery but attainable, reasonable degrees of control. They must outline levels for learner progress in various dimensions. Grammatically, that outline must specify which structures and functions learners will have under full control, which under partial control, and which only under conceptual control (as recognition). Similar decisions need to be made for content. Learners who intend to apprentice abroad in clothing design will require full control of the nuances of clothing words, partial control of day-to-day language, and conceptual control of business letters (for comprehension, since secretaries, not necessarily designers, write them).

Other goals may be set for a given program or course sequence, such as the inclusion of particular content areas (e.g., preparing for junior year abroad) or genres that suit particular learners' career objectives. Such considerations may lead a department to concentrate on language comprehension initially, postponing extensive oral practice. In that case, oral production can be initiated by reintroducing a reading or video excerpt taken up earlier for comprehension only. Reintroducing content and assessing learner progress in making such reiterations will encourage students to recognize and ultimately produce different speech acts using familiar vocabulary and concepts.

For example, warm-up exercises can use pictures of familiar items in different frameworks yet in ways that require learners to manage the new frameworks with old language and content materials. Describing such objects may be turned into a dialogue that enacts their purchase. At a later phase in the class, those descriptions may appear in a short quiz or an assignment for a formal oral presentation (e.g., recommending the place shown in a picture as one desirable for a vacation); next they may be used in a composition whose genre helps specify different communicative intents— a letter to a friend, a travel postcard, an advertisement, or something more formal, like a petition to ban a product or save a park or historic building. To be able to shift contexts in this way and to produce such extended forms, learners may need as models lists of discourse markers, a short text on the topic, or an outline of content for their production. Such repetition is critical in extending basic language use into different cultural contexts, an extension that learners experience as increases in cognitive demands placed on them.

The initial years of language instruction thus move FL learners from narrowly monologic language production (such as descriptions and the expression of opinions), into dialogues and other strategic forms of discourse (petitions, recommendations, reviews). To achieve negotiation skills in a FL, learners must move from language centered around themselves and their world toward more content- and interaction-oriented engagements with that language and toward the context of the FL world as well. A series of assignments that move from comprehension to production along this pattern in several dimensions might rework text materials over two class days. In such a sequence learners first identify a related set of ideas and vocabulary from readings, listening, or their prior experience in and outside the class. Then, using that language, they produce simple descriptions and opinions and, with the introduction of specific expressive genres or interactive scenarios, move to more structured comparisons, recommendations, and the like. Whether the progression occurs in speaking or writing depends on the learning framework that the individual program wants to uphold (Doughty and Williams).

Such practices can be found in an increasing number of programs with a focus on text or content (see Krueger and Ryan; in particular Baker). For instance, Georgetown University's German department has implemented assessment for each level of its text-based program. Those tests are designed to evaluate student performance in terms of that program's expectations for learning language through content. Eastern Michigan University's programs in language and international business and Minnesota's work in the social sciences have performance and assessment features in common with the University of Utah's classic Immersion/Multiliteracy Program (Sternfeld), where beginning students read authentic materials, have short prereading discussions, and are assessed with the use of subject matter rather than formal-linguistic quizzes—another example of a small but growing number of programs that use performance-based instead of normative tests.

To build on such policies in lower-division programs, articulation between learning levels demands that FL programs establish the outcomes for the advanced learner, a category subsumed under the concept "upper division." In most institutions, that level lies on the far side of a divide that the majority of language learners choose not to cross. For students with a language background in interactive communication such as we have described, some curricular practices for advanced course work can prove frustrating. For example, the convention of tracks inherently works against holistic learning, because language courses become separated from content courses as parallel but not necessarily equal curricular entities. Another "apples and oranges" problem for many advanced learners is the way reading material changes in different sections of the curriculum. Some upper-division language courses (among them the familiar conversation-and-composition or stylistics courses) use popular- or mass-culture texts (newspapers, films), while literature courses stress reading high-culture texts, often in a lecture rather than an interactive format. Literature courses in particular often shift from shorter, annotated texts to reading much longer works (or other high-register or high-status texts, including specialist material in various subjects) whose content and concepts have not been introduced to students in previous classes. The point here is simply that the expanded, holistic curriculum we advocate, in which content and discourse remain mutually informing at all levels of teaching and learning, needs a richer, more coherent curricular and pedagogical configuration (Davis).

Literary or other high-register texts assume pride of place in upper-division classes not because of cultural elitism but because they represent more complex, more sophisticated, and more carefully targeted examples of a culture's habits of mind and expression. Needless to say, the upper division will draw more extensively than the lower division on authentic texts for listening, video viewing, or reading. Yet those texts cannot be exploited for language learning or for their literary-cultural value alone. They are used to create building blocks to help students cope with multiple literacies: systems of social behavior and knowledge that reveal culture-specific functions.

Multiple Literacies to Bridge Cultural Gaps

In the holistic curriculum, the multiple literacies that upper-division courses offer the advanced learner are not just building blocks to be managed but also a set of gaps that competent, literate speakers are able to negotiate with reasonable success. To be literate in a foreign language, learners need to see the patterns of messages within cultural contexts of communication, textuality, and negotiation, to manage them and their implications in various situations. That is, they need to see how these building blocks interlock in the target culture—how situations refer to one another across time, space, and user groups.

As an example, most cultures have marriage rituals, but the specific significance of a ritual may diverge radically from one culture to the next. The learner is confronted with a classical intertextual situation, where the text of an FL marriage does not match up with that from the home culture.

Research confirms the difficulties readers have in bridging these gaps. Margaret Steffensen and her colleagues did a now-classic study over two decades ago with Americans and English-speaking readers from India who lived in the United States (Steffensen, Joag-Dev, and Anderson). Both groups read two letters that described weddings, one occurring in India and one in the United States. Although the two texts were in English, each group's recall was consistently higher when the wedding remembered originated in its own culture, its C1.

Those differences in recall were also qualitative. Both Indians and Americans understood, for example, that the bride wore something borrowed and that the bride's parents failed to exchange gifts with the family of the groom. But these features, tagged by American readers as positive or neutral, were viewed by readers from India as signs of poverty and hence regrettable. What for American readers was a typical way to celebrate the occasion, following conventions that did not include the exchange of gifts between parents, was read quite differently by members of a culture for whom the bride's affluence, demonstrated in her family's ability to give lavish gifts, predicts her chances for future happiness.

This case may not at first seem generalizable. Both passages were fairly short letters (about 700 words). One would presume that after reading additional texts about American wedding practices, the Indian readers would find their earlier inferences, which were based on a single reading of a single text, inadequate or inappropriate. However, subsequent research on FL reading suggests that students resist correction of first impressions, that initial misapprehensions about textual features can become entrenched misreadings across intertextual and intercultural maps. Elizabeth Bernhardt illustrates how a reader who initially mistakes the German cognate *Rat* ("advice") for the German word *Ratte* ("rat") entirely misses the point of a story describing a child's view of devastation following an air raid ("Model").

Apparently, without prior orientation to key vocabulary, FL students' faulty cultural schemata can result in their maintaining a flawed reading despite subsequent textual cues to the contrary. To be learned from effectively, then, texts need to be read as cultural artifacts and explicitly treated as systems within a FL context so that they may forestall misapprehensions that derive from a reader's native culture. Learning to transpose the meaning of a text into another culture is an act unto itself. Misreadings and faulty inferences, which superficially appear to occur on the basis of a language deficiency, reflect cultural blind spots instead. Not only must FL learners identify differences between texts in individual customs or languages; they must also learn to overcome their strong horizon of expectations for culturally based phenomena, attitudes, and perceptions. To overcome these gaps and develop broader, more flexible conceptual contexts, they must engage in multiple literacies about texts.

This engagement is a demanding task. For one thing, categorical thinking about Americans, Italians, Scandinavians, Chinese, or Latinos can easily obscure the cultural multiplicity within each society. Such obfuscation would reduce phenomena to unconnected events, turning the text of a culture's interactions back into isolated points of information. The "something borrowed" difference between the two weddings points to larger patterns of variance between the two cultures: the status of the bride in each society determines what is implied by the isolated facts of borrowing or not borrowing, wearing something old or something new. Cultural stereotypes are constructed, not truths, and the learner needs to negotiate both generalizations and more specific and informed instances of cultural patterns. As a further example, a stereotypical postcard image of a *mercado* in a Central or South American city square may provide enough information for a learner to comprehend incidents taking place there, in a site of commerce. But in such general form, the postcard *mercado* is little more than a template for a physical organization and a few basic facts (buying and selling food). Only when students begin to see how the *mercado* also functions as a sophisticated text of social behaviors and attitudes (e.g., about money, status, or authority) within a town can its significance be read. When the stereotype of a general outdoor market appears in an authentic text as a reflection of more nuanced cultural values, now as a specific type of marketplace, then students can move toward active negotiation with the foreign culture—they can learn to collect and de-code the data in the text, as the stereotypical template of "market" becomes a stage for a particular cultural performance and negotiation.

A stereotyped assertion like "French families drink wine" is minimally meaningful in itself. But it can become meaningful as a kind of cultural lit-eracy when students read about how particular groups define and evaluate drinking behaviors, including getting drunk. In America, where children consume only nonalcoholic beverages at the dinner table, drinking alco-holic beverages away from home often signals bonding with a (male-stereotype) peer group. In France, drinking is embedded in family ritual and other well-circumscribed and well-conventionalized settings, and so it is less likely to be refigured as a kind of exotic, liberating bonding behavior for groups outside the family. Accordingly, inebriate behavior is a social blun-der in France, a faux pas rather than a sign of purported manliness. In this fashion the cultural generalization "wine drinking" assumes appropriate so-cial meanings only when imbibing alcohol is linked to a more nuanced con-sensus about valued or discredited behaviors within specific cultures. The bottom line: even familiar cultural behaviors have different implications in different social relationships. Even in France, whether to tag drunkenness as manly or a social embarrassment may depend on the company one keeps (working-class vs. white-collar). Distinctions in cultural typing change with history and locale as well—the texts of the behaviors within the larger cul-ture may vary also and often do.

Another case where overgeneralization can hinder a learner's negotiat-ing the gaps between two cultures' systematic knowledge involves Ger-many's public transportation system. As a fact in isolation, the system's en-viable performance—German trains run on time—is trivia or a lifeless cliché. However, when that knowledge is linked to demographic changes or personal stories, FL students can begin to think about how the presence or absence of public transportation radically alters individual and family life. They can then consider costs of private against public transportation in so-cial as well as fiscal terms—how, for example, Germany's public transporta-tion network provides senior citizens with mobility and independence un-available to their counterparts in the United States.

Upper-division classes should enable responsible cultural readings of this sort for learners to grow past the basic literacy of language into vari-ous literacies of social practice and texts. These classes should promote a discernment of patterns within more complex cultural performances and texts: their narrative point of view, structure, content, and context (macro-systems within the culture). These texts (performed, spoken, behaved, written) all have known patterns of sentence- and paragraph-level discourse markers and forms of coherence and cohesion at all levels of the system of language, from vocabulary and grammar to genre-based characteristics. For students to be able to transfer their own perception of cultural invariants (e.g., needs for survival, group identification, marking and exercise of dominance) across a gap into new cultural situations, they must read texts in ways that reveal how those functions are variously created and enacted in different times and places (see Geertz for classic formulations of this phenomenon). Learners need practice in decoding and encoding such textual information about behaviors, attitudes, and values.

The particular challenge in designing courses for advanced FL learners is, therefore, to encourage them to recover patterns out of texts by, for example, ascertaining what behaviors appear in a novel, story, or film and how those behaviors are judged by others in the work—that is to say, judged in their respective cultural contexts. That students will initially identify a movie's noble heroine according to their own value scale is probably unavoidable. But to attain a more appropriate interpretation and, by extension, a flexible cultural literacy, they must learn to identify the patterns of, say, noble features represented in the film, not as they themselves would represent those features. Which characters in the movie are noble, who finds them noble, and how are the patterns of nobility different for a North American viewer? The interpretation process is less that of a correct reading than the ability to negotiate cultural gaps, accessing real-life situations through careful comparisons. What, in turn, the learners are to retain from those negotiations will depend on the curricular goals set by the department. If an upper-division class is focused on learning cultural patterns, a checklist can help students structure their reading as they collect data about, for example, rituals or play activities (drawing on Geertz or other sociological or anthropological typologies). Other goals may be more language-driven or reflect other aspects of competency about culture, information, or cross-cultural literacy.

The chart in figure 2.2 is an example of such a content-based exercise in data collection, based on a book (or one of several movies) whose plot and characters are relatively familiar: Jane Austen's *Pride and Prejudice*. Offering a

FIGURE 2.2. Abstract Social Typologies and Their Instantiated Tokens
in *Pride and Prejudice*

Social Function Valued in the Era	Specific Manifestation
Pleasure and enjoyment	Dinners, card playing, balls, conversation, being invited, being admired
Pain and suffering	Lack of parties, loss of social status
Social rituals	Men decide, women complain and manipulate; breeding reveals real class
Governance (who's in charge); class structures	People of noble birth, wealth and leisure, good breeding
Manners, etiquette	Breeding, enforced by legitimacy of title and bloodline
Sustenance-survival needs	Provided by others, presupposes independent wealth

well-known cameo portrait of English landed gentry at the turn of the nineteenth century, the novel provides a picture of a culture foreign to us in
time and locale. Leaving aside the question of language, students can easily
correlate data in this chart, which matches abstract constructs about social
performance to their textual instantiations, types to tokens, thereby uncovering the variant and invariant social functions in that culture. If students
use text information to document cultural systems in this way, they can
substantiate their assertions with quotations drawn from the text and thus
enter the language and cultural space of that other world as they learn to
label behaviors appropriately.

Students will need to identify, for example, that only after Mr. Bennet
visits Mr. Bingley is it proper for Mr. Bennet's five daughters to be introduced to that eligible young man. Men decide who will meet whom. Im-
plicitly, Mrs. Bennet's ceaseless complaints prompt the visit; Mr. Bennet
acts to please his insistent, nagging wife. Later in the novel, the motive behind Mr. Bennet's fateful decision to let Lydia visit Brighton is expressly
stated when he tells Elizabeth "We'll have no peace . . . if Lydia does not go
to Brighton" (246). Thus, consistently, although men decide, their decisions
are not unilateral; women have input. If the man in question is weak or

indifferent, that input will be decisive. The patriarchal social order governs, but women may dominate through manipulation.

By completing an integrative task such as this one, students are forced into learning systems rather than individual items. A set of who-does-what observations points toward an overarching interpretation of male-female behavior. If *Pride and Prejudice* were no more than light entertainment, an inventory would suffice. Popular literature, after all, reaffirms a particular cultural myth—pretty women get their man, hard work pays off, breeding tells. But in the category of texts that are more challenging (to which *Pride and Prejudice* certainly belongs), cultural changes, conflicts, and shifts are signaled. Individual deviations in behavior assume significance as indices for social change. Precisely Mr. Darcy and Miss Elizabeth Bennet's ability to see alternatives to the status quo suggests where larger public or cultural consensus in that society may be in a state of flux, where what is stated in the text may not reflect the society's real values. At that point, the work opens itself to history (literary and otherwise): Was the story of Mr. Darcy and Miss Bennet popular at the time, and did it seem popular? Why or why not? As stereotypes interact, one can read a culture negotiating its values, as a text represents and comments on norms of behavior and deviances from it.

Here, extremely high-order social knowledge emerges from a careful reading for details, details creating a sensitivity to, knowledge about, and literacy in another culture's behaviors and values. The marriage between Elizabeth and Darcy is potentially transgressive, since she is a woman of lesser estate (with an aunt and uncle from the merchant class). But how the story negotiates this match makes it clear that Darcy's nobility will triumph as a social principle, not as just an empty form. In his judgment, Elizabeth's propriety and ability (her "liveliness of mind" [403]) ennoble her. Darcy's behavior and his society's attitudes point the way for a Disraeli and eventual knighthood for a host of England's public-schooled entrepreneurs—a statement that nobility is behavior and disposition as much as it is an inherited birthright.

The concern for propriety as the hallmark for social acceptability remains a prominent theme in English culture to this day, furnishing versions from Oscar Wilde to John le Carré, from *Chariots of Fire* to *Monty Python*. This trope continues into the televised *Upstairs, Downstairs*, where, since Lady Bellamy is a duke's daughter, she and Lord Bellamy are a social mismatch. His political skills, however, overcome their social disparity, and the two forge a union acknowledged in England's most exalted circles.

This approach to reading as a key to systems of cultural knowledge—to defining a cultural outcome for a third- or fourth-year course—asks students to think about difference and even learn to negotiate it. It also requires beginning and intermediate levels of a curriculum to give learners exposure to representations of the FL culture, especially to the popular literature, which has more in common with their own culture than does elite literature, which trades in nuances. A student who understands how a Harlequin Romance book works will be much better prepared to deal with Mr. Darcy and Elizabeth, because popular romances establish the expectations of readers (star-crossed lovers; poor or otherwise disadvantaged girl and rich, seemingly unattainable man). With their grasp of the romance-novel schema, Harlequin readers are poised to discover what nuances and variants Austen introduces to the genre (e.g., humor and wit count more than money and position).

Such approaches to the various texts of culture facilitate learners' comprehension of cultural patterns because they demand macrolevel understanding, an attention to systems. But they do so with disciplined attentiveness to texts. Just how that attentiveness can be acquired and taught is discussed in chapters 4 and 5, with exercises based on a text matrix and the précis. For now, it suffices to say that any advanced-level or upper-division program requires some version of this kind of learning: either one uses popular texts to chart the road toward more challenging texts or one picks texts in order to practice how to recognize patterns in their actions, events, and outcomes. When familiar with cultural networks, students have less difficulty identifying ruptures in a pattern that indicate a shift in the network as a whole. They have developed a set of tactics for analysis and in future work will be more sensitive to how different personality traits, actions, and appearances that violate or reflect norms of a social class, gender, or age of characters affect perceptions and outcomes in narratives from different times and places (see Iser, *Act*). They will be working toward managing the multiliteracies inherent in their own and FL cultures.

Applications of Literary Theory to Foster Multiple Literacies

Other categories besides the social-anthropological question of proper behavior can be used to direct cultural meanings; among these categories are various kinds of cultural and literary theory, each of which searches in its own way to describe the production, representation, and reception of meaning in cultural contexts. Theory, broadly conceived, also enables students to address systematically the questions of how and why artifacts of culture can be understood, questions that do not need to be isolated from the learning of language. The models of understanding outlined in theory, therefore, may be used as guides to structuring learning in other ways—as regional ontologies (Husserl's term [663]) that allow the mind to understand fields of data in various ways, as structures of mental representations that enable FL learners to move beyond the kind of fossilized stereotyping that Steffensen, Chritra Joag-Dev, and Richard Anderson spoke of in discussing reader responses to descriptions of two weddings, one in India and one in North America.

While a more expansive treatment for using literary theory as a tool for learning language and culture occurs in chapters 6 and 7, today's literary and cultural theories address four coexisting realms of cultural representation: language, discourse, behavior, and knowledge. In general, these theories cast the study of culture as the study of how images, sounds, words, and other signs are arranged to convey meaning and create social literacy in the form of rule-bound utterances, social performances, and products—as discourse in contexts. Learners study discourse to see how language functions as a set of cultural practices, negotiating power and social position, planning and building worldviews, and dealing with the codified and uncodified rules of social practice. Behaviors and other forms of nonverbal communication work as systems in culture in ways parallel to those of language and other sign systems, and thus they also constitute boundaries within which human beings all build their identities, often on the nonverbal level. Finally, systems of knowledge, as codified in traditions, institutions, and disciplines, constitute perhaps the most culture-specific configurations that affect language use and understandings of culture.

For language teachers of advanced FL courses, the challenge is to bring these realms of data into focus as patterns of cultural literacy, using various theories as the basis for coherent curricular praxis. Figure 2.3 is intended only to stimulate further thinking in how one might go about identifying underlying and pervasive patterns in the textual, visual, and spoken communication found in a given culture.

Figure 2.3. Domains and the Theorists Who Inform Them

Domains	Theorists, Works in a Curricular Progression
Knowledge	Barthes, *The Fashion System* Eco, *A Theory of Semiotics* Kristeva, "Stabat Mater"
Behavior	Foucault, *Discipline and Punish*, "What Is an Author?" Fanon, *Black Skin, White Masks* Lacan, "The Mirror Stage"
Language	Mukarovsky, "Standard Language and Poetic Language" Hjelmslev, *Principles of General Grammar*
Discourse	Bourdieu, *Language and Symbolic Power* Derrida, "Structure, Sign, and Play"

For example, in *Principles of General Grammar*, Louis Hjelmslev declares that no positioning of the speaking self exists outside the rules of language use and that no system of language exists outside that positioning. This model can constitute an ideal point of departure for language learning. While beginners learn to use pronouns with the correct cases, identifying whether the actors are enacting or receiving action (e.g., "I see you—you see me"), intermediate and advanced learners need to locate the patterns of language in more abstract contexts, in genres like extended conversations, interior monologues, sermons, political speeches, or works of poetry. Hjelmslev's model of a general grammar might require the learner to follow the position of the subject/I in an extended conversation. Two people discussing what they liked and disliked about a movie are in all probability going to express their selfhood overtly in a series of opinions whose grammatical options involve frequent use of modal auxiliary verbs ("he should have . . . I wanted to see . . .") and negation ("I did not like . . . she could not").

Alternatively, if one took Jan Mukarovksy's "Standard Language and Poetic Language" as a guide for conversational analysis, nonstandard uses of these pronouns would be taken as moments where a speaker's intent breaks down or a strategy shift occurs—as moments of linguistic innovation. In contrast, the analysis of a lyric poem or song and its lyrical I would lead to a study of self-representation and the experience that is staged by the utterance around it.

Any such discourse can be analyzed as part of cultural studies (Swaffar, "German Studies"). When the study of a nation's language becomes associated with cultural studies, the link between discourse and content becomes more straightforward: the advanced-level sequence focuses on cultural literacy, a process of learning register and discourse strategies that are both culture- and text-specific. Such courses are about how cultures evolve and influence one another and about the multiple domains of culture (e.g., Asian, African, American, or European ideas; history, philosophy, architecture, music, and art).

The challenge is to design tasks that guide learners in applying strategies that reflect, among others, reception theory, new-historicist analyses, reader-response theory, semiotics, and cultural sociology—tasks that foster the problem solving and creativity that can be defined as multiple literacies. Designing a course guided by theory involves more than choosing contents. Such a course must convey a cognitive style, revealing how disciplines produce knowledge out of individual bits of information and how they inform one another. In practicing not only a language but a discipline's pattern, students can practice two discourses, one from a discipline and one from its cultural context. Each frame uses particular structures, signs, and strategies for comprehension and communication (Derrida, "Structure").

Redefining advanced curricula in terms of theories or cultures brings with it specific linguistic challenges, as well as the cognitive-cultural and disciplinary ones on which we have focused. The multiple literacies involved in such an enterprise serve language-learning goals by affording repetition and elaboration of key concepts in different frameworks to enhance language acquisition at all levels. In a history course, for instance, learners can practice ascertaining what is different when reading two texts written from two different perspectives and for two different audiences and thus seeing what is said and what is not (and speculating why). An essay by a German historian and an interview with a NATO commander can both discuss the German army's participation in NATO, yet each uses different rhetorical strategies to establish the rapport sought with the intended audience, and each does so in a different disciplinary register (a historian and a general speak differently as professionals). To read either one, learners need to identify the phrases that tag each discipline and how the structure and focus of information, in and of itself, reveals the field's discourse goals (Bourdieu, *Language*).

A German instructor situated in a school with a strong fine arts program might construct a course on Freud's Vienna to offer information about city planning, art, history, the emergence of Freudian psychology, and its links to Austrian literature and theater. To be responsive to potential audiences in an institution with a strong architecture or public affairs college, that same instructor might design a course entitled City Space as Cultural Space, comparing Vienna and Berlin as great cities of central Europe and as planned cities. Such an approach would focus less on art and particular intellectual movements and more on public responses to the pressures of population growth and industrialization, thus appealing to students in urban studies, regional and city planners, and architects. The qualifications necessary to create either course would be anchored in the instructor's grasp of the German language and culture—and eventually in the student's mastery of language. A single context can, in such reframings, be the basis for tasks that force learners to negotiate multiple discourses and multiple ways of organizing simple to complex utterances. Yet ultimately these courses must expand to include interrelations of content, register, and discourse, to allow students to respect alterity, the otherness, of the text's cultural world.

As today's departmental configurations suggest, the studies of theory, culture, and literature are natural allies with language studies, since they share a common search for the production, representation, and reception of meaning. Theory, broadly conceived and applied, can enable a FL program to address systematically the question of how and why artifacts of culture can be understood. Theory sets the paradigms where individual scientific and humanist disciplines are conceived.

The Space for Literature in the Era of Popular Culture

Each theory pulls learners' focus to specific systems of meaning and to varying types of comprehension and production learning. Yet cultural theory also argues that literature, film or video, and other extended forms of narrative need to take pride of place in any program for advanced learners, to aid them in bridging gaps between two cultures that exist in all FL learning situations. We discuss in greater detail below how to integrate literature into the curriculum. At this juncture, however, we wish principally to argue that literature is central to the holistic learning environment. An extended text like a novel or period film provides a particularly useful simulation of culturally anchored affective, cognitive, and language systems. That simulation in turn speaks to an audience, within its L1 culture, at a certain time and with certain intentions.

Still, like other curricular goals, a successful reading of a literary text can be defined in various ways. For an audience of contemporaneous readers, the text's culture is presumably familiar, and so its context, discourse, and contents likely pose few difficulties in understanding. When the readers are further removed from the text—by cultural position, by time or geography, or by language—they will have greater difficulty in recovering the text's meaning successfully.

The initial statement in Kafka's "Metamorphosis" is paradigmatic: "Gregor Samsa awoke out of uneasy dreams in his bed one morning and found he had been transformed into a cockroach" ("Als Gregor Samsa eines Morgens aus unruhigen Träumen erwachte, fand er sich in seinem Bett zu einem ungeheueren Ungeziefer verwandelt" [56; trans. ours]). This sentence is incomprehensible if a reader does not know the language in which it is written, but it is almost equally so if that reader does not understand the whole premise of human-to-insect transformations as a kind of psychological or social metaphor. The first incomprehension is a problem with the language of a text; the second is a problem with patterns of metaphor and allusion available to the world of 1915—with the idea that a text can express a psychological state as a physical form. Other comprehension problems may arise in film adaptations of novels. Austen's *Emma* has been filmed several times, each time for a different audience.[2] Readers-turned-viewers of these various films are in a situation parallel to that of L2 readers: to understand what an adaptation means, they must evolve systems of comparison among the texts on paper and on the screen. Works of literature and films are both culturally embedded texts requiring multiple literacies in their readers or viewers and, from them, extended work with systems of information and signification.

The first, simplest level of text comprehension is based largely on familiar systems, such as anthropology. Where lower-division learners reading or viewing sections of an extended text might be able to identify and comment in general terms about characters and their lives, upper-division learners moving toward cultural literacies have to pay more attention to extended systems and their enactments in contexts to make anthropological sense of a world apart from their own. They may, for example, be asked to assemble patterns of actions or speech that make individuals see others as irritating or desirable. This task focuses their attention on how characters in *Emma* express their likes and dislikes instead of on the learners' own opinions. The task opens up new connections between language and social structure, since such an inquiry is not complete until readers know what each character says in appropriate language and also who each character is. If learners repeat this exercise for various film versions of one novel, they will be practicing listening comprehension in particularly intensive ways that point to additional social knowledge about manners—that politeness is also a question of posture, inflection, and volume, not just of word choice. Readings of the novel or film will treat the work as representative of culture: figures from another historical era behave in ways that may or may not differ from ours.

A learner's approach to a text, in addition to being informed by such social-anthropological references, can be specified by a certain branch of theory, such as feminism or Marxism. Two versions of a story can be compared along the axes of representations of female disempowerment or empowerment or class biases. Such comparison represents the kind of synthetic learning appropriate for the upper division, stressing systematic cultural knowledge as well as extended language performance.

This example is in English, but parallel sequences can be evolved using the FL, as we demonstrate in the next chapter. The examples that the FL learners collect may be shorter, depending on their learning level and commensurately restricted language, but learning proceeds in the same way. Learners will practice speaking in the voices of the various characters before they begin to collate larger patterns. If not yet able to compare a book and a movie in an essay, even relative beginners can write contrasting sentences on the basis of carefully targeted bits of information. For instance, they can list which likes and dislikes confer prestige on a speaker in *Emma's* social milieu and which tend to lessen that person's position (the elements critical to a semiotic reading of actions and the responses to those actions). When students re-create the hypochondria of Emma's father ("He always thinks he's sick") or the arrogance of Pastor Elton and his wife ("They think they are better"), they learn to appreciate nuances of character and intention in the Austen novel while they are enriching their language resources. This act of reading therefore expands their language register; their reading will be a success when they can retell the story in recognizable terms at their language level, respecting the anthropological difference of Jane Austen's world from their own.

Learners can choose to read, and teachers can use to evaluate their success in reading, texts that provide many different patterns of literacy. Students can look for patterns of ideas and values in order to compare them with their own, culturally familiar schemata—not just read examples of sociolects (socially discrete conventions of speech and writing) out of a text. If they work with a film based on a novel, they might profitably make connections between the eras of these two versions of a story, or they might view two film versions from different eras and made for different audiences. Acknowledging the differences between their own site and that of the texts, they could then bridge the historical distance between the two by drawing parallels to fill in their gaps of knowledge and vocabulary. They might identify the protagonists in *Clueless* who parallel figures in *Emma* but then distinguish the 1990s language and behavior in the film from those of the novel. These two versions of the story come from two different cultures (current teenage middle America and pre-Victorian England). Their different norms of expression reflect different value systems as well as different kinds of language use.

When students read a historically and culturally distant text like Kafka's "Metamorphosis" with its bug protagonist, they confront many of the same problems, albeit with heightened language difficulties since readers lack visual reinforcement. Yet they can overcome that distance by making other content connections between the situation in the story and their own lives—the frustrations of living with parental restrictions, for example, or a teenager's anxiety about peer acceptance ("feeling like a worm"). In either case, two versions of a story separated in time, space, or language help students build vital bridges between how the text presents concepts or information (as a pattern based in culture, not as information bits) and how readers recognize patterns of culture for their own purposes. By connecting the familiar and the new, a fundamental strategy of reader-response theory in Wolfgang Iser's phenomenological approach (*Act of Reading*), learners make the text's contexts and integrity the primary norms against which to gauge their success in reading. To succeed, they must recognize that stories like "Metamorphosis," *Emma*, and *Clueless* play in worlds with very highly developed, albeit differing, social patterns. That is, they must both realize and be able to articulate that the daily experience of any culture has a distinct structure and a system of appropriate or inappropriate behaviors. They must learn to read the systematic otherness of worlds with different languages or simply different times and places.

Readers pursuing such comparisons will not read a text like *Emma* only as a filter for understanding the relations between cultural practices and perspectives of early-nineteenth-century England (an extreme version of an L2 culture). Instead, *Emma* is now conceived of as a message based on typical patterns within a cultural context, patterns that need to be compared systematically with the reader's context, requiring explicit bridges between the two. To fulfill the objectives for a reading task formulated in this way, readers must be cognitively mature enough to grasp two distinct language and cultural contexts simultaneously—to construct a logical comparison between two cultures on the basis of content, linguistic form, or other variable. A functional bicultural perspective must evaluate each culture on its own terms.

Necessarily, bicultural perspectives involve having learners participate in two cultures by joining schematic knowledge and language production. Learners look at how speech and behavior in texts are marked by a combination of distinctive key rhetorical features, specific genre conventions, and personal intent. Those readers may also move beyond re-creating the cultural and linguistic patterns of a text as it speaks in its own context and apply them in their own lives, integrating them into their own contexts.

Such tasks exemplify how readers at the upper-division level can use a literary text to become empowered in two different language contexts, learn how to negotiate many factors in language and cultural knowledge simultaneously, and hence prepare themselves to be independent readers. The outcome of such encounters and negotiations may not be the full language competence of the native speaker or the full knowledge of another time and place, but it does offer learners multiple encounters with the systems of culture, their own and that of the FL. Even when students seek only a limited competence in an FL, such as in a course for language for a special purpose, they must see how a doctor, lawyer, or businessperson is represented in contemporary films, how documentaries speak about artists and musicians. The material studied will differ from that in a generalist or humanities-based course, but to develop strategies for bridging gaps in their ability to use a foreign language appropriately in its cultural context, such students still need the fuller exposure to how cognitive, language, and cultural knowledge interact.

BEYOND THE FL MAJOR

The examples offered here are representative only of the kinds of tasks appropriate to a holistic undergraduate curriculum for majors and nonmajors alike. We present them to show the rethinking necessary to redefine language learning within a more comprehensive humanities context, to suggest the quality of comprehension and production that is desirable and possible for adult learners at various levels in an FL program. Later we make more specific recommendations for particular types of programs within different institutional contexts. We also address specific differences between lower- and upper-division undergraduate levels.

NOTES

1. These are student writing samples based on the initial statement of a newspaper article from *Die Frankfurter Allgemeine Zeitung*, entitled "Jeder fünfte Baum geschädigt." In the original German their comments read, "Bäume sterben überall auf der Welt. Ökologische Probleme töten Baume [sic] fast überall. Umweltschmutz tötet alle [sic] Art Bäume." These statements were the result of an assignment asking students to reduce the information in the initial paragraph of the article to its essential topic and comment.
2. *Emma* was chosen as an L1 example familiar to most readers from recent film and video versions (most notable are three versions: dir. Douglas McGrath in 1996, with Gwyneth Paltrow; another 1996 version, starring Kate Beckinsale [A&E Network]; and a 1972 BBC miniseries [dir. John Glenister]) as well as from the rewritten and updated version represented in the popular teenage film *Clueless* (dir. Amy Heckerling, 1995).

The Holistic Curriculum: Anchoring Acquisition

Chapter 3 | in Reading

Designing a holistic curriculum requires structured decision making on the part of a program. This chapter moves through the levels of a typical undergraduate curriculum for both majors and nonmajors and argues how reading of texts (and, by extension, viewing films or videos) can be factored into staged learning. We discuss in greater detail how to select and sequence texts within a curriculum in terms of their readability and how to create assignments that fill specific goals within a holistic approach to FL learning.

SPECIFYING READABILITY

Selecting readable texts is the first stage critical to ensuring that study in the FL leads to the desired outcomes in language and cultural learning. But what makes a text readable? Two conventional answers have been a limited quantity of material (a certain number of words familiar at any level, texts not over a certain length) and conformity to student interest. Those answers are insufficient in a holistic curriculum, because the readability of a text is only partially due to its language materials. Consistency in point of view; coherence; text layout on a page (including the use of subsections); the use of diagrams, maps, charts, or other illustrations also make the text more accessible as a system of information, not just as a system of language. From the reader's standpoint, interest, familiarity with the topic or with the context of the text, prior knowledge and ability to activate a schema that helps organize incoming information and fix it in memory all make a text more readable. Physicists read physics texts more easily than others do, no matter in what language.

A more readable text usually

- is more redundant or longer, having more than one point at which readers can access it (including illustrations, titles, restatements, and the like)
- is organized around concrete situations or references rather than around abstract principles (unless the abstract principles have exact equivalents in L1 topics familiar to the students)
- identifies the unfamiliar—obscure, alien, or taboo activities, situations, and responses—with reference to the familiar, again in order to facilitate the readers' connections and comparisons (what is concrete and familiar to one reader may be abstract to another who has not experienced it)
- deals with topics of interest or familiar to intended readers (so that it allows for communication and expressions from within their frame of reference)
- fits reader demographics (e.g., is age-appropriate) according to the norms of both the L1 and FL cultures

As factors for selecting texts, these criteria have interlocking influences that should be weighed against one another in terms of student populations and program needs. They can be weighed along the following lines.

Length and Readability

A long text, if it has enough redundancy, can be more comprehensible than a short one, especially if the short one is conceptually inappropriate for a class that has mastered its language complexity. Advertisements, for example, are often linguistically simple but culturally-cognitively too complex to be intelligible to an outsider. Similarly, learners often need cultural knowledge to understand the message of a parable. For this reason, readability commences with a teacher's assessment of the student population; it hinges on the match of a text's presentation of material with that population, with the joining of two cultural communities. Longer texts with more clues to content—cognates, logical connectors, restatements, sentences of varying length, a fuller argument, a broader scale of information—are often easier to read than shorter ones, even if the details of syntax are unknown formally. To be sure, to overcome syntactic limitations, readers will have to be keyed into the topic to actualize what they know, but then the reward will be greater.

Short texts, particularly those from popular newspapers or magazines, often combine several topics into single paragraphs, because they know their readers are familiar with them, and so the texts can jump around through various topics. They become unreadable to groups who do not know those topics or who have not been following the discussion. If too many topics are summarized in too short a space, brevity can create an unbridgeable gap; the deciphering depends on embedded clues instead of general knowledge or reading acuity. A short text with short sentences can be completely unreadable to a novice reader who does not understand its cognitive coherence or its cultural reference. Directions for playing cricket make no sense unless readers know that cricket involves some features of baseball (and thus is not a board game or a card game). In contrast, directions for baseball written in Spanish can be easily deciphered by the most elementary class that already knows the rules of the game: there will be cognates or patterns that key what sentences are about for such readers.

Degrees of Concreteness or Abstractness and Readability

Texts also differ in how their content is presented: a text that has concrete examples or that speaks about specific persons, places, and things is usually much easier than a text organized around abstractions—especially for first-year students, who may not yet have reached full adult cognitive abilities. If a text is organized around abstractions—"Five Problems for Today's Environment" or "Avoiding Bankruptcy"—there is no necessary connection among its parts: a list of avoidance strategies has no narrative continuity, no transition from one to another.

To figure out such texts, readers must burrow deeply into their content or rhetorical organization. Also, readers are not immediately set up in a concrete context, in a known place and time, with known characters. Who or what is "bankruptcy" and for whom? Where is today's environment, everywhere or just in one's backyard? What is the authorial intent? Who is the intended audience? When and where (in what time frames) is the issue relevant—is it about today or the future, in a foreign country or the United States? Such specifics are often implicit, abstract, in texts written for specialist audiences. It may help if a text has many cognates, but the main issue remains: Do the students know about environmental issues or what bankruptcy is, in more than general terms?

A text that starts with a story, then moves to the abstracts, is much more appropriate for beginners. A text that talks about concrete situations or that is framed concretely (with a distinct who, what, where, and when) is generally easier to understand than one that refers to abstractions or frames its issues in an unspecified time and place and with unspecified actors—for example, a philosophical, emotional, opinion-based, ethical, or other theoretical debate with no indication of who is on which side or of where and when the debate occurs. Concrete references to context make understanding a text easier.

The Learner and Readability

The concreteness criterion is not in itself determining, because readers' familiarity or unfamiliarity with the text topic also affects readability. As in the baseball-cricket example above, a reader who does not know about baseball will not be likely to learn about it from an FL text. Even the most concrete text will be incomprehensible if the topic is unknown. Similarly, suitability plays a determining role: texts that are age-appropriate or gender-appropriate, for example, are more likely to be easily comprehensible to their readership—if only for motivational reasons. Moreover, the definition of a category like "age-appropriate" may be as important as a reader's language competence, because appropriate texts help readers engage in activities and communities.

Conjoined with considerations about length and concreteness or abstraction is the fact that texts chosen for instructional purposes need to reflect the demographics and social mix of the class. Are the learners older or younger (socially, physically)? Is the student body predominantly male or female, preprofessional or pre-art or performance-oriented (what do students plan or want to do after they graduate)? Are they familiar with high culture or with popular culture? Are there particular community values served or countered by the text?

Tasks and Readability

Yet the factors discussed above, in and of themselves, need not eliminate a given reading selection. While age, gender, educational background, educational goals, regional variation, and other social variables (e.g., a department's student demographics) all affect how readable texts are, deficiencies in reader background or text format can be offset with prereading activities that set the stage. Adding a parallel text in the L1 or adding a bit of history to reinforce context sometimes renders readable texts that might remain obscure to a particular group of readers.

There is scarcely a right or wrong text for a particular learning level, but there are definitely right or wrong tasks applied to a text. A common practice has elementary-level students discuss personal ads or short texts about different types of celebrities, such as those in *People Magazine, Time,* or *Newsweek*. Most often, such texts are used to review personal attributes. Yet a simple twist on the task makes the text appropriate for more advanced students or for elementary-level students being moved toward a greater degree of cultural literacy: comparing celebrity articles in the foreign language with those they know from their L1, as evidence of the celebrity game, yet played out with global cultural nuances. When students consider the lifestyles of the rich and famous across national lines, they are opening up a cultural-cognitive space that requires them to move beyond description to comparing ideas—a task that is linguistically and culturally more complex. All countries have celebrities, but what can make or damage a celebrity varies: British actors move to Monaco for the tax shelter and are lambasted in the British press, while American actors living abroad do not face such attacks by American journalists.

Pointing even beginning learners toward this complexity in cultural attitudes has an additional positive result: it allows sequencing different tasks for the same text. The first-semester class can focus on the more concrete task of remembering how to describe individuals, while the second-semester class can reread the same text to move beyond that level of language command toward comparing cultural references or to identifying what is familiar and unfamiliar about such international texts. For example, paying taxes is seen in some countries as patriotic and contributing to the national good (Scandinavia), while in others it is seen as an infringement on individual rights and opportunities (USA). To understand the existence of and basis for such difference is part of understanding an FL culture.

At times, providing clues to a limited number (usually about five) key nouns or verbs will overcome learner difficulty in identifying cultural references, as such clues signal unexpected shifts of topic or solidify a reading hypothesis about the content. When students are oriented to the major who, what, where, and when of the text, they will be able to hypothesize more effectively. A familiar parallel to an unfamiliar historical incident orients readers to content or context. For example, a picture can direct a reader into an unfamiliar cultural venue (What is the difference between a café and a coffeehouse?). In other cases, warnings about differences in tone and cultural value may set the stage by helping readers avoid misreadings that stem from cultural expectations (e.g., journalistic practices in two different countries can vary widely because of legal systems and social traditions).

Introductory tasks might orient readers by addressing questions of typography or visual language. If students are to learn to read in a way that eventually fosters joining an FL community on any level, they must read not only the written foreign language but also the visual language of its culture. To the discerning eye, that visual language is often as foreign as the verbal language, and it can be read for its own characteristics. When a reader realizes that a fairly consistent pattern of difference exists between the visual languages of two cultures, then that pattern can lead to inferences about cultural difference as well.

German and French books, for example, tend to have fewer graphics and larger blocks of text in their layout and typography. Their graphics will also tend to be more technical (and often more technically detailed) and less colorful. Web sites seem to be slowly developing such distinctive national "dialects." Often, comparing and connecting such texts can reveal culture-specific patterns of communication. If novice readers lack a point of view (e.g., a clear cultural or grammatical goal) from which to approach predominantly print texts, their working memory may be overtaxed. Graphics, however, speak for themselves only if readers can encode them. For example, readers must understand how to read charts or maps in general before they approach charts and maps from other cultures and other eras. Similarly, pictures can add points of view—specific cultural references—that must be understood as their own systems of meaning. Thus paintings from an era will help readers comprehend texts from that era.

In a real sense, every reader is a novice reader of texts on some topics: most readers lack cultural background, key information, or certain kinds of language knowledge in one area or another. Moreover, the customary aids to learning, word lists or glosses, often do not exist for particular classes of texts—or those glosses may not match the needs of that reader. In the worst case, a traditional gloss on a text tempts novice readers to translate rather than read, making the process of reading laborious (because it slows them down, while creating the impression that the linear sequence of words is the only way to understand a text's sentences). Rendering a text readable in the ways suggested above rather than through reliance on dictionaries and glosses creates a cognitive support system for the learner and, consequently, encourages reading for messages, not just translating word for word.

Another way to render a FL text more readable is to have it preceded by an L1 text on a similar topic. That prior reading experience will not only help overcome a reader's language difficulties, it will also lead the reader to make comparisons and connections with another culture more easily. The L1 text can orient the reader to a text's topic and point of view more effectively (more pleasurably, more in tune with cultural comparisons) than can other kinds of language aids (e.g., dictionaries), because it focuses the reader's attention on appropriate connections of language and cultural elements, on culturally similar or dissimilar patterns between the two texts.

It makes pedagogical sense that when a language program deliberates about the wisdom of using a particular text at a particular point in its learning sequence, the readability of that text should be judged not on the text's own terms but according to the environment of support (facilitating tasks) needed to make the text readable. For example:

If a text does not have a clear point of view (e.g., as a weather report does), can it be given one easily?

If a text relies on simple language but contains complex concepts, can those concepts be introduced in compressed form (e.g., in a list of 3–5 important dates of events in World War II) or through an illustration (e.g., a painting)?

If a text relies on familiar (if complex) concepts but uses difficult language, can one introduce those concepts through other readings or media (e.g., a parallel text presentation in English or a graphic version of the same topic) instead of having students rely on extensive dictionary use or glossing?

If a text has an illustration, does that illustration enhance the text or add
little to it? Is there a better illustration (chart, etc.) that could
substitute for the original or be added to it? Do students possess
strategies for unlocking the message systems of those illustrations?

These are the ancillary materials needed and the considerations that
should be made when a department undertakes text selection for a holistic
program.

DESIGNING LEARNING OUTCOMES TO INTEGRATE TEXTS AND LANGUAGE PRACTICE

Once texts are chosen, graded, and put into a learning sequence to achieve
overall objectives, questions arise about how to spiral students' abilities to
work with the materials, how to develop sequences that scaffold materials
and strategies, propping up students' abilities so that students can move to
more complex tasks and outcomes. Most languages have well-evolved pedagogies for teaching their linguistic forms. What must be added in the framework of a holistic curriculum is a strand of assignments that help integrate
comprehension (reading, viewing) into the curriculum at the earliest possible stages, especially as part of language production practice and of cultural
learning. Most of these tasks are familiar to FL instructors. What is less well
known is how to go about linking them or how to structure their recurrence,
since a task introduced at length at the elementary level of instruction to
identify messages (a recognition or comprehension task) can profitably recur
as a warm-up or as a preview for later tasks in the learning sequence that express the implications of those messages (production tasks).

To begin the planning process, one should select tools pointing to text
and task types that help students achieve both comprehension and production goals set for them at particular levels. To illustrate this point, let us take
a hypothetical case study of how the specification of an audience and the
choice of outcomes lead to a structured curriculum. The venue is a liberal
arts college that has a two-year language requirement, with students scat-
tered across all the traditional majors.

In the first weeks of classes in a Western language, the students have
few if any language resources. They are following a standard grammar textbook and so have been practicing forms of the verbs "to be" and "to have"
and various adjectives describing people and things. But this curriculum

FIGURE 3.1. Goals at Holistic Level 1: First Five Weeks

What Is Asked	*What Students Do*	*Language Goals Achieved*
Students find ads for specific products in a given array (virtual or real) of magazines.	They start to recognize how verbal and nonverbal clues reinforce each other in the L2 culture. Their approach to text styles also begins.	Linking known L2 vocabulary to concepts; establishing passive recognition of cognates
Students write an ad text in the L2, describing the product, using words they know.	They practice sentences with familiar items. Known language resources are tied to new contexts.	Reiterating limited, familiar materials in new contexts; increasing interest; tying words to culturally appropriate visualizations
Students read around in text of ad for cognates, compounds, words they can recognize.	They practice recognition problems in known texts.	Comparing; getting used to how the L2 uses the page
Students describe how they (or people in their family) use the product.	They shift focus or address. They may use change of case. Creativity with limited language material is encouraged.	Opening the question of cultural demographics and age and considering the speech and behavior appropriate to them
Students engage in modified read-alouds: for example, they order another person to use the product in a certain way, or they decide if that way is a good use for the product.	They gain the ability to lexate (use words). They get oral comprehension practice. They learn how to interrupt or get information.	Enforcing community standards for pronunciation, etc., as part of an act of communication

also includes authentic texts, because having students bring in advertisements is appropriate to start their cultural learning as well. Figure 3.1 illustrates what kind of cognitive demands might easily be added to the linguistic demands familiar from those first five weeks (demands that can be met by specific exercise types, as discussed below). These tasks correlate with easily designed short class activities or assignments, and they rely on the fact that the FL shares a typeface with the L1. This chart begins to outline a curriculum that integrates social-anthropological learning into the more traditional language-learning framework.

For elementary instruction at virtually any institution, texts need to be selected to echo the kinds of language found in the basic textbook (if one is used); but they should have greater density and explicitly address the native speaker in the FL culture. Such supplementary readings constitute first steps in approaching the foreign culture through its language and the foreign language through one's own sense of culture. Students who only partially comprehend the language of texts written or spoken in the foreign language can begin to look at genre structures and other main indices of meaning; the tasks that ask them to do so also develop their abilities to make these connections outside the classroom.

Once the learner has a certain amount of language under control, so that simple sentences come more naturally, the topics in supplementary texts can be revisited in more sophisticated ways. By the end of the first semester, more-coherent or -extended tasks become possible as curricular goals. These tasks capitalize on the earlier comprehension and extend initial learning by taking the additional materials as the basis for more nuanced comprehension and expanding written work and speaking. Possible learning goals for the end of the first semester may be outlined as in figure 3.2. The general comprehension tasks suggested above set higher goals for the learner with respect to communication, cultural knowledge, and logic than do the ones set for the earlier level.

After a semester, learners are expected to interact with the text directly and to understand it in something more like its own voice (instead of simply appropriating parts of it for their use, as the earlier tasks require). At the same time, these simple acts of comparison and acquisition of cultural knowledge are carefully isolated, so that learners are called on to exercise focused, limited language competence. Nonetheless, the focused language will lead to culturally sophisticated acts of comprehension and communication, so that students with less familiarity with the L2 can use their greater intellectual maturity and cognitive resources to engage with the FL cultural contexts. The kinds of tasks that might first be introduced using advertisements can be replicated with all kinds of genres: short interviews, film clips, sections of novels, or short stories (discussed in the next chapter). Negotiating between the difficult language that learners read or hear and the simpler language that they can produce is critical—a fundamental task in literacy at all levels that points toward intermediate levels of language-learning proficiency.

FIGURE 3.2. Goals at Holistic Level 1: End of First Semester

What Is Asked	What Students Do	Language Goals Achieved
Students compare short L1 and FL genres, or they compare FL genres written for different countries.	They increase their ability to decode and speak of what practices are implied by these products and their marketing.	Cultural sensitivity: becoming aware of verbal and nonverbal cues used in different cultures or for various demographic groups; developing a sense of register and appropriate language use
Students relate various opinions about typical people, products, or events supplied by the teacher or collected from source materials. They identify who said what, where, when, to whom.	They are enabled to identify the most probable speaker on the basis of a description, then create sentences justifying their choice.	Practice in identifying age- and situation-appropriate language; practice in expressing difficult concepts (justifications) in simple language
Students get an FL text in which a familiar person, product, or event figures prominently (e.g., a movie review, a page from a mail-order catalog, an encyclopedia entry). They scan first paragraphs for language to serve a particular task: to identify what is good or bad about the text or to recommend it.	They reframe information in an article. They work on creative reuse of known language.	Making logical connections— recognizing how different speech acts relate to given language material; practicing flexibility in reusing known language and applying it to new contexts
Students read further in the text to build up patterns specified: multiple terms for "who, what, where, when" or other specified reading goals.	They build up patterns in ways appropriate to the L2, not to the L1.	Differentiating what is the same or different across cultures—using content and language as keys to cultural differences
Students read texts for idioms, then go back to ads: which visual ads reflect the point of view of the text. They write ads or diary entries for the text's readers.	They adapt language to specific target audiences. Short texts recycle known language, transfer language from a text into another context.	Communication: building up sense of what speech communities exist in the L2 culture or of what might be differences between the L1 and L2 cultures

By the time most FL students are in the second year, or whatever counts as intermediate in the curriculum under development, they have been presented with the fundamental language resources needed for rudimentary comprehensibility: the basic grammar and the vocabulary that anchors nascent language use in the FL. But except in very special circumstances, the intermediate curriculum in most institutions must work consciously toward the integration of more complicated textual materials as well as toward more extended and better-controlled language production. If written texts in genres close to everyday speech and contents (like diaries) are used in elementary instruction, the next step is to ask students to read a contemporary story or view a contemporary film—something that illustrates everyday life in the FL culture in greater detail and that presents everyday life contents in context.

Let us assume, for instance, that the students have been assigned a contemporary short story about an FL student trying to survive the first days at a small liberal arts college in the United States. The comprehension goals in this situation lead more directly to structured production outputs, since the learners have certain language resources at their command, as shown in figure 3.3. These tasks move most explicitly toward requiring age-appropriate production of language and cultural behaviors that grow out of reading activities. They build on the earlier reading goals, in terms of language and cultural knowledge, but require engagement in a larger variety of tasks of self-expression (different ways of speaking and writing) and more conscious control of cultural context and knowledge. To be sure, the upper division needs to go still further (as is discussed in the next two chapters), especially in moving learners' language production toward formal registers. Such progress will require decisions about learning outcomes. Beyond this, one must underscore that exercises alone do not suffice; they must be supported by consistent checks on learner progress.

Figures 3.1, 3.2, and 3.3 summarize initial steps for any course design in known curricular frameworks. It is crucial for course designers to be able to identify which learning aims need to be realized across their program levels and how to do so. For example, an assignment that tells learners to skim an article, comparing titles and subtitles with illustrations, gets learners to activate their background knowledge. But in a holistic curriculum, the evaluation of success will be different: student outcomes must be weighted in terms of the specific knowledge they convey, not just for language correctness. In consequence, a statement that identifies several new phrases or vocabulary items in proper relation will be worth more than a grammatically

FIGURE 3.3. Goals at Intermediate Holistic Levels

What Is Asked	*What Students Do*	*Language Goals Achieved*
Students scan the first paragraphs to identify what characterizes the foreign student's world—what the foreign student notices, wants, misses.	For a homework assignment, they write a coherent description of the school or of the student's letter home.	Practice in coherent discourse and in how to acquire vocabulary and syntax from context; practice in informal writing
Students collect phrases that represent the world of the foreign student before and after entering school.	Small groups work together to decide what problems the foreign student might have (they develop a hypothesis).	Informal communication—because students work together: cognitive synthesis of text language with ideas
One episode is reread as the basis for a debate: Was it a good or bad idea for the foreign student to go to that school?	They establish contrasts between the two worlds—one group recommending one world over the other. This discussion is followed by an essay on the topic	Evolved sense of sociolect and social structure in established culture; strategic management of debate (formal communication)
Students reread an episode as the basis for an essay comparing that college to the one the foreign student came from.	They write a formal essay on the theme: they gain practice in writing contrasts, in arguing a point of view.	Intercultural knowledge, comparing L1 and L2 cultures
Groups playact what being in the dorm at that college would be like, using the text as a springboard for a new episode.	They gain practice in register, in age- and gender-appropriate discourse.	Practice in informal communication; integrating details from everyday life using the L2

correct simple sentence based on cognates. Similarly, if the purpose of an exercise is communication—picking out words from the context of a dense text and using them—then credit must be given for use of grammatical elements from the text, even if in sentence fragments, as long as the answer is comprehensible. If a task requires learners to identify synonyms or cognate words out of a text, then the task can be assessed for correctness of content or according to grammar accuracy.

Such assessment choices/requirements also indirectly raise questions about what classroom praxes should be:

What is the role of the L1 in the classroom? of the FL?
When should language accuracy be a chief concern in outcome
    assessment? What other factors should be assessed?
What can students do with texts that are too difficult for them to
    translate?

These questions can be answered first and foremost by reference to the learning goals set for the curriculum. But the answers, like program goals for any particular institution, change with learning levels.

Spiraling the proficiencies represented in any language-learning sequence (revisiting earlier materials, yet each time at a higher level of performance demands and learner command) requires teachers to be aware of their students' developmental and social needs as well as of the goals set for the kind of holistic language learning at play here. At the same time, they must be aware that cognitive, social, and language skills require practice and refinement at all levels; that cognitive skills lead to ever more complex production; and that, as tasks recur across the curriculum, the performance of them may need to be assessed differently.

ITERATING LEARNING GOALS INTO CURRICULAR TASKS: FROM COMPREHENSION TO PRODUCTION

The examples above speak to the earliest introduction of authentic texts into a holistic FL program as a complementary activity for acquiring grammar knowledge and a supplement to overt grammar learning. We do not believe that holistic language learning is possible without such early introduction of reading or viewing tasks (books or films), since cognitively challenging materials speak to the background and thinking capabilities of adult learners.

Yet to enable students with deficiencies in the foreign language to engage productively with these texts, the cognitive demands we have just outlined need to be addressed in a classroom pedagogy. The most effective sequence of learning, the research has long argued, proceeds from comprehension to production. In general, this sequence recommends an approach to cultural texts that leads learners from reading and listening into various forms of production. Each of the five stages we suggest introduces different activities that move learners from comprehension to creative language production. Especially in early and intermediate language instruction (but the approach is not limited to that), learners must be led through the following phases:

1. Prereading, to anchor the themes or topics of the text in students' conceptual framework
2. Initial reading in a text for 5-10 words that anchor its global ideas
3. Rereading to identify and reproduce textual messages gleaned in initial reading
4. Rereading to express messages that the reader has appropriated from textual information
5. Rereading to create discourses that express an independent viewpoint vis-à-vis textual perspectives and that negotiate among communities

Each phase deserves independent note, since adherence to this checklist allows a classroom to realize the learning goals outlined above, starting with reading comprehension and culminating in communicative, potentially interactive language production.

1. Prereading for Topic Orientation

Prereading, as initial exposure to text concepts and genre, sets the stage for reading by helping learners connect the known to the unknown. By comparing ideas or language usages in the L1 and the FL, learners will be introduced to new concepts, vocabulary, pronunciation, or morphosyntax in the text to be read; will contrast their social practices and attitudes with alternative ones; and will integrate an understanding of the FL culture into their own identities. The less prepared (or younger) the learners are in the FL, the more necessary it is that they engage in prereading rather than reading, so that their cognitive load is lowered.

Prereading activities should never be synthetic (asking for new knowledge). They should ask learners to speculate analytically about patterns of information rather than draw conclusions, for instance. They should ask for minimal-pair discrimination (does this item belong to category x or y? true or false?) to locate members of a category; to parse, connect, or identify stages in a linear way; or to ask about genre and general setting. Such exercises move from the concrete to the abstract, from the general horizon of expectation to the particularities of this text. Most important, a prereading introduction consists of creating a framework of expectation of general and prior knowledge that will guide the readers' first work with the text.

Some prereading activities may even include the introduction of a limited number of new words—especially for an unfamiliar set of who, what, when, and where words. The caveat in using word lists, however, is that extensive new vocabulary lists may be counterproductive. More than about seven or eight new words produce an overload for most students. Ultimately more words are remembered if students are confronted with a smaller number of them. But even if the number is appropriate (5–10), teachers must remember that lists foster reliance on lists instead of on a learning-to-learn praxis in contexts that reflect real reading. Extensive glossing seems to yield only a short-term benefit. It may make students more comfortable initially, but it is not clear that any long-term advantages accrue from it.

2. Initial Reading for Orientation to the Topic Focus in a Text

Initial reading leads learners to orient themselves in the text. In most cases, that first orientation consists in locating the global or macro-issues: Who or what is the text about, and where and when does the action take place? Those facts usually are found in the initial paragraphs or sequences. Titles and pictures (and sound track, if the text is a film) generally provide at least one or two of the five or six concept words that will unlock the text in an initial reading. The goal of initial reading is to help students learn to identify the ballpark in which the text plays out and to orient them to the information systems that it will build.

Newer approaches to reading take initial reading as a classroom activity. It can also be set up as a homework assignment, as a carefully built series of tasks to be completed before any extensive reading or viewing is undertaken. The caveat here is that the traditional skimming and scanning activities often advocated in textbooks are not helpful in themselves unless learners know what they are looking for. For FL readers to avoid cognitive overload, they must understand the framework of what they are about to do: seeking differences among people, the boundaries of episodes, or the main setting and objects the text depicts. Only when initial reading is conducted to aid the learners in establishing a mental map will they have a better chance to reduce their uncertainties and make better use of their prior knowledge and experience—to apply their prereading orientation to the text systems.

Initial reading thus functions best when learners approach a limited amount of the text, armed with a focused task, such as identifying in the first paragraphs the who, what, where, and when of the text; figuring out the relation of the illustration to the text; or, in a longer reading, discovering where episodes change or when speakers or narrators alternate. Initial exposure to the text, after all, is just that—the first attempt to get an overview of how the passage presents information. Hence the teacher might want to choose one of two options: (1) have the learners read an initial paragraph or two (or view an opening scene of a movie) for language that introduces the information that will be read in the passage as a whole; (2) scan somewhat more extensive passages to assess the text's rhetorical construction. Initial reading should ask learners only for what can be done relatively quickly (in less than five minutes) in class, to confirm and expand on the horizon of expectation first hinted at in the prereading.

What makes any initial reading task effective, however, depends on the text's particular difficulty. If the selection is longer or complex, then identifying its segments (its speakers, episodes, time frames, changes in locale, and the like) is important. Some of these segments may even be marked with nonlinguistic features such as quotation marks (or their absence), visual differences in blocks of text (dialogue versus commentary or descriptions), scene changes (in a play), and speaker designations. Often, identifying the text's genre, in and of itself, sets up expectations of a sequence of events (e.g., a mystery novel and romance novel have different focuses).

Yet not all texts have such prominent rhetorical differences. Some may more profitably be approached through shifts in topic rather than in rhetoric. Ultimately, the initial reading should be designed to help learners get *something* out of a text, so that the reading task becomes feasible. When chunking passages (dividing them into groups either in terms of rhetorical organization or for concepts), learners are establishing a crude but crucial road map of the entire text, a sketch that they will fill in as they reread for additional comprehension. The initial reading, therefore, sets up the text systems that will be followed in subsequent stages.

3. Rereading to Identify and Reproduce Textual Messages

The next stage in the sequence from comprehension to production is rereading to elaborate, modify, and augment ideas. In this stage, often considered the only reading activity by instructors who follow a more traditional, language-driven curriculum, readers attempt to retrieve textual messages in order to reconstruct them in their own language, not just to comprehend them. At this level, tasks must link content to language choice. In chapter 5, we elaborate on the content matrices and précis that we have already exemplified (fig. 2.2), a task format that we believe is optimal in this situation.

The beginning FL learner will most likely conceptualize the text in the L1, so it is critical that ideas be linked to the specific FL used in the text; the link fosters a kind of comprehension that is more than recognition and recall (Kern, "Role"). To encourage conceptualizing and expressing concepts in the foreign language, both in class and out of class with independent reading, the readers' main activity is building up sequences of text information to prepare for production in various L2 forms. That is, prereading, initial reading, and reading to identify and reproduce textual messages must be extended into production tasks.

4. Rereading to Express Textual Messages

Tasks identifying and reproducing textual messages ease the learner's transition to forms of rereading for expressing textual messages, that is, to acts where sequences of text information are built up and reshaped into a student's own expression of a text's message. Such tasks ideally require learners to return to the text to increase their language and content resources and to engage more fully with the target culture.

If, for instance, a learner is reading a play, then the story can be reworked linguistically by retelling it as prose; or by interpolating new scenes; or by writing postcards, letters, or diary entries in the voice or name of one of the characters. Note, however, that this production phase focuses on shorter discourses: paragraphs, short interchanges, retellings, and summaries. Those rewritings must also be thoroughly connected to the FL culture—preferably, to examples of the language production in that language, so that the literacy of the culture the learners are re-creating is one that natives would identify as possible.

Learners using reading materials in these ways will not only have learned to engage in short exchanges, they will also have gained a measurable degree of flexibility in their command of language and content. As tasks require them to reread and to adapt textual language (e.g., writing personal letters, short book or movie reviews, diary entries, or informational oral presentations), learners will practice not only comprehension but also production, in written as well as spoken expression. The language choices they learn to make in managing the content of the texts must reflect the different audience for each type of writing or role or play change; each choice is a different speech act.

For example, the content and tone of a personal letter depend on the person addressed in that letter: a grandmother, a child, a close friend, a wife or husband. A book review can be written for specialists or the popular public. While many cultures share those forms, they differ nonetheless in the treatment of them, aspects that intermediate and advanced learners particularly will need to negotiate.

5. Rereading to Create Longer Discourses

Such work in shifting between genres need not stop with short exchanges. It foreshadows rereading to create longer discourses, the later phases of learning from texts, the moves beyond comprehension and simple verbal exchanges to longer language production, in the same or related genres, where students do more than play with the language of a sample selection. Within the flexible boundaries of those genres, students can introduce new ideas and intentionalities.

The personal address of a letter will contrast with the confessional address to oneself in a diary entry. An expository speech will not be argued using the contrast logic and rhetorical markers of a debate. The third-person summary of a book report will foreground representative details that the reviewer finds positive or negative about a work, whereas an informational presentation will present a neutral summary of the main ideas (the informational talk may well be biased, but it must not sound that way!). Such genres are used in the various speech communities of a language culture, and sensitivity to their provenances is encouraged as the learner advances.

MOVING TO EXPLICIT CURRICULAR DESIGN

The holistic approach to FL learning aims to move a learner from comprehension to production of an increasingly more complex and sophisticated
set of language uses. Basing that move on a selection of texts is especially
necessary between intermediate and advanced levels. Comprehending or
creating a longer spoken text, for example, involves more than length; it requires students to understand in new dimensions. Students who base their
language learning and production on a variety of texts that reflect the FL
culture also move toward creative, analytic, or expository writing, the
rhetorical abilities needed to assume and hold a position in communication. The goals set for each level in a program's sequence must be designed
to provide practice in comprehending and producing language reflecting
the kinds of control a student must exercise over the language, content, and
communicative situation. The goals should also reflect the values of the
program—specifying what outcomes students will be evaluated for—and
some version of the multiple literacies valued by the FL culture.

Literacy requires such practice in all the dimensions of language control, including the ability to work in specific cultural contexts and to exercise appropriate speech acts. The key to success in all longer production is
the ability to move from a seemingly neutral summarizer of content to one
who takes an unambiguous position vis-à-vis the text and the text's culture. The case we have made here for anchoring a holistic curriculum in
reading thus sets certain requirements into place for curriculum-design
projects:

that all curricula be based on readable texts of various genres
that readability be defined according to a curriculum's goals and the
    programs' learners
that those goals be defined in terms of cultural comprehension as well as
    linguistic forms, and
that texts be carefully sequenced in a curriculum and pedagogically staged
    in a series of cognitive steps that make it possible for learners to profit
    from complexity rather than drown in it

We next describe how a content matrix, the précis, serves to elaborate
curriculum goals into learning stages based on texts and reading. We illustrate how a matrix exercise can be used to enable discovery learning and
equip FL students with the tools to become strong readers with multiple

literacies, readers who can identify patterns of information in a text and discuss their implications in the context of a foreign culture as well as their own. Because of the centrality and complexity of these issues, we have divided our treatment into two chapters: chapter 4 discusses the application of the précis for beginners and intermediate learners; chapter 5 addresses the advanced learner.

A Template for Beginning and Intermediate Learner Tasks: The Text Matrix for Staging Genre Reading

Chapter 4

To the FL program whose goal is to enable students to move toward comprehension and culturally appropriate production of extended language in creative ways, literature offers texts that are particularly well suited to foster the kinds of multiple literacies that education needs and today values. Whether serving as a focus for a program or as a culturally significant complement to content approaches, literary genres and texts related to them (reviews, interviews, Web pages, critical essays, and film versions of literary works) can function as a springboard for a holistic curriculum.

Developing this curriculum is not necessarily simple. Many departments are caught between traditional and new missions in their institutions, between old images of high-culture literacy and newer visions of education relevant to the here and how. Unfortunately, all too often, programs accomplish their transition from the first to the second of these two value systems by simply excising literature from many courses as too difficult or as irrelevant for the average student—or they maintain literature in ways that do not necessarily serve students' learning. That is, they respond to pressures about what to teach instead of setting new goals and rethinking how to teach the texts, contents, and contexts they have decided are central.

This chapter makes the case for reading as the key to cultural and language literacies and thus to new curricular sequences. Using the reading of a short literary work, it demonstrates how a challenging text can be incorporated advantageously from the earliest phases of foreign language instruction as an ideal model for both comprehension and production activities. Our focus here is the beginning and intermediate learner; our pedagogical approach is the précis.

THE CASE FOR LITERATURE

Increasingly, FL acquisition research suggests that literature is the necessary textual environment for creating strong readers, readers who have the cognitive strategies and linguistic resources to comprehend and interpret a work as well as an aesthetic object as a complicated act of communication within a culture. That literature (and not other kinds of texts) seems too difficult to teach in today's FL classroom may be evidence of not so much a language barrier as a practice common in first language reading. In many English classes, students are inadvertently trained to read for details in bottom-up fashion in a class that shares a literacy; thus, inadvertently or not, this approach privileges model readings, often teacher interpretations or generalized student reactions, instead of teaching the principles of independent reading and evolving interpretation. Few teachers educate their students to apply top-down processes that yield original, grounded interpretations—and literacies—rather than to recall facts and decontextualized opinions.

For students who lack advanced language proficiency and extensive FL background knowledge, however, the strategies for interpretive, top-down processing of texts prove particularly helpful, as we have noted above and argued elsewhere (Swaffar, Arens, and Byrnes 115–16). Teaching top-down strategies for global processing of textual detail can help FL readers compensate for insufficient language mastery by prompting them to apply the organizing tools found in leading literary theories. But teaching students to apply such tools involves approaches that are very different from those needed to interpret. That distinction has not been adequately addressed in research, but classroom experience supports the claim that using theory and teaching others to use it call for different pedagogical strategies.

Precisely because literary theory is the mainstay of a great deal of graduate study and subsequent publication for those in the field of literary and cultural studies, our discipline has assumed that teachers know how to teach students to use theory to read independently, as a path to various literacies. But often what is taught is only the teacher's application of a theory in the context of an expert reader producing a finished interpretation, not the operational theory, the theory turned into a tool for the learner, or a reading strategy (Marshall, Smagorinsky, and Smith). This lack appears not only in English and cultural studies. Foreign language teachers generally present literature in similar and similarly inadequate ways: they fail to help students learn how to identify and systematize textual data in meaningful patterns, and they focus on product—"correct" interpretations—rather than on process, not teaching the strategies learners need if they are to bridge their lack of expertise and generate readings of their own. Not surprisingly, that situation has particularly negative consequences for students in the FL classroom.

Even when FL students are articulate enough to react to texts and discuss their emotional impact, they are rarely taught how to develop and express stronger, more organized perceptions about what a text says—to become literate about a text and not simply opinionated. Text-based reading addresses this lack by structuring classes to avoid misreading and by teaching students to attend to one pattern of textual messages at a time instead of falling into gaps of knowledge and culture. Their background knowledge can inform those messages, but it should contribute to a detailed interpretation only after they examine what the text actually states and how it organizes that statement—for instance, as a chronological narrative, causal argument, problem and solution, contrast or comparison, description.

A pedagogical imperative in creating such a curricular sequence is to remember that cognitive overload occurs when the learner fails to grasp the norms of communication embedded in a text's messages. Many students, whether in first or second languages, find the study of literature frustrating because of a gap in knowledge: the social and psychological references are unfamiliar to them. For this reason, prereading in a classroom (see ch. 3) is critical to prepare learners for subsequent stages and help them deploy their existing knowledge of contents and contexts, their literacies in the problems presented in a genre. When one is orchestrating an initial student-structured reading, theory can be a valuable organizer, since, virtually by definition, it encourages a top-down approach, setting up patterns of textual information that yield discrete systems of meaning. Theory can therefore serve in classrooms, for example, when it helps learners forestall misreadings by enabling them—almost compelling them—to recognize unfamiliar contexts and behaviors different from the ones their experience leads them to expect. In literary as in all other forms of reading, attention to textual patterns helps readers see how the presentation of events in a text can challenge their cultural assumptions.

This kind of literacy cannot be achieved passively. Comprehension is in its way as active as production. Cognitive scientists have proposed that reading is a process of reconstructing. Consequently, the approach to reading and language learning we have outlined to this point emerges as particularly useful for tying literary readings to goals of cultural literacy and to individual empowerment in expression. In the optimal situation, the teacher avoids telling students how to reconstruct the text, working instead to enable them to discern and understand its structures. The ultimate goal, in general and in the case of literary readings, is to turn readers into independent, articulate interpreters who can find macropatterns without help from an instructor.

Whatever pattern a reading starts with to point toward a goal (be the goal drawn from aesthetics, contemporary theory, or a contemporary issue), it is crucial to add only one element to what students already know. When a literary theory is used as an organizer helping learners reconstruct the text's macrostructure as a precursor to their own production, then that theory must be broken down according to the systems of information that it favors. A deductive and bottom-up teaching approach must accompany a top-down and interpretive one, if learners are to join the conversation as empowered speakers and writers. This process can be undertaken in the L1 or FL, from beginning stages on. The cognitive load problem can be managed in steps that build up literary and theory comprehension, just as they build language ability and cultural literacies of various sorts.[1]

The initial stages of that building up are exemplified by a first-semester Spanish class that reads as a literary work Enrique Anderson Imbert's short tale "La muerte" for language use and cultural sensitivity. It is an example of what the author styles as a miraculous story—an everyday, plausible, and familiar situation into which the fantastic intervenes. That link of everyday perceptions and a culture-specific fantasy allows a particularly fruitful meeting place between two cultures, which even beginning FL readers can uncover.

IDENTIFYING PATTERNS IN INITIAL READING

Initial reading activities can help learners negotiate moving from simple comprehension of content to a more careful look at the literary techniques of the story and to various production activities in which learners articulate, argue, and substantiate their readings. Teachers should plan curricula that include such texts in introductory instruction. Initially, the time commitment will seem substantial. The instructional sequence most successful in working with texts to open up multiple literacies requires about ten minutes of group activity to introduce it, with follow-up stages of homework and a class or small-group activity for fifteen to twenty minutes in at least two subsequent periods. From the first class activity on, the process insists on meaning making anchored in textual information and hence in the target language, first through verbal responses about what is understood, partially understood, or guessed at and then through structured observations about textual information in oral or written forms. When introducing these techniques in the first semester, the teacher may want to use English. After clarifying procedures and goals (one or two sessions), the switch to the foreign language should pose no problems.

Each of these activities can choose to stress more content comprehension (cultural literacy goals) or more formal grammar (language literacy goals). A teacher interested in formal literacy, for example, might ask learners to identify in the text and use features of grammar recently introduced, such as adjective endings or verb forms. In order to further the goal of cultural literacy, however, teachers will also want to integrate such an emphasis with the literary features of the story, such as its repetitive or striking language or its use of motifs from established literary traditions. Such activities combine teaching language with preparing students to undertake text-based, independent ("strong") readings at the upper-division level. Any prereading activity must therefore draw students toward the kind of expert readings set as goals by the program, not by telling those students what to think but how to build up, for example, what a critic might say about what makes a story fantastic. At the same time, an initial reading activity must implement the concepts schematized in a prereading discussion.

Several established classroom techniques serve well as initial reading strategies. A directed reading, directed thinking activity (DRDT) offers feedback in the classroom (Stauffer). This task interfaces well with other approaches to organizing student responses (e.g., the matrices we present in this chapter). Allowing teachers to provide structure for initial encounters with texts encourages learners to engage in strong reading, to identify what they do or do not know and what they misread or fail to grasp as a result. Since this activity involves mainly recognition and some reading aloud of words and phrases that students consider meaningful, it represents a nascent step in language production as well.

Designed to distinguish pure speculation from text-based inferences, directed reading asks students to express their thinking about how a text presents information, to confirm or disconfirm what has been said, and to make predictions about forthcoming information. A true exercise in reader response in the sense of Wolfgang Iser (*Act of Reading*), this pedagogical task has no right or wrong answers; it honors any attempt to draw meaning from the text that is based on any facet of textual language practice. If augmented by students' preexisting knowledge, directed reading allows readers to exercise agency, to verbalize their comprehension without anxiety about giving wrong answers, and to receive immediate feedback from peers or the instructor to confirm or disconfirm that thinking.

To implement directed reading, the teacher simply asks students to read the title, then the first paragraph or two, pausing after the title and each paragraph to give them time to make notes, consult with others, or respond immediately to what they think the segment says, substantiating their views by referring to language in the text. The teacher may also ask students to identify what genre they are reading or which stylistic or linguistic features strike them. On the basis of everyone's observations and the teacher's minimal comments when questions arise, students will then predict what the next paragraph says. Commonly, the class as a whole makes at least three or four predictions, but only one is confirmed and possibly modified after further reading.

The title of the story, "La muerte," elicits even from beginners responses such as "death," "dying," "murder," or possibly a misreading such as "corpse" (*muerto*), "pattern" or "sample" (*muestra*). Eliminating initial misreadings, a kind of scaffolding help offered by the teacher-expert, focuses learner attention in subsequent reading, an important step toward fostering a strong reader, since misreadings made at the outset have been shown to persist as interference factors when the reader progresses through a passage.

Once students identify that the title has several optional meanings around the idea of death or murder, they read the first paragraph together (most easily on a transparency or computer projection screen) to see whether it offers clues for choosing one definition over another and to see what additional ideas establish the setting or scenario for a particular definition. While reading from a book or photocopy is also effective, the focus on a screen provides immediate pinpointing of what students identify as important in the text. To exemplify, the first paragraph of "La muerte" and typical responses are given below:

> La automovilista (negro el vestido, negro el pelo, negros los ojos, pero con la cara tan pálida que a pesar del mediodía parecía que en su tez se hubiese dentenido un relámpago) la automovilista vio en el camino a una muchacha que hacía señas para que parara. Paró. (47)

> The driver (black her dress, black her hair, black her eyes, but with a face so pale that despite the noonday sun it looked as though it had been struck by lightning) saw on the road a young girl who was signaling her to stop. She stopped.[2]

As the class engages this task, the teacher monitors its progress, reminding learners to work with what they know rather than to worry about what is unfamiliar. Their first job, one conducted in the FL, is to identify language features that seem important.

Beginners, for example, will not recognize verb forms such as the past perfect subjunctive (*hubiese*) of the auxiliary "to have" (*haber*), the imperfect (*parecía*) of "to appear" (*parecer*), or the preterite form (*vio*) of "to see" (*ver*) but should have no trouble identifying the presence of a vehicle with a driver (*la automovilista*) and descriptors of the driver's appearance—black clothes, black hair, black eyes ("negro el vestido," "negro el pelo," "negros los ojos") or relatively common nouns such as *el camino* ("street" or "road") and *una muchacha*. Some may even know the verb *parar* ("to stop"). They probably will sense that the repetition and position of *negro* ("black") in the parenthetical phrase are an echoing ritual language, not characteristic of normal speech rhythm.

Research findings suggest such tasks prove efficacious for retention of language (Hulstijn). Student comments typical of those documented in think-alouds (research that asks students how they decide about text meanings while reading) often reveal that readers learn through puzzling out words in context (Hosenfeld). After noting such responses, teachers may want to elicit English-language speculation about the meaning of the terms identified. They can expect comments such as "an *automovilista* is a car or a driver, maybe a woman driver," "the driver is dressed in black," and "I think there's a girl on the road." With a record of assertions on a transparency or the blackboard, teachers can prompt other students to agree, disagree, or elaborate.

By helping the class pool its knowledge, these tasks offer the teacher several pedagogical advantages. First, it becomes evident what the class as a whole does and does not know; the teacher has feedback about students' language and cultural knowledge alike. Second, the teacher has focused attention on students' cognitive processing and hence maintains their interest in resolving remaining problems as they continue reading ("Read on to decide whether *la automovilista* is a vehicle or a driver"). Finally, by leading them from conjecture to confirmation of hypotheses, the teacher has modeled how an interpretation is constructed but without providing an interpretation.

This initial reading exercise has numerous possible follow-ups. Rather than continue to read to resolve problems or puzzling information, which means focusing on the plot, teachers may, depending on their pedagogical goals and the text itself, choose in subsequent sessions to ask the class to reread for specific literacies. If the goal is to highlight the functional load of grammar, a brief reminder that the feminine endings accompany noun gender addresses the question about whether the driver of the car is a man or a woman. To emphasize writing style, instructors might want students to look for redundancies ("¿Qué se repite?" / "What's repeated?"). "Negro el vestido, negro el pelo," and so on will doubtless resonate with some students as a trope of folk songs or ballads in their own culture ("Black, black, black is the color of my true love's hair"). In this way, a grammatical exercise has functioned as the basis for identifying a literary technique.

What the teacher is responsible for in leading learners from initial reading to more complicated literacies is to find out what they know and do not know and, on that basis, to encourage predictions about what will happen next. In turn, the readers are engaging in response processes that literary scholars identify as critical (Rosenblatt). Reading on in "La muerte," for instance, students discover that it remains unclear whether the reference is to a death or a murder, whether the driver is a man or a woman. But they will probably see that *la automovilista* is a person, because s/he talks with *una muchacha*. The scaffolded insight they gain in this case is tuning into a dialogue as the heart of the story.

The questions of whether or not the *automovilista* is a person and whether or not s/he has stopped boil down to an understanding of narrative style. As so often happens in literary works, obscure or peculiar grammar converges with narrative manipulation or genre moves. Thus if, in their initial reading, learners have been directed to decide whether the first paragraph is a monologue, a first-person description, a dialogue, or a third-person description, they will be attuned to what turns into the literary considerations of genre, as they determine whether that description, dialogue, or monologue continues or not.

The first paragraph is followed by exchanges:

—¿Me llevas? Hasta el pueblo, no más—dijo la muchacha.
—Sube—dijo la automovilista. . . . (47)

—Will you give me a ride? Only as far as the village, no further," said the girl.
—Get in, said the driver. . . . (47)

The dashes and question marks in the text illustrate Spanish typesetting conventions that differ from those commonly used in English-language texts. Their brevity and the repetition of *dijo* ("he said," "she said") conveys the sense of a dialogue even if students are unable to identify the preterite form of the verb "to say" (*decir*) or *sube* ("get in") as the imperative form of *subir*. These grammar cues are tied into this short story's narrative structure and thus integral to its genre conventions.

Working from what they do know to what can grow out of that knowledge, readers learn to inventory episodes, just as they learn to continue reading despite gaps in their language knowledge, to avoid relying on a dictionary to address uncertainties that cannot be resolved by retrieving individual items of content from outside the text's structured world. Subsequent paragraphs of the story help clarify what was unclear at first or at least expand on patterns noted, which will eventually emerge as structures of meaning—as readers' interpretations. Students also learn that, in literary texts particularly, opening paragraphs introduce rather than explicate. First speeches of plays, first paragraphs of stories, first pages of novels set the stage but rarely identify overtly all the uses and permutations of theatrical props that will be essential in acts 2 and 3.

IDENTIFYING TEXTUAL PATTERNS: CREATING A MEANINGFUL MATRIX

At the next scaffolded stage of engaging with the text, learners focus on pattern identification, usually by means of a matrix that steers them toward data that can become a pattern. After monitored feedback on their initial reading, a class can be guided by a matrix to more informed reading—a rereading—that establishes the meaning of text structures as logics (keyed visually) and as data sets. Such work at pattern comprehension is necessary for the FL learner to overcome the temptation to read word for word. Indeed, without a matrix, the illusion that understanding every word yields a meaningful reading is difficult to break.

A text matrix helps learners join syntax and general (macro-) propositions with supporting details or micropropositions that elaborate them in the text (Kintsch and van Dijk). Macropropositions are the main ideas or gist features of any story: the tokens of heroism, villainy, or nurturing, the compass points of human experience. Each is necessarily articulated into a topic (fairy-tale princess) and a comment about its nature, goals, or results (rescuing the princess). Micropropositions add texture and meaning to the general outlines, making them part of a specific world. For beginners, a partial fill-in-the-blank matrix (prestructured as a worksheet) helps sort details of textual information in ways that foreground their relation to details of text content and to the language used to express those relations. In figure 4.1, some details from Anderson Imbert's text (tokens) are arranged into categories by type; details supplied by the teacher are italicized, while the students fill in further examples. The column "Scenes" is an additional advance organizer, in recognition of the difficulty this text presents in dividing one episode from the next. A binary organization of categories or

FIGURE 4.1. Matrix Sample: "La muerte"

Scenes	Familiar	Unexpected
Picking up a hitchhiker	la automovilista ("driver")	negro, negro, negros, pálida ("black, black, black, pale")
Conversing	varias preguntas ("various questions")	"¿pero no tienes miedo?" (repetition of the question "Aren't you afraid?" and denial three times)
Dying	el auto se desbarranca; la muchacha queda muerta ("the automobile crashed; the girl lay dead")	voz cavernosa; automovilista desapareció ("sonorous voice"; "driver has vanished")

types, like the familiar-unfamiliar contrast between events and behaviors here, generally proves easiest for readers to sort. Two columns indicate a topic-comment logic for the conceptual typology of this text's data: the behaviors, problems, institutions, ideas, persons, or events talked about and the contrasts, solutions, features, goals, or causally related events that illuminate each topic's significance. Such elements constitute the most basic forms of propositions (Kintsch). Even readers with minimal command of the FL will be able to use the matrix to understand a given passage's conceptual fundamentals and to supplement the gaps in their understanding of details about facts or language. The matrix can therefore help learners read for meaning without extensive command of language.

Syntax practice is also implicated in such a matrix, in all the potential questions and answers, including inappropriate ones. For example, some readers might erroneously suggest that "¿Me llevas?" ("Will you give me a ride?") is an unexpected exchange between a driver and a hitchhiker. They are making a cultural content mistake but also a mistake in selecting a grammatical form that does not fit the category. After the matrices are completed as homework, misidentifications can be clarified as a group when individual results are compared in class. Here, the opportunity for feedback on process comes to the fore. If, for example, classmates do not object to the inclusion of "¿Me llevas?" in the "Unexpected" category, the instructor will need to point out the meaning of the verb *llevar* as "to carry, take" and ask the class to speculate about a probable translation in this context. Students then understand that "Will you give me a ride?" belongs in the "Familiar" category as an anticipated inquiry from a hitchhiker. They have begun to monitor their own production and cultural literacy.

Clarifications could also occur in a synchronous chat room in a computer-assisted environment. No matter what method is chosen, by associating the question with its appropriate referential system, learners begin to link individual words to the macropropositions of the passage—and to patterns of cultural literacy. Since they make these distinctions to clarify global meanings, memory of the specific meanings of words should be facilitated (e.g., see Parry).

Dictionary correctness may not apply once words are put in discourse contexts. Consequently, feedback must validate the learner's effort at communicating appropriate messages about the text just as much as it must attend to developing correctness of form. The nonproficient reader attempting to construct propositional systems must still be valorized as a potentially strong receiver of a literary work. Cognitive engagement, identified in research as essential for success in reading comprehension, lays the foundation for exposing the strategies the text uses to mean.

This approach speaks to active as well as passive memory. The more words are used and thought about in different modes, the greater the likelihood of their retention. A further advantage of this task is that while moving pieces of text from their original contexts into logical categories is a sophisticated cognitive act, it requires few new linguistic tools. Thus this iteration of text meaning focuses on applying what is known about language rather than either simply recalling language or learning new usage. Regardless of the specific matrix format or of where group decisions occur, learner efforts to construct this level of expressive complexity in a foreign language need to be reviewed and discussed as legitimate stages in the process of moving toward more complete comprehension. Discussions of misreadings are useful to clarify language use and reinforce ways in which micropropositions support or fail to support a particular column of meaning in the matrix.

When language and content of a text are reinforced holistically through extensive reading, learners are prepared for subsequent tasks that guide them in thinking about the text and its culture and expressing that thinking by using its language. The matrix task of reproducing a text's micropropositions in terms of textual logic encourages learners to arrange the surface language of that text in associative schemata. Having linked details to larger patterns, they are also prepared for specifically literary discussions. In "La muerte," the juxtaposition of the real and the supernatural is, after all, a familiar narrative strategy in the Latin American literature classified as magic realism. Despite language deficiencies, a learner can become a potentially strong reader of literature by using a matrix whose theoretical, macropropositional construct is designed by the instructor.

FROM STRONG READER TO AUTHORITATIVE INTERPRETER

Once a matrix has been completed with representative entries from a story, it can be utilized in several ways to prepare learners for their next stage of development. Its precise use depends on the goals set for the class. If the goal is language practice, for example, then a graduated sequence of tasks can lead to more sophisticated spoken and then written expression of the language patterns learners have found in their matrices. Even beginning students can write and act out more dialogue between the characters they have met, reflecting the characters' voices and modes of being yet preserving the everyday setting with which the students are familiar.

Sentence building emerges from propositional logic in more complex ways, so it is crucial to link matrix information to students' existing command of grammar, to practice how to generate various sentences off the same content base. If beginners know how to match gender endings for nouns and adjectives and to manipulate the present-tense forms for the Spanish verbs "to have" *(tener, haber)* and "to be" *(estar, ser)*, they can be instructed to use their matrices to describe the two figures or objects mentioned in the story—thereby changing the point of view in the discourse. They can be directed to decide which verbs the text uses for "to have" and "to be" and then to think about which form *(tener* or *estar)* is appropriate for their present-tense descriptions. This way of focusing on grammar and meaning at the same time fosters learning to learn from the earliest phases of instruction.

Anchored first in semantics rather than in formal knowledge about tense markings, such a writing task links morphological features in the story's language to its content. The story itself uses present-tense forms of *tener* and *estar* several times but only in the first and second persons. In their versions, students must apply the third-person forms, precisely because they are shifting from dialogue to a description. In doing so, they take a first step away from repeating the exact language of the text. At the same time, any nouns and adjectives used will be drawn from their matrices, and observations about parts of speech must be anchored in the content of the story. Typical answers for a task asking for simple sentences based on phrases selected for the matrix categories will be *La automovilista tiene ojos negros* ("The driver has black eyes") and *La muchacha no tiene miedo* ("The girl is not afraid"). The linguistic material thus achieves a new dimension as it is given a different affective purpose: expressing readers' intent (to describe) as they recall textual information.

Despite the relatively limited linguistic repertoire of a first-year class, instructors will discover that students are indefatigable players with language and can, if asked to do so, write from six to eight simple sentences using the format above, all of which express a cultural insight. They might then be ready to write a longer description that contrasts the familiar with the unfamiliar using discourse connectors such as *pero* or *aunque*. Given the topic sentence, "This story is / is not very mysterious, because . . . ," students have the linguistic tools to express a point of view, for example, *Este cuento es / no es muy misterioso porque la muchacha hace varias preguntas peculiares pero la automovilista no tiene miedo* ("This story is / is not very mysterious, because the girl asks peculiar questions but the driver is not afraid"). Playing with attributes mentioned in the story, students practice a speech act while optimizing their linguistic resources.

For more advanced students, these steps from comprehension to basic production may seem minimal or redundant. That perception depends largely on the incremental learning an instructor builds into the task by developing elaborated scenarios. The challenge posed by asking students to change verbs from the indicative to the conditional or to introduce negation depends on the conceptual material students are poised to tackle in accordance with their particular learning level and the learning objectives set. In minimally revising simple statements, as illustrated above, students practice expressing their own point of view, which is a useful warm-up for even advanced intermediate learners. They practice becoming strong readers who are also articulate readers, able to exert agency over the story material from the very first, beyond the level of reproduction. They begin to identify the holistic significance of textual details and the language used to express those details as tokens in the text's larger pattern (typology) of meaning.

This type of task is an essential intermediary step between comprehension and the creative language expression that can become literary interpretation. The usual format of grammar exercises does not contextualize language practice as part of systematic interpretation and reading. Instead, most reading exercises remain unrelated to the messages of a literary text. Small wonder that students guided only by such strategies prove unable to discuss texts at more sophisticated levels. They have been denied the building blocks necessary to achieve sophisticated expression. Even when learners have adequate language skills, they rarely have the reference tools of larger proposition building with which to ask literary questions and begin to develop literary interpretations.

Of course, part of learners' failure to interpret literary texts originates in language deficits. Without intermediary-practice stages with building-block vocabulary and variation of expressive options aimed at making the options automatic in culturally appropriate contexts, students all too often resort to English or, particularly in writing about a literary work, to translation instead of linking what they see in a text with their own language resources. In other words, they need to practice modifying textual language to create individual speech acts.

Ultimately, the task variation described above can be interesting only as long as tasks are not purely mechanical. Minimal variation and recursion must be among the speaker-writer's options for expressing significant cultural content. Creative tasks can provide cognitive and affective interest even though students are reworking language in relatively simple ways. The kinds of grammar, discourse, and propositions practiced must be the same as those that students will be required to produce at the end of their study.

After the grammar framework for these expressions is established and validated at the sentence level (e.g., tense; mood; voice; and such morphosyntactic complexity as appropriate use of verb condition, adjective endings, negation), students are poised to use the texts as the basis for self-expression. At the next stage in their development from production to interpretation, they will interpret a work primarily through their own point of view and in extended forms of discourse. Such movement of course depends on the pedagogical objectives of the teacher and the desired juncture between practices at the lower- and upper-division levels. Students can develop their abilities even in the context of more traditional conversation-composition classes, if they repeatedly retell stories read in lower-division courses, reproduce them as minidramas, provide variant stories using the originals themes and stylistic devices, conduct mock interviews of figures in stories, submit police reports, or express a point of view in a written paragraph or short essay. The language used in these different genres will be largely repetitive, but speaker intent and message shift.

In lower-division courses, the first more complex speaking and writing tasks succeed best when they are preceded by sentence-level practice linked to the propositional meanings of specific reading materials. With sentence-level practice based on the discourse patterns in those materials, the grammar of and matrix for a story provide a safety net for students' linguistic accuracy by setting limits to linguistic innovation and avoiding the risk of introducing dictionary- or translation-based infelicities (e.g., Anglicisms).

If the earliest use of a matrix involves lexation practice (practice using new vocabulary by confirming or disconfirming which examples go in which categories), and a later use is minimal communication of text materials, then the next step is a more explicit link of such micropropositions (a text's surface language tokens) to macropropositions (a text's conceptual typology). In the transition from beginning to intermediate phases, learners interpret, making more extended judgments about what the elements of the matrix tell them about the text. They will work not only at the text's logic (in the example of "La muerte," on the contrasts implied between columns) but also on the categories themselves and their implications as part of cultural literacy. One column lists familiar features of the world: drivers of cars who ask questions and have car crashes in which their passengers are killed. But the patterns of a story must also be interrogated for what they do not say and how they differ from events reported in newspapers or on TV (in attitude; in formal features; in cultural types, tropes, or stereotypes traded on). The same interrogation must be made for the second column, with its strange questions, cavernous voices, and disappearing drivers.

The difference here in task difficulty is principally a cognitive one: these questions involve higher-level analytic abilities and discourse strategies more than they require such specific language abilities as command of vocabulary or syntax. Students must learn to generalize, to use details or tokens to illustrate a gist or typology. The language necessary to express the differences between the "Familiar" and "Unexpected" columns in figure 4.1 is rarely complex—with minimal linguistic resources, the differences can be expressed clearly if not always completely idiomatically. Most students who complete a matrix for "La muerte" will eventually note that none of the references to people in the "Familiar" column are personalized with a name or other specific identity. That the driver and the girl remain types rather than particular persons is an insight that can be expressed with simple sentences in Spanish.

Addressing cognitive complexity brings the reader close to what scholars like to call a literary interpretation instead of simply reading for pleasure or some practical purpose: the real and the unusual emerge as the discourse of magic realism. The "Unexpected" column throws new light on the lack of personal names, as the reader tries to keep track of various things that do not take a normal course. Even who is speaking to whom is unusual, particularly when after the driver repeats for the third time that she is not afraid, laughter is suppressed and the girl in a cavernous voice declares herself to be death. Only the early, ballad-like description of the driver ("black her dress, black her hair, black her eyes") and the driver's repeated answer foreshadow her threatening potential as a personification of death—adding up to a domain that evokes magic. The story's narrative, however, does not make that domain clear until the last line, although the text has worked toward building that interpretation from the first. At the close the driver got out of the car and vanished upon reaching a cactus ("siguió a pie y al llegar a un cactus desapareció"). Once it is seen that a supernatural being of some sort is probably involved, a logical approach to the reading may well turn into a more affective, aesthetic pleasure.

For beginners, such insights that synthesize the verbal movement of the matrix chart into deeper cultural or literary meanings will probably be most productively expressed in English. But before many months of exposure to the language have elapsed, making that kind of synthesis while using Spanish should prove feasible: learners will be able to exemplify the style elements of magical realism, even if they can't use all the rhetoric a scholar would to talk about it. Students can draw from their everyday experience to identify distinguishing features of a particular literary work. A student might say, *No sabemos los nombres de las dos personas, solamente las características. El artículo en un periódico da nombres.* ("We don't know the names of the two people [in the story], only their traits. An article in a newspaper provides names"). Once students see that the story's use of typological characters reflects a pattern, they have uncovered one key to interpreting Anderson Imbert's aesthetic in this short work.

Learners will then be poised to draw inferences in a variety of ways. Some may recognize that the narrative system in its juxtaposing of the everyday with the surreal suggests anthropological generalizations about attitudes and behaviors. From this perspective, the tale presents a young girl who possesses the bravado and daring typical of youth. Others may be aware of Anderson Imbert's expressionistic style and its reductive gesture toward basic human experience, echoing ballads and fairy tales in its repetition of questions. Still others may wonder why the young girl keeps asking the driver variants of the same and, by implication, frightening question. Is this act like the proverbial three questions of a folk tale? Moreover, who is asking and who is answering may not be clear until the sequence of the conversation is carefully established—a strategy that is important yet frequently overlooked when determining agency in a literary text.

Anderson Imbert's omission of explicit references to speakers underscores the subtle way the author creates uncertainty in the reader. What is implied by the playing of this series of little tricks? What do these narrative ploys add up to, and how do readers revise the assumptions they made at the outset. Is the reference to *muerte* one of death or murder? Is the young girl a victim of cosmic chance or complicit in her death? and if complicit, how? Whether the answers are searched for in-class, through directed reading, or found at home using an information matrix, students are prepared to think about and argue their own views. Such acts of synthesis begin to be literary interpretations.

Again, for the teacher of strong readers, no right answers exist. Indeed, the teacher must stress that the questions themselves initiate interpretation, that reading literature involves interrogation of the text's underlying messages and appreciation of how those messages are constructed through consistent patterns in its surface language. For learners to behave as adults in cultural contexts, they must learn to negotiate cultural differences, not expect absolute consensus, for example, about the meaning of a literary text. Strong readers have earned the privilege of deciding what a pattern they identify says to them, of drawing an inference and articulating an implication they see. As long as students' questions are text-based and their answers intelligible, their insights at this stage should be valued as significant steps toward the multiliteracies of culture.

AFTER EARLY LEARNING: MOVING TOWARD DEVELOPMENTAL SEQUENCES

After the act of interpretation has been initiated by tying grammar practice to content knowledge in holistic ways, learners at the second or third level can take on an additional challenge. Using their learning background, they will be able to put their earlier interpretations of texts into larger frames of reference, seeing those texts as cultural or aesthetic artifacts with specific (and multiple) text-extrinsic dimensions; as reflections of timeless truths; as engaging particular social or political issues; as cultural documents; or as well-wrought urns of great beauty.

The teacher who wants to prepare students for advanced literary or cultural analysis will encourage them to consider more dimensions. Is "La muerte" an example of magic realism, or is it a subgenre of the fantastic, as some critics would have it? Are such stories distinctly Latin American, or are there parallels in English and other literatures with which students are familiar? What kinds of cultural, class, or gender biases might such parallels reflect (for good or ill)? Alternatively, with the increased emphasis in many foreign language curricula on cultural studies and content-based course work, such literary texts can be read in conjunction with other cultural documents to encourage students to reflect about how social problems and attitudes have many facets.

Such learning goals must be fostered across the curriculum by using a variety of text combinations. After progressing from factual reading to interpretation, from simple to complex comprehension to production as recall, and from production as application to synthesis of language, the next move is from a text to intertextuality. Parallel fictional and nonfictional accounts of an event or subject exemplify how literature lends meaning to real-world experience. Using such a parallel leads to a set of pedagogically sound choices from the standpoint of FL development, because the resulting comparisons work with redundant vocabulary and contexts. Parallel accounts from both L1 and FL cultures can open up visions of intercultural or multicultural literacy, depending on the goals of the course. If a teacher selects a Spanish- or English-language text about the incidence of fatal accidents among different age groups in the United States, readers of "La muerte" might consider youthful attitudes of invincibility as promoting the disregard for risk illustrated in Anderson Imbert's tale—a sociological more than an aesthetic reading.

If course goals stress cultural dimensions, a parallel text or film clip (documentary or fictional) might depict social conditions in a South or Central American countryside and the practice of hitchhiking as an accepted means of transportation. Students would then consider the reasons for this acceptance and the reasons why hitchhiking is now relatively rare in the United States and becoming less common in Latin America. Student attention would be drawn to economic differences among regions in the Americas, the greater likelihood of car ownership in the United States, the banning of hitchhikers on North American and Pan American throughways, and how economics affects social praxis and cultural attitudes. Should aesthetic features be emphasized, fictional and nonfictional accounts of a hitchhiker's experience could still be compared—but with a different goal, that of distinguishing between literary conventions and actual events. How does the narrative of a story differ from a newspaper report, for instance?

What information is conveyed and aesthetic objectives served by the underlying ambiguity in Anderson Imbert's story?

This chapter has explored how holistic reading tasks can lead to multiliteracy throughout the FL curriculum. We have identified the matrix as the anchor for a series of tasks that can serve as the basis for exercises that enable adult learners to become multiliterate in a foreign language by applying their cognitive sophistication to the reading of culturally marked texts. Our illustration was a short short story. Using a matrix to stage learning that moves from comprehension of textual language to comprehension of how that language is used to create patterns of meaning, we have argued that this process situates learners to think for themselves in systematic fashion and to become strong readers as a result. Rather than search for a single right answer, learners identify answers that convey meaning to them yet are verifiable in the text and in the text's culture as well as their own. We have shown how the pieces of that meaning become the basis for a FL student's independent language production.

In the next chapter we turn to an expanded exercise type that uses a matrix as its fulcrum: the précis. We illustrate how, in the context of a holistic FL program whose goal is to foster multiliteracy, the précis can facilitate the reading and interpretation of longer genres, from interviews to novels and films.

NOTES

1. For detailed lesson plans describing in-class activities and related assignments, see Kern, *Literacy*.
2. We are indebted to Sharon Foerster and Delia Montesinos for assistance with the Spanish-language use in this chapter. A longer version of this argument is found in Swaffar, "Reading."

A Template for Advanced-Learner Tasks: Staging Genre Reading and Cultural Literacy through the Précis

Chapter 5

An information matrix, described in chapter 4, can become a fully developed exercise form, the précis, understood here as a template for a series of pedagogical tasks that integrate comprehension and production practice. The goal is to enable learners to identify the messages, obligatory textual moves, and language features of various genres holistically, as part of cultural literacy.

Exemplified with reference to both fictional and nonfictional genres, which are thematically connected in Laura Esquivel's novel *Like Water for Chocolate* (*Como agua para chocolate*), the précis tasks we suggest here originate with specific genre features, such as the distinction between formal and informal, between private and public discourse, and between the language of the sender and the language of the receiver. We argue that only after identifying characteristics of the media presentation, genre conventions, and handling of stereotypes are learners in a position to analyze and articulate textual information in a culturally appropriate fashion, because they have begun to engage in simultaneous negotiations with more complex forms of discourse.

Students who engage in comprehension-based tasks, such as comparing thematically related genres, can construct verifiable bases for drawing inferences about the broader cultural implications of genre-based changes, thereby becoming competent advanced users of a second language. The curricular units described here apply to intermediate through advanced FL learners, defined principally as those college students whose abilities in a foreign language qualify them to take courses at upper-division levels and whose cultural knowledge qualifies them to take sophisticated content courses as part of their undergraduate experience. In many course sequences, this level is the point at which extensive reading commences. It is also the moment when learners inevitably confront rhetorical organization, since a text's choice of words; the topics raised; the order in which points are addressed; the degree of directness or obliqueness with which exhortations, complaints, or eulogies occur all involve distinct discursive and rhetorical patterns that are associated with different genres in public and private settings. Knowing these associations is part of cultural literacy.

This chapter uses a short novel to exemplify pedagogies that will support learners in taking this step toward advanced comprehension and production in their developing FL literacy. These pedagogies rest on a broader notion of language as a set of culture-based discourses than is currently in play in many upper-division offerings. For purposes of our discussion, a variety of texts—the novel, the book review, the movie synopsis, the interview, and the film—are discussed as genres, *genre* understood as an oral or written rhetorical practice that structures culturally embedded communicative situations in a highly predictable fashion, thereby creating horizons of expectations for its community of users, to use Hans Robert Jauss's terminology. Such patterns of discourse—discourse genres—enable comprehension and communication in culturally valorized ways. Working out from that definition of discourse genres, we present a broader use of the précis as a template for sequenced advanced-learner tasks. The inherent predictability and cultural embeddedness of genres make them ideal pedagogical tools to facilitate learners' more advanced analyses of textual information and their use of more complicated forms of expressive production.

We chose Esquivel's novel not only because it has become a popular text for advanced classes but also because it has enjoyed a wide reception in the United States beyond the classroom. For that reason a large set of texts in various genres have been generated around the novel, a naturally occurring cluster, each with different communicative purposes. Our goal is to show how an instructor's understanding of the précis can aid students in uncovering a genre's multiple message patterns and the linguistic foundations of those messages. Through the kind of cognitive and linguistic engagement with texts, language, and culture that précis-structured curricula can offer, students will learn to link their existing knowledge to the content-form patterns instantiated in the FL text. That linking leads to the capture of essential qualities of advanced learning and the advanced learner.

CHALLENGE FOR THE ADVANCED LEARNER: GENRES ENACTING COMMUNICATION SITUATIONS

The advanced learner can be variously defined by programs and departments, depending on how they place and sequence students. For this book, we define advanced learners as those whose language competencies enable them to enroll in the typical nonsequenced topic courses (not just in major courses) that a department designates as advanced or upper-division. Presumably, such students have in their lower-division studies encountered many genres, from simple conversations, letters, and newspaper articles to films and short literature. They are not necessarily familiar with how to use the structures of genres in context as the basis for their reading comprehension and as models for their speaking and writing. Nor do they necessarily know how these structures should be weighed, as optional and obligatory textual moves valued in a culture and alluded to in each realization of a genre, directly or indirectly.

These typical advanced learners have had little, if any, systematic practice in recovering, replicating, and reproducing the formalisms that define genres in the target culture (if, indeed, they have had such practice in their own culture). Also, they have probably not worked extensively with extended discourse—texts of more than a few printed pages—and have rarely been asked to do more than describe or possibly contrast genres or to discuss genre use as a culture- or community-based communication activity. As advanced learners, however, they now confront such daunting demands. Taking these objectives as defining upper-division curriculum goals does not mean that a program is simply recognizing a need for more vocabulary and more sophisticated use of grammatical forms. These demands also stem from the cognitive claims that longer texts (whether read or verbalized by students in spoken or written form) make on student recall and student ability to synthesize information. A longer FL text often challenges readers to interpret its unfamiliar cultural parameters in a larger, sociohistorical context.

The point of departure for advanced students' learning is that the genres used in lower levels of the curriculum have not differed much from those in general use in the West. Students have read, listened to, and talked or written about advertisements, nursery rhymes, songs, soap operas, fairy tales, newspaper articles, and Web-based texts. But they have not been challenged in any systematic way to confront the systems that produce two different cultural products from genres that on the surface seem alike or to confront the meanings of genre structures as social-cultural practices. In the upper division, then, an advanced learner may face cognitive overload. In Western languages with shared Latin alphabets, many genres seem alike at first glance but actually differ from country to country, even familiar soap operas or fairy tales with their stock characters and repertoire of predictable behaviors. A magazine article or biography originating in a foreign country often contains moves and sequences that are unfamiliar, specific to its cultural location.

To take genre into the advanced curriculum is necessary, because genres exist at the intersection between linguistic expression and social convention. The tools to help learners make the leap across gaps of practice and understanding, however, exist in theories about genre and textuality (albeit often formalist text theories) but not about FL reading. For example, in his essay "The Problem of Speech Genres," Bakhtin looks at the way texts represent the normative and at the same time more complex ways people and groups speak to one another. Tzvetan Todorov points out that literary texts in particular include representatives of different social classes, different positions vis-à-vis the messages of the text, and different degrees of formality in utterance (*Poetics*). Such theories thus lead from individual texts and language use into cultural worlds, especially if genres are considered not as literary-aesthetic but as forms of communication.

A diary entry or a letter, for example, has more than one set of characteristic formal features; the features depend on the context of use. Both genres may be considered private if their authors intend them only for personal reading or an intimate circle. By contrast, the diaries and letters of well-known writers, captains of industry, or politicians are often written in full knowledge of their eventual disclosure or use as a basis for subsequent public writing (e.g., memoirs). Degrees of formality, register choices, and topics reflect decisions about the discourse situation that the text enacts. For the FL learner, becoming aware of the text's function or audience, as marking the social situation, may well be the most important factor to guide the outset of reading. That is, the form of a genre may be less revealing to a novice reader than the knowledge of how certain markers are used in the text to indicate, for example, how public or private its use is intended to be.

How to define genres in use rather than as formal entities is illustrated in figure 5.1, which is organized according to the demands of the communication situation that the genres enact. Note that this graphic defines genre forms in terms of the sender-receiver relationships they enact. Genres are more private when written than when spoken, because written texts are more easily controlled and configured as private. The sender-receiver relationship for informally written letters differs from that for business letters. The receiver of a personal letter is specified, profiled as a distinct individual, therefore the learner needs to know in what kind of relationship writer and recipient are engaged. In the business letter, the receiver is impersonal, generic—a bureaucrat at another agency or a customer type—and not a discrete individual with whom the writer has a specific, nuanced relationship.

FIGURE 5.1. Discourse Genres

Type of Communication	Informal Examples	Formal Examples	Sender-Receiver Relationship
Written and personal	letter	business letter	specified sender to receiver
	blog	diary (esp. publishable)	specified sender to generic receiver
	montage, scrapbook	business diary	generic sender to generic receiver
Spoken	conversation ad hoc speech, monologue	debate oratory, homily	face-to-face equivalent monologue, one-sided
Printed or published	letter to the editor	review.	Implied readership is the general reading community of the medium involved.
	expository prose: general periodical, self-published nonfiction book	expository prose: specialized periodical, book from established press, handbook, encyclopedia	Implied readership belongs to a specialized community.
	fiction and other literary genres in limited-use contexts (chapbook, small press)	popular fiction, driven by formulas	

↑ Private

↓ Public

FIGURE 5.1. Discourse Genres (*cont.*)

Type of Communication	Informal Examples	Formal Examples	Sender-Receiver Relationship
Electronic publication or broadcast forms	sound only: radio, Web-cast	sound only: radio, Web-cast	forms with known sender, generic and media-specific audience demographics
	call-in show sound bytes, short reports or announcements, DJ or hosted format	interview, news show	two speakers, one speaker, generic audience
	downloads	variety or news digest (Fresh Air, ATC), audio CD, finished collections	one uniting voice or context; included materials marshaled into that single context
		public Web site, e-zine, other electronic forms	
	print and graphics mix: personal Web site, electronic discussion list, newsgroup		All the subsequent forms are specific and content-driven or use-context-driven modifications of the above.
	broadcast TV: drama, comedy, variety, serial, soap opera		
	film, video, DVD, on-demand media: special features, voice-over commentary, outtakes, director's cuts, speed up and edit out commercials		

Private ↑

Public ↓

The learner will thus in many ways have easier access to the business letter, once language formalities are cleared up, since the purpose of business letters is fairly straightforward. Some genres blur the distinction between public and private differently, but they do so in consistent ways.

As shown in figure 5.1, a blog (a Web-based diary or Web-log site where authors express personal feelings and events in their lives) and a diary written for publication both have generic receivers: people are interested in the senders' personal reflections, but the receivers are not personally specified, since the messages are posted or published, not sent to individuals. The blog, however, is typically less formal in style and register than the for-publication diary, since it is often structured as completely personal or to be shared with friends. The diary intended for possible publication or wider reading will have more formalized obligatory moves. It will frame topics ("Today was one of the happiest of my life"), explain references ("because . . .") and define terms, while the blog can skip from one topic to the next without transition markers or structured entries, even to the point of including pictures or media clips. "Went skiing. What a bummer those prices are. . . ." The receiver of a blog must often create links to ideas and the senders' situation or remain a reader at the purely factual level, while the reader of a published diary is initiated more systematically into understanding a text's intent as the author reflects and elaborates on topics.

For the advanced learner, awareness of such distinctions, of such differently configured sender-receiver relationships, can ease reading comprehension significantly. For teachers, it helps pinpoint which texts will probably work for their learners and which, despite ostensibly simpler register, sentence style, and subject matter, will not. This approach also explains why genres need to be examined carefully for their readability for the advanced learner. A blog entry can have simple subject-verb-object sentences on a known topic like hobbies, but its intent may be utterly alien to an uninitiated readership. Some blogs are relatively easy, with clearly signaled purposes ("Jerry's Favorite Movies"); others are virtually opaque, since readers must use their background to fill in the gaps in style and content characteristic of this genre.

An Example: The Encyclopedia Article

The need for careful differentiation according to sender-receiver issues in genres defined as formal types holds true for letters or any of the genres listed in the second column of figure 5.1. Sender-receiver relationships reflect the fundamental premises of communication in cultural space. When a text's setting is construed as formal, for example, readers are more likely to be able to follow its messages and their implications without much advance preparation, because *formal* often means the signaling of overt intention. The genre of an encyclopedia article implies a reader who is a member of a generic (standard, demographically mixed and thus unprofiled) community. Such an article has few hidden agendas. The writer of a typical encyclopedia entry must abstract the age, gender, dialect, and regional location of its receivers (or implied readers), precisely because the genre functions to provide for a broad audience the information required about a subject. That objective necessarily prescribes the text's formal features and responsibility in communication. In other words, the sender operates under syntactic and information constraints that characterize the resultant text. An encyclopedia article is seldom calculated to rock the boat, to challenge the status quo by introducing new knowledge. Its obligatory moves—its standard pattern of communication—thus are conventional and straightforward.

The obligatory moves of a typical encyclopedia article involve locating a specific person, work, event, or concept historically and providing an account of its origin, representative functions, and products. The entry on an author will usually not contain multiple voices, whose multiplicity might challenge a master narrative; at least the entry will not do so without an overt negotiation ("Two theories exist about why she did this . . ."). While its readers might expect to find brief citations reprinted to reflect assertions about an author's life or established reactions to an author's writing, the very definition of the medium and its speech situation (the way it is designed to communicate) make this genre likely to conform to the master narratives of the culture it serves, at least to established views about cultural achievements.

Written for a demographically mixed audience, the encyclopedia article is relatively predictable in register and structuring of messages for a novice learner, particularly when it concerns subjects familiar to the reader, where topic familiarity can overcome a large quantity of unfamiliar vocabulary. More important, the degree of interest or discussion arising from such an article in a class is generally restricted, because the article has condensed a broad, potentially multifaceted subject into a succinct summary. Neutral, often immediately comprehensible, and having little communication value in a class beyond its content, it can be used to inform learners about salient facts but rarely to engage them, unless they approach it with a specific task in mind.

By contrast, an entry in an academic handbook for specialists in the field may generate greater user interest, inasmuch as it is engaged in a more challenging exchange: it claims for itself the voice of the expert, the ability to set professional norms. Designed to serve a particular readership and thus assuming a certain level of professional knowledge on the part of that readership, academic handbook articles often include the pros and cons of a subject, its nuances, and controversial features while relying on the reader to take a position, albeit one within the parameters of areas of disagreement in the field. Although also directed at generic receivers, handbook articles serve a specialized audience that has expectations that differ from those of people who consult a comprehensive encyclopedia entry. Such articles are engaged in different speech situations, with different degrees of publicness and authority and thus different formalisms (different obligatory moves in the organization of information and rhetoric).

Genres and Predictability

Genre factors into the success of courses in another way: where FL students have a horizon of expectations that parallels that of the target language audience for a text in question, especially one designed for a special niche audience. Genre formalisms work to convey meanings for those students whose background knowledge derives from their membership in a specialized reader community, such as the business world or the medical profession. Predictable sequences occur in most essays, textbooks, professional correspondence, and research reports written for the fields of science, social science, engineering, business, and the fine arts.

When a special field is less public and authoritative, however, the formal features of its characteristic genres tend to be less predictable. Readers of literature or TV viewers have a wide range of texts from which to select, and their tastes, despite sometimes vigorous marketing efforts, are not always homogeneous. *TV Guide* is shared by all as a horizon of expectation, but *Soap Opera Digest* does not reach the same audience as *Tiger Beat* (a preteen magazine in which teen idols are profiled). Many genres—sometimes the richest, from the standpoint of cultural information—have limited audiences. Hence the text and its readability for a learner exist in a context of limited use, a use that depends on the cultures of both the learner and the author. Diversity in an audience often signals that a genre will be less predictable than one that is authoritative.

When an instructor confronts the choice among literary genres, the situation changes somewhat. Many forms of fiction and other literary genres stress originality in limited-use contexts. As Janice Radway specifies in *Reading the Romance*, particular genres often appeal to niche audiences. Original fiction, like the nonfiction that interrogates dominant expectations about a language community's behaviors and values, can confound novice readers' expectations about word choice and style as well as content and the obligatory moves with which it is presented.

Such works contrast with popular fiction driven by formulas (the horror story, the romance, the detective novel). Writers who produce books in series (in the vein of *A Is for Ashes* through *Z Is for Zeppelin*) and publishing houses that specialize in formulaic series like Harlequin romances provide a specialized reader community with culture-specific versions of their individual genres. Such literature is so predictable that FL readers with relatively meager vocabulary can nonetheless begin reading it for main ideas, gradually acquiring vocabulary as they progress through a work.

While the same obligatory moves characterize classics of a particular genre (Dashiell Hammett's mysteries or Graham Greene's spy novels), the measures of predictability about plot development, register, tone, and style do not apply as fully to such complex masterpieces of the genres as they do to their more conventional companions. *The Maltese Falcon* (Hammett) and *The Quiet American* (Greene) are novels that made demands on reader attention by disrupting the expectations of their day. They intentionally disconcert readers, who are ordinarily complacent in their understanding of the power of wealth or in their judgment about the ethics of spying, with humor or irony that questions such attitudes. Purely imitative or formulaic genres simply confirm readers' expectations: boy meets girl, boy loses girl, boy finds girl again after surviving tribulations.

Small wonder that advanced learners of a foreign language can find themselves challenged even by genres that seem to instructors to be relatively formulaic in language and typical for the foreign culture in content. Of course, audience expectations differ from one culture to the next, even when genres are virtually equivalent. But the result of a relatively minor deviation might be that the predictability of a genre is easily reenacted by native speakers of the FL while posing significant problems for the novice-to-advanced learner. Kafka's "Metamorphosis" will not communicate if a reader does not understand that a bug can think logically in this text's world.

The question of audience expectation plays into considerations of genres in another way, as a problem of intertextuality as well as one of spanning communication situations. Perceptions about an audience's cultural literacy, often termed its "horizons of expectation," influence the way a genre is translated from one modality or medium into another, such as a novel's being turned into a film or video. The content cannot be rendered literally in the new medium, because *literal* means something different in each.

In recent decades, for example, novels of magic realism have been widely accepted in the United States, as indicated by the best-seller status of work by Carlos Fuentes, Gabriel García Márquez, and Isabel Allende. Despite the acceptance of this genre in written form, films based on the books of these authors have not fared well. The star-studded film version of Allende's *The House of the Spirits* (1993), turned into a Hollywood costume extravaganza, decided to excise most of the magic of the novel. The producers left the event structure of the story with only a few fantastic scenes, in which young Clara moves objects by telepathy. The adult Clara (Meryl Streep) depicts a protagonist as "sensitive" rather than as the clairvoyant of the novel—a semantic possibility (because sensitives or empaths may indeed be thought of as related to clairvoyants) but by no means an equivalent cultural meaning. Apparently, producers felt that United States and international audiences would be discomfited or alienated by the novel's magic dimension and its ambiguous implications: they didn't want to make a ghost story. Their decision may well have been influenced by the failure at the box office only a few years earlier of *The Milagro Beanfield Wars* (1988), which maintained the grandfather's ghost as a real character in the novel's present.

Teaching genres, therefore, means teaching more than the formal features of a text type. Learners must be sensitized to the culturally significant elements of the text's horizon of expectation as well as to its syntax and semantics. Similarly, familiar genres will not be familiar to learners if the cultural differences of the texts are too great. By the same token, difficult texts emerge as considerably more straightforward if the cultural bases offer few stumbling blocks.

THE PRÉCIS AS CULTURAL ENCODING OF A TEXT:
FROM GENRE TO READING

The trick of getting learners into more complex communicative situations is to sensitize them to the implications of the communicative situation, not just its language materials. Part of that work must be done, as we have suggested in previous chapters, in a careful cognitive and linguistic staging of phases in reading, moving from the collection of details to the building of patterns that ground comprehension into production.

To empower advanced learners to read genre features systematically (for their formal as well as for their semantic or content messages), teachers need to create reading assignments that emphasize how formulas in cultural data, communication situations, and sender-receiver relationships work in the target culture. That is, they must teach learners to comprehend and acquire the formulas that constitute literacy in the target culture. As advanced learners encounter increased demands on their language competencies, they need structures that keep them from becoming mired in translation efforts, in the frustration of partial comprehension, and in false analogies between cultural settings. The structures they need most will often be related to communication in cultural context.

By using textual language to articulate the ideas of the text, as we have proposed, learners strengthen their grasp of a work's language usage. They also strengthen their grasp of the obligatory moves of a genre and of the larger cultural patterns in which that genre functions, as they reflect about the specific meaning of a text. At the very least, tasks that have learners use facets of texts they read as the basis for personal expression afford practice in sophisticated language use—a use that is patterned according to a set of cultural expectations larger than one imported from the learners' own culture. It is a particularly felicitous way of teaching cultural information by having students encode the interlocking relation between formal and semantic features of texts in culturally appropriate ways: learning not only an FL but also its cultural literacies.

We have already introduced the information matrix as an exercise element that fosters holistic learning (see fig. 4.1 [p. 87]). An information matrix can be embedded into a longer series of exercises, in an extended form known as a précis, a composite exercise that leads from focused tasks in comprehension to specific tasks in production. To illustrate how the précis can help advanced students identify and utilize the information that genre provides about a text, we now consider how genre literacy leads to broad cultural literacy for the advanced learner, to multiple literacies of cultural content and familiarity with the conventional moves that structure a genre in public horizons of expectation.

Because teaching related content by using different genres builds vocabulary while offering distinctly different applications of that vocabulary (i.e., it uses the same or similar vocabulary in different communication contexts, with different intended receivers), we have selected not only a Spanish novel to use as an example on how to build an extended exercise sequence but also a movie based on that novel (its screenplay written by the author), a film review, and an author interview. This juxtaposition shows how attention to genre literacy fosters extended literacy in language and rhetorical organization as well as in cultural norms and expectations. We demonstrate how teachers can use the précis template to have students work with both literary and linguistic features of a text and at the same time uncover for themselves a variety of cultural implications.

A précis has four distinct parts, each addressing a different aspect of the reading process. Part 1 identifies the topic or content of what is read. Part 2 states how the reader sees that content organized as a pattern of textual information. Part 3 gives a few examples from the text in a matrix format. To this point in the typical précis, students have used the language of the text almost exclusively. Therefore the first three parts constitute a replication of text language as well as textual messages and the particular cognitive strategy of the text's organization (its typical moves). Finally, in part 4 of the précis, using the language they have identified, students can articulate thoughts about the patterns of that language. It is here that they explore what the chosen examples say to them—their implications and significance.

The specific direction taken by the précis to guide learners in selecting and organizing textual language and innovation depends on what they want to find out, on their reader perspective or point of view, and on how the instructor directs their attention. Consequently, when not constructed by the teacher or as a class activity (hence very carefully staged, albeit still leaving leeway for reader variability), independent précis vary among readers.

That variance can be reduced when instructors specify particular parts of the précis in assignments, as was shown in figure 4.1. Such specification in turn depends on the needs of learners and the goals of the course. Advanced students unfamiliar with reading longer authentic materials need assistance in constructing précis, because their reading comprehension can break down under the processing demands of details in the text. Unfamiliar vocabulary and grammar tend to distract their attention from main messages (top-down processing). However, with focusing guidelines built into the précis matrix, they can attend to major episodic stages in the narrative development of holistic ideas.

When applied in a classroom setting in the context of a cluster of genres and communication situations such as that occurring around *Like Water for Chocolate*, the précis is more than an assignment tool. Its format can serve an instructor as a pedagogical template for discussing a text in culturally sensitive ways. A guided précis in particular, one for which an instructor provides categories, can help the novice-to-advanced reader stay on track in negotiating cultural and linguistic differences, because it focuses attention on the story line and the text's rhetorical structure as a reflection of the text's cultural communication horizon. Once completed, a précis can be the basis for both written and oral work. To maximize a précis's benefits in promoting multiple literacies, class time is necessary to identify and utilize its key constituents.

Let us now turn to how a précis can open the richness of a literary text into the text's culture. We hope to show the ability of the précis to capture a variety of approaches to the reading of a literary text; we hope also to offer convincing evidence for the particular suitability of a literary text in advanced classes, inasmuch as it invites just such a multiperspectival engagement in ways that a nonliterary text does not. The sample précis are in English for illustrative purposes. An advanced class would have Spanish versions and respond orally and write in Spanish.

Pedagogy of the Précis: The Novel

The first stage in the sequence presented here is introducing Esquivel's novel as a particular form of cultural communication. It is the source text of this example text cluster, a proven text of interest nationally and internationally, that can bridge cultural horizons of expectation. That it is subtitled "A Novel in Monthly Installments with Recipes, Romances, and Home Remedies" suggests from the outset a domestic setting for a romance genre.

Published first in Spanish in 1989 then in English in 1992, the book became a success in both English- and Spanish-speaking countries, was a best seller in the United States, and was made into a movie in 1992. This trajectory from text to translation to film is not unusual for modern Western cultural knowledge: a topic of interest will recur in various forms and be adapted by various user groups for their own purposes, in their own voices, and in their own preferred genres.

Esquivel's work intersperses actual recipes with events in the lives of women living on a ranch near the border between the United States and Mexico: the formidable Mamá Elena, her three daughters, and their loyal female servants. Set at the turn of the century, their story takes place against the background of the Mexican Revolution.

If students are to read an unedited or lightly edited version of *Like Water for Chocolate* without heavy reliance on a dictionary, a précis for preassignment work as an in-class activity is essential. Long texts need to be previewed, or they will overwhelm less-than-fluent readers. For initial in-class reading, establishing the content and patterns of information in a text provides practice at the lexicogrammatical level and strategies for identifying the macropropositions of any text. It will help students identify the obligatory moves of a given genre, as well.

To build a learner-centered approach into this exercise sequence from the outset, readers of the novel are not told in detail what to expect.[1] Instead, the teacher introduces the text with a preview, reading a paragraph, page, or specific set of textual features, and has students react to that reading by focusing on what readers identify as content and on the pattern of that content, helping them assemble and begin to deploy their own cultural literacy. In a novel whose chapters commence with organizers like months of the year and recipes, a brief perusal of chapter headings suffices to suggest their importance. The headings show how food in general, not just chocolate, organizes the text. Then students are prepared to read the first two paragraphs of chapter 1 ("January: Christmas Rolls") to see how food relates to the story the text wants to tell.

The first sentence is in the present tense, as readers throughout the West would expect from impersonal recipe directions: "Take care to chop the onion fine." But then the cook herself intrudes with a private observation by line 2 ("To keep from crying when you chop it [which is so annoying!], I suggest . . ."), and by the end of the paragraph, the recipe itself has been forsaken for discussion of a shared family trait (5). Both the unnamed author and her great-aunt Tita have cried excessively when cutting onions. The first sentence of the next paragraph focuses on Tita and the story of her birth, childhood, and early womanhood. Students see that the initial obligatory move of almost any novel, the introduction of characters, occurs here in the context of culinary events.

Using about ten minutes of class time to elicit such initial perceptions from learners before they go to the book on their own, the teacher enables them to uncover the narrative strategy they will encounter throughout the text: the links between cooking and its impact on the lives of the characters. Equally important, readers will have distinguished the voice of the present narrator (the "now," the present tense) from the storytelling voice, the one speaking in the past tense with the full authority of total recall. Using the Spanish imperfect, the storytelling voice knows what Tita thinks and feels as well as what she does and says.

Developing a Matrix for the Genre's Content

The communication pattern—the language pattern of the text—has been established in the classroom preview. Readers can now ascertain independently how it plays out in the novel, in several culturally significant dimensions. The organization of textual information reflects this pattern consistently with grammar signals. Using a chapter of *Like Water for Chocolate* in a course in style or composition on the advanced level would take the précis in a distinct direction, capitalizing more on the grammar aspect of the novel's pattern than on the cultural nuances. The actual précis task could begin with a matrix in which students are keyed to contrast usage in these two voices: present and imperfect tenses, shifts in narrative focus, the particular events or moments in Tita's life in which the recipes are embedded.

If the class interest is on grammar logic, the basic elements leading to the structure of the matrix are given in figure 5.2. This matrix is purely descriptive and is structured around the text's grammar rather than its cultural context. More culturally relevant and concrete versions are possible, as we show below. The items collected in this matrix, however, because they must be sorted by syntactic markers, can lead to systematic sentence practice of the relations of past and present tenses and to systematic retellings of each story component in its own time frame (not interspersed, as in the original).

FIGURE 5.2. Grammar-Based Précis Elements for *Like Water for Chocolate*

Grammar focus: how episodes shift between two time frames

Grammar logic: how past events correlate with activities involved in preparing a particular recipe

Past Element	Niece's Present-Tense Description of Aunt Tita's Recipes

Moreover, the complex language of the story can be taken apart into various simpler production activities, all of which help clarify nuances in the original, naturalizing them into the learners' own usages.

A course that has as its goal comprehension of longer texts will likely want to concentrate on extensive reading, on practice in assembling and understanding the genre's obligatory moves as a culturally familiar pattern for literary works. A grasp of narrative strategy is also essential, because readers are not yet fully in command of the language. Knowing the major techniques the narrator uses helps them account for shifts in story line or context that might otherwise derail their comprehension. In this way, they can keep more of the text's global genre factors in mind (here the sequence of events) while trying to grasp the local details (individual words and sentences) of the narrative. The teacher might assign the first chapter by focusing reader attention on the text-linguistic features that forge these global-local links. The introductory reading and discussion in class have yielded a partially completed or guided précis to ease students' reading comprehension by providing them with a macropropositional matrix for the unfolding of the story.

This introductory in-class reading also identifies the novel's cultural content in terms of a message pattern: Tita's life as experienced through her cooking and intense relation to food preparation. In chapter 1, the storyteller moves in stages from birth to early childhood to young womanhood. In each stage, the culinary situation is linked to a critical experience. Rather than make discrete point questions (What causes Tita to be born prematurely?) or multiple-choice questions that ask only for specific facts, the matrix connects facts with the expositional logic that casts light on authorial intent. It thus helps reconstruct a time line out of a text that is nonlinear.

The time-line matrix also asks students to approximate closely the language of the text as a reflection of how they perceive the textual logic, a first stage in appreciating the author's discursive choices to convey meaning. If the instructor devises a précis to encourage focus on such structural propositions of the genre (its macropropositions), novice readers of a longer text in a foreign language will be in position to have the textual logic that was established through in-class reading reinforced by a writing assignment.

The guided précis in figure 5.3 illustrates how a précis with an analytic focus on text information can function as such a writing assignment, as a kind of open-ended and discovery-oriented worksheet that provides a holistic reading of the text rather than a collection of unrelated information. Items in italics are given by the instructor; roman typeface indicates student work. As is always true for précis answers, any student selection that matches the logic of the text is considered correct. Students are told to select actual phrases from the text where possible. These references help them attend closely to the language use of the text, they ease teacher assessment by identifying the place where misreadings occur, and they facilitate exchange of ideas in subsequent class discussion. In an advanced Spanish-language class, the format would be completely in Spanish.

FIGURE 5.3. Information Matrix for Chapter 1 of *Like Water for Chocolate*

Period in Tita's Life	*Culinary Context*	*What Results for Tita*
Babyhood	*"onions . . . being chopped"* (5) *"Nacha offered to take charge"* (6)	*"brought on early labor"* (5) "Tita's domain became the kitchen" (7)
Childhood	Sisters "felt playing in the kitchen was foolish and dangerous" (8)	"Nacha became [Tita's] playmate then" (8)
Mid-teens	"When Tita was finishing wrapping the next day's Christmas rolls . . . Mamá Elena informed them that she had agreed to Pedro's marriage to Rosaura." (14)	"Tita felt her body fill with a wintry chill." (14)

Although a preinterpretive task leading to a specific kind of comprehension, this précis also orients students to some key features of Esquivel's
use of magic realism. It teaches them how to do traditional text-centered
readings, associated in the United States with New Criticism. Their reading
of chapter 1 prepares them to see how the novel interweaves the relation
between food and the human condition in aesthetically well-crafted acts of
language. This formalistic, language-based matrix takes more concrete
shape as a cultural understanding.

Developing a Matrix for the Genre as Art

Subsequent assignments stressing this text-centered approach to *Like Water
for Chocolate* as a repository of aesthetic relations validate it through systematic reading. They reveal the work's status as art—as a particularly individual version of a culture's communication norm, as an example of poetic
language set off from standard language (Mukarovsky).

The reader has been prepared for the exaggerated effects of Tita's food—
from mass fits of grief to sexual orgies. Using the implausible circumstances of
her birth as a starting point, a teacher might construct a Spanish-language
précis designed for close reading of magic realism. For chapters 1 and 2, which
deal with the events leading up to the marriage of Pedro, the man Tita loves,
to her sister Rosaura, such a précis is given in figure 5.4. As with the Anderson
Imbert story, discussed in chapter 4 of our volume, by focusing on the scenes
that use techniques of magic realism, students can more readily uncover the

FIGURE 5.4. Précis on Literary Style for Chapters 1 and 2
of *Like Water for Chocolate*

Literary-historical focus: Illustrate the semiotics of magic realism.

Logic: Compare the plausible with the implausible and consider the message system
that results.

Plausible Event	Implausible Result
Tita, "already crying as she emerged" at birth, "washed into this world on a great tide of tears." (6)	"Nacha swept the residue of tears. . . . enough salt to fill a ten pound sack. . . ." (6)
"To make the cake for Pedro and Rosaura's wedding, Tita and Nacha. . . ." (25)	Rosaura eats the cake and leaves, "swept away by a raging rotting river" of other people's vomit. (40)

implications of features that critics define as part of the art of prose. After juxtaposing an event as realistically depicted and its outcome as comically exaggerated, they can interpret that relation in a variety of ways, as indeed critics of New Criticism have done and would recommend.[2]

Such interpretation requires that learners move from the individual phrases and sentences in the matrix cells into more connected discourse. To explain what the matrix means to them, they will have to use more than a single sentence (even when they are prompted to move in a certain direction). One implication statement (for an advanced Spanish class, it would be written in Spanish) might be along the following lines, using more literary vocabulary:

> The matrix reveals a pattern of ordinary feelings and events that become extraordinary and powerfully felt. For the reader, the relation between psyche and soma acquires power as the intensity of the felt experience becomes a palpable reality. At the same time, the implausible extremes are funny, because they reflect and allow release for suppressed feelings, psychological reactions many readers have themselves experienced under similar circumstances.

Other readings are possible. A plot-oriented approach, for example, would simply require students to assemble the story correctly, not considering what kinds of correlations the author uses to create unique statements. There are a myriad links to culture that these exercises might explore.

Developing a Matrix for the Genre's Cultural Patterns

If a course for advanced learners is oriented along the lines more of cultural than literary history, the teacher might use the implication section of the précis to ask students to assess the novel as a document of the social power relations and structures that characterize its episteme: the belief systems implied by the institutions and practices of the place and period in which it was written. The patterns collected in the matrix section of the précis will quite naturally expose social relations of the two time periods involved. A précis designed to help students interpret a text in this way would require them to focus on different aspects of the text, less on the correlation of character development with the text's language, more on how the social standards that motivate the characters are set, manifested, and violated and how the characters relate to real social and historical settings.

These issues are very much the concern of cultural theory since post-structuralism. Most often, poststructuralism points to the gaps between what people believe about their lives and the forces that actually control them. In *Like Water for Chocolate*, as in many romance novels, there is a pronounced gap between the implicit and explicit social rules of the culture. In Tita's world, for example, daughters must obey their mothers unquestioningly or be cast aside. Servants live under a similar constraint. Whether explicitly stated or not, what is considered allowable and what is not show how a dominant order imposes itself on individuals, revealing the class- and gender-bound ideology behind its maxims.

Students can find illustrations of the obedience maxim and its consequences in every chapter of the novel. When Tita questions her mother's demand that she, the youngest daughter, remain single to care for her mother in her old age, her mother doesn't speak to her for a week. The aged servant Nacha, herself a victim of the same injunction as a young woman, dies when her surrogate child Tita loses her suitor at Mama Elena's order.

What the little rural society described in this novel considers true or proper and what it rejects are revealed most explicitly in what happens to those who break the rules, which is another face of the correlations between the two time frames.[3] When the sister Gertrudis runs away and works in a brothel, not only is she ostracized by her mother but all traces of her existence are destroyed as well. She can return to the ranch (and to the narrative) only after her mother has died, but even then she is only a visitor. Her ties to the past have been effectively severed, and the break between the two time frames emerges as a new life and new options for Tita's sister.

To see whether such moral, legal, and social codes are firmly established in the other characters' lives, readers might look at how the text articulates the impact of rule breaking on different groups (e.g., by class, gender, age, wealth) in the society. A text-centered reading reveals that *Like Water for Chocolate* abounds with examples of social rules that are challenged or broken. A focus on aesthetic structure shows how characters' value systems are built up for the reader gradually through their actions and the way the characters are described and articulated (as would be exemplified in précis for successive chapters). A poststructuralist reading looks at social codes and their practical consequences, as actions and reactions or as power patterns. Such a reader correlates winners and losers of power games with espoused codes for behavior in order to establish how social rules operate under different constraints and which codes are more subject to revision.

An even more explicit poststructuralist précis might be based around social power rather than time frames, asking readers to look for social relations that prove problematic for the novel's heroine and then expand that focus to the logical correlative of social expectations and Tita's (the subaltern's) resistance to them. The matrix part of the keyed précis would require readers to identify behaviors that other characters in the text object to or that result in profit or loss for those individuals or groups.[4] A possible matrix that points to the issues highlighted in poststructuralist theory is given in figure 5.5. Viewed typologically (in categories of rules broken, as summarized in the matrix's vertical columns), the social strictures violated in these examples can be read in multiple ways. At this point, the empowered student reader will draw reasonable inferences from the examples selected and placed horizontally to suggest a cause-and-effect relation.

The student might infer that all Tita's responses involve a suppressed resistance to a social injunction and might conclude that Tita, the victim or object of social constraints, passively resists public pressures for accommodation. She is not visibly or publicly in violation of any social expectations; instead, she subverts them privately, through transgressive thinking, thereby insulating herself from social retribution.

The production exercises in the implication section of this précis would differ from those of the time reconstruction of the first matrix and from

FIGURE 5.5. A Poststructuralist Matrix for Initial Chapters
of *Like Water for Chocolate*

Social Power Exercised	*Resistance Undertaken*
Mamá Elena: "You being the youngest daughter means you have to take care of me until the day I die." (10)	Tita wanted to know "who started this family tradition? . . . What happens to women who can't have children?" (11)
"The wedding guests were not performing a social act, they wanted to observe her suffering. . . . " (36)	"She was not meant for the loser's role. She would put on a triumphant expression." (37)
"With a look, Mamá Elena sent Tita away to get rid of [Pedro's] roses." (48)	"It was as if a strange alchemical process had dissolved her entire being in the rose petal sauce. . . . That was the way she entered Pedro's body. . . ." (52)

those of the illusion-reality comparison of the artistic précis. If the advanced class continues through the novel using a matrix focused on issues of social power, students will have both the textual language and the propositional information to draw individual inferences about the larger cultural horizons represented in the text.[5]

Some might conclude that Tita's passivity ultimately betrays her. The power inequities are present in each chapter but in somewhat different form. Tita escapes her mother's overt tyranny, for example, but not the covert tyranny of Pedro's physical attraction. Conditioned to subterfuge and reacting outside the pale of social acceptability, Tita is unable to recognize the exploitative parallels in the two tyrants in her life, across gender lines. She ultimately rejects her mother for indirectly killing her baby nephew but fails to hold the father, Pedro, accountable by that same standard. When Tita has a chance for marriage and a family with a man she cares for, Pedro seduces her and ruins her relationship with her prospective husband: she may have escaped matriarchy, but the patriarchy that dominates even that authority ultimately triumphs.

Using précis information in this way, the reader is in a position to argue that the story deplores overt, publicly sanctioned sacrifices but valorizes the sacrifices arising out of illicit passion and that there is evidence of gender inequity in the culture. The comprehension activity sets up options for sophisticated production activities—for example, an analysis of how, in this culture, the private domain takes precedence over the public sphere. If love does not conquer all, it seems to rationalize all. Matrices may lead other readers to assess the novel as a critique of the very cultural characteristics it purports to mythologize.

With rich literary texts, which are relatively informal and have several layers of meaning, the précis often yields as many text interpretations as there are readers. The patterns evolved suggest different interpretations to be made within the horizon of expectation of either the source or target culture. Students soon become adept in developing their own theses and arguments for individual chapters, because comprehending a longer text becomes easier for them as they proceed. Familiarity with an author's use of genre, plot line, and lexicogrammatical options enables students to take full charge of their reading and articulate their own horizon of expectation.

The chapters of Esquivel's novel documented in other student-generated précis may be read and discussed in many ways, yet all are anchored in textual evidence and textual language. Such plurality reflects the moves of artistic genres, moves that are seldom standardized, unlike those in encyclopedia articles or travel brochures. The possibilities in reading a novel open up many forms of cultural literacy that are less prominent in the personal voice of a diary or the public one of an encyclopedia. A novel contrasts the values and behaviors of a society. After locating passages about the passionate, food-producing Tita; the inhibited sister who cannot cook; and the uninhibited one who dances in the kitchen, student readers of Esquivel can contrast the three characters to make statements about their characteristics and gender stereotypes. Related language production exercises may take different forms, but they share the key facet of being based in the text's representation of its culture rather than drawn from the students' point of view alone.

Readers might find exaggerated the descriptions of the grief, joy, and passion experienced in the wake of eating Tita's food and consequently write or talk about the novel as a parody of magic realism or as a cultural critique, as noted above. Those who argue for the seriousness of these experiences could, on the basis of similar précis documentation, view them as metaphors for the power of sensual experience. Whatever the interpretation, as long as it is grounded in the language and message systems of the text, students are engaging in an exercise in cultural literacy: exploring and evaluating the social and aesthetic semiotics of a text written in another language for another ethnographic community, a different communication situation.

USING THE MATRIX FOR COMPARING GENRES: THE NOVEL TURNED INTO A FILM

When viewing the film version of a literary work, students engage in yet another type of cultural literacy, needing to negotiate both visual and aural message systems that belong in different communication contexts and have different obligatory moves. Even a film that seems to exhibit great fidelity to the print text necessarily alters the reader-viewers' experience of the novel in a variety of ways, once a director's vision is added to the author's words (to say nothing of the intervention by screen writing).

First, a film is not only a different material mode of communication, it also has its own genre characteristics and hence introduces new obligatory and optional moves into any strategy of storytelling it may have borrowed from its source text. For example, it must emphasize dialogue over monologue, showing over telling. Films tend to condense and propel episodes through visual rather than verbal means. Similarly, the camera rather than the narrative voice controls point of view, and the background film score and sound effects can intensify or contrast with the visual scenario.

Second, films guide the reader-viewers' point of view covertly, through these various, almost independently manipulative systems of meaning but with greater specificity than a novel or short story can attain. By showing concrete images of people and places, the film version restricts viewers to its, rather than their, construction of the story's context. It is inherently more controlling of its viewers' expectations, as film theorists like Laura Mulvey underscore. Such images can reconfigure the audience's horizon of expectation through a range of options, from camera angles and color coding to casting.

Cast with well-known, largely Anglo-American actors such as Meryl Streep and Glenn Close, the film version of Isabel Allende's *The House of the Spirits*, for example, became less South American and more international in its cultural framing. Echoes of previous roles played by these stars necessarily influence audiences' and critics' perceptions of their roles in a film about military oppression and class struggle in an unnamed South American country. The politics of the story might have been more evident had the film been cast with unknowns instead of stars.

If the adapted print text belongs to the canon of high culture, the film drawn from it often alters the original in a third way: it generally strives to reach the widest possible audience. Popularization involves using film features designed to appeal to many, whereas a consciously aesthetic novel will highlight the particularity of its narrative voice. Most films reflect the producer's awareness of the target audience's capacity to accept or reject a specific cultural point of view. A mass-market film version's inevitable weighting and addition or omission of elements from the print text alter the message systems of the print version.

Equally predictable special effects broaden audience appeal yet maintain the cachet of a European film when it is remade for a domestic audience in the United States (e.g., *La femme Nikita* [1990] became a TV series in 1997) or when it is made for international distribution by known directors of, for instance, European art films (e.g., Volker Schlöndorff's *The Ogre* [1996], with John Malkovich, who is an international star of independent films, and Arnim Müller-Stahl, who is a known quantity for German audiences). When such "foreign" films have been made not only to be viewed by native speakers of their maker's language and culture but also to reach lucrative United States and international audiences, they provide advanced students with excellent case studies in cross-cultural literacy.

Como agua para chocolate was not such a film. Made in Mexico, it featured actors known largely to Mexican and Central American audiences. Consequently, only the first two types of moves characterize the adaptation of this novel from print text into film: obligatory changes conditioned by the genre (visual versus print) and changes in point of view for different audiences, underplaying the specific Mexican quality of the cultural references in favor of a more general Latin American quality. Space prohibits a detailed analysis of these shifts, but their implications for framing pedagogical tasks that explore some cultural implications of these changes can be briefly addressed.

As already noted in our discussion of the novel, Esquivel's text is divided into monthly installments, each introduced with a particular recipe germane to that episode. Given its time as well as media constraints, the film reduces references to recipes and the implications of food preparation and consumption; it overlooks the detailed time frame in favor of the more general statement that time passes. Consequently, not only the recipes but also the character who plays the narrative voice of the print text, Tita's niece, appear less frequently in the film, and so the typical viewer's focus of attention is more on historical events and a realistic Tita than on the tension between each event and its meaning as a mythic story for future generations.

Even more significant for those readers who saw the function of recipes in the story as parodying clichés or stereotypes about Latin romance novels, this element is reconfigured through visual emphases that viewers may not see as equivalent to the descriptions in the text. A real kitchen does not convey to a film audience a sense of parody; instead it fosters identification with the culinary culture of a sociological group.

Perhaps most striking to viewers who have read the novel will be the film's depictions of relationships between key figures. Whereas the novel describes Tita's mother as despotically matriarchal, repeatedly punishing and even viciously beating her daughter for minor offenses, in the film this woman is merely stern. As a result, film viewers are more likely to read Tita's verbal resistance to her mother as petulance and the meaningful glances and verbal exchanges with her sister's husband as engagement in reprehensible collusive behavior.

The novel, making many more references to the ways and means of Mamá Elena's virtual enslavement of Tita, provides legitimacy to Tita's subterfuges: the reader sees them as essential for the young girl's psychological and physical survival. Instead of petulant and underhanded, the novel's Tita can be read as both long-suffering and courageously independent. As noted above, the movie script is attributed to the author. As often happens with film adaptations, authors sanction changes made to accommodate media and production needs. Isabel Allende, for example, also has author credit (as novelist) for the movie version of *The House of the Spirits,* although it changes her work's messages.

If asked to look for contrasts between images in the novel and those depicted in the film, students can identify them as evidence of the film-maker's effort to make many aesthetically exaggerated features of the book more palatable to a larger viewing public. A student précis comparing images might note that where the book has guests spewing rivers of vomit after eating the wedding cake Tita has helped prepare, the film's camera looks down at a discrete distance on the backs of people lined up along a fence over a riverbank while a soothing narrative voice announces that they are vomiting. Where the novel has Tita, the presumed culprit for this poisoning, receive a "tremendous hiding from Mamá Elena," for which she needs two weeks in bed to recover (41), in the film even the mother's barely articulated verbal remonstrance is cut short by Tita's announcement that their chief cook (Tita's surrogate mother) has died.

Students who find such shifts between these different versions of the same scene—in terms of media presentation, genre conventions, and handling of stereotypes—have the basis to draw inferences about the cultural implications of the changes. For example, they might conclude that the novel with its critique or parody of patriarchal myths prevalent in Central and South American countries has turned into a film about a mother-daughter relationship whose archetypal conflicts are embellished with trappings of magic realism.

If supported by careful attention to these contrasts (elicited by précis tasks), students will be able to analyze the cultural positions of the two genres in a sophisticated fashion. The novel depicts a landowner's tyrannical cruelties, thereby implying a need to reassess patriarchal norms (whether embodied by a man or a woman); the film tells a bland fairy tale about the eternally human. By directing viewer attention to mothers and their pasts, the filmmakers have shifted the novel's focus away from its Mexican-specific messages about daughters and their futures against a specific political background. Instead of being introduced to a particular tradition, the international cinema audience views a universal, humanist message.

The pedagogies associated with the précis apply in other, mostly nonfictional genres, though with less variety and more predictability—in general magazine essays, in biographies, autobiographies, movie reviews, interviews. That nonfictional texts are formal generally makes them easier to read (easier in intention and content but not necessarily in grammatical form or specialized vocabulary) than those genres that are marked by originality and hence have fewer obligatory formal features. But increasingly authors of all stripes aspire to a global audience, so their obligatory moves and registers (formal features) are relatively predictable to audiences across cultures.

A Movie Review

A movie review of *Like Water for Chocolate*, particularly one published on a Web site, would be an easy read in comparison with the novel: the reader knows in advance that the review will be for or against (aspects of) the film. Movie reviews commonly begin with a judgmental statement that frames the subsequent synopsis of content and genre features in conjunction with an assessment of the work. Depending on the complexity of the review, the précis format for this genre can ask students to look for descriptive features and reasons for accepting or rejecting them or for the reasons for accepting or rejecting features and the judgments that result. In either case, the reader is to ascertain the reviewer's criteria for recommending or rejecting the book or film. From the standpoint of fostering students' cultural literacy, reviews offer fairly transparent windows into perceptions about different segments in a larger cultural community. Their structures are very common across cultures, while the contents often reflect a specific culture. United States reviews, for example, are much more likely than European reviews to fault films for ethnic and gender insensitivity.

Reading several reviews with differing assessments will help students learn how to look for the basis for judgments in this relatively formal genre and to identify the accepted values of the reviewer and the review's audience. Such an exercise provides practice in ascertaining how individual statements are made in formulaic genres, in particular cultural contexts.

An industry or studio Web site for the movie version of *Like Water for Chocolate* will predictably provide readers with an advertising variant of a review stemming from a disinterested source. Note the example in appendix A. An obligatory move for such a Web site, the review-promotion, made by the company advertising the movie, commences with a paragraph synopsis that stresses the role of the smells and flavors of the traditional Mexican kitchen ("los olores y sabores de la cocina tradicional mexicana") joined to the theme of eternal love ("un amor que perdurará más allá del tiempo"). The five paragraphs of comments that follow each pick up a different theme: the significance of the novel on which the film is based, the personal history of the director, the international appeal of the film, its audience appeal, and its artistic merits. The segments are anonymous, signaling a generic rather than a personal sender of these messages, an everyone's review designed to interest the maximum number of viewers for the film.

Since the intent of the review is evident from the outset, even novice readers can note each paragraph topic (what aspect is discussed) and the particular virtues praised. They could easily create a précis whose logic revealed the review's bases for praise and the rationale for such praise. Thus the topic of paragraph 5, the aesthetic value of the film ("un éxito a nivel artístico") is supported with phrases like "an interesting story, well executed . . . marketed in an intelligent way" ("historia interesante, bien realizada, . . . comercializada de manera inteligente"). The sum of such a system of features and inferences from all five paragraphs enables students to see how moviemakers in our neighboring country to the south try to position themselves as culturally unique, both independent of and competitive with Hollywood. Students encounter a completely familiar formula from Hollywood marketing yet used in a different way.

An Author Interview

Other genres related to book or film promotion are equally formulaic but focus on other content areas: plot, personal stories, quality, social messages. An author or actor interview, for example, has aims similar to those of the production-sponsored appraisal of the movie, but such an interview can be more challenging to read because of its dialogic structure. The interview must be framed by the interviewer, usually with a colorful description of the subject, then followed by questions and answers in which the subject lives up to or counters that description. This format, the leeway afforded verbal exchanges, and the inflated claims that celebrities often indulge in can become more comprehensible if the genre is read using the strategies of a précis format reflecting the interview's obligatory moves.

An illustration can be taken from an interview in *La jornada* in 1995, just after the appearance of Esquivel's second novel, *La ley del amor* (*The Law of Love*; see appendix B).[6] Laura Esquivel is briefly introduced as a person "conscious of the energy of the universe" ("Consciente de la energia del universo") yet as a modern woman who loves movies because they are "the artistic manifestation of our century" ("La manifestación artística de nuestro siglo"). The subsequent exchanges are grouped by the subtitles "The Story of a Passion" ("La historia de una pasión"), "The Invasion of Time" ("La invasión del tiempo"), and "Just Laura, Nothing More" ("Laura, nada más"). The interviewer has set up a grid that keys a specific ideology about what an author is: timeless elements of the woman as artist ("energy of the universe," a metaphor tapping into certain gendered ideas of what a female-creator must be) yet engaged in this century (making a space for a modern woman, who is nonetheless anchored in traditional values—perhaps a good space for a Mexican audience to learn to listen to a younger female author who is social-critical) ("Laura Esquivel").

The subtitles prepare the reader for a broad range of serious topics but relatively little substance. Comparisons with United States counterpart interviews in *People Magazine* or on *Entertainment Tonight* could point to differences in self-fashioning as culturally marked realizations of audience expectation. A recent United States interviewer would scarcely consider it appropriate to hint that a woman should be inward-centered, a force of nature, instead of social-critical. Even without such cultural comparisons, a précis structured to follow the internal logic of such an interview could lead to a matrix following the structure of the genre by noting two or three "typical stereotypes imposed by the interviewer-author responses that deflect (or support) such insinuations."

Students might observe, for example, that a single reference to *La ley del amor* turns the interview into a promotion of Laura Esquivel the person and not her new novel. This impression is reinforced by the pattern of questions and answers, with most questions in the vein of "Do you believe you are the same Laura Esquivel who gave us *Like Water for Chocolate?*" (". . . crees ser la misma Laura Esquivel que hace años nos entregó *Como agua para choco-*

late?") and answers such as "No . . . [that book's] immense success changed my way of life and automatically changed me as well" ("No . . . Su éxito inmenso cambió por completo mis circunstancias y automáticamente yo también cambié").

Such exchanges reveal less about the novel than about the interviewer's assumptions regarding female authors: what facets of Esquivel's life are worth noticing or asking about and what stereotypes of authorship Esquivel accepts for herself, an essentialist definition of woman-artist that seems dated to many United States audiences. Filling out a matrix that illustrates this tension could prepare students for a short writing assignment on the implications of the sample queries and responses students select (fig. 5.6).

Students who have examined the interview from this perspective of contrasting Lauras are poised to write about or discuss intercultural play in the content of this exchange. In the interview's emphasis on Esquivel's personality, the author's observations about herself follow a pattern of enthusiasm

Figure 5.6. Sample Information Matrix Contrasting Agendas of Interviewer and Interviewee

Interviewer: The Intimate, Personal Laura	The Interviewee: The Outgoing, Community-Oriented Laura
"Esta relativa demora podría leerse como cierto temor." (question 1)	". . . sólo disfruto de la posibilidad de tener . . . una relación directa con el lector."
("This relative delay [i.e., the gap between your first and second book] could be read as a certain fear/ timidity.")	(". . . I just enjoy having the possibility . . . of a direct relationship with the reader.")
"¿También [cambió] tu relación con la literatura?" (question 4)	"Lo que cambió fue mi ritmo de trabajo. . . ." ("What changed was the rhythm of my work.")
("Has it [success] also changed your relationship to literature?")	"Me gusta hablar por teléfono. . . ." ("I enjoy talking on the telephone.")
"En Nueva York . . . ganas algo: el anonimato." (question 10)	"Las personas se acercan a mí sólo porque soy otro ser humano y ya. Allá lejos me vuelvo Laura, nada más."
("In New York you gain something— anonymity.")	("The people around me [in New York] know me for myself, because I'm just another person. There I can revert to being Laura, nothing else.")

about the vicissitudes of living in the real world that contribute tacitly to any debate about her choosing to live in the United States and about the domestic norms and values she experiences in Mexico.

Typically, the early dusks of winter depress her in New York ("en invierno, la noche llega a las cuatro de la tarde. Eso me deprime"), but the anonymity she enjoys opens up a different style of relationship to others, one freeing her from the artificial life of the celebrity ("me encanta [el anonimato] porque me permite establecer un contacto más espontáneo y natural con otras personas"). Perversely, after her literary success, she can be "more real" in a United States urban environment than in a Mexican community.

These contrasts provide the basis for an implication statement that assesses Esquivel's interaction with the interviewer. A class discussion of the matrix leads to a paragraph or essay that addresses stereotyping most explicitly. Such an assignment might direct students to describe the exchange using forms of negation (what Laura denies or how she differs with the interviewer) or have them explore their interpretations of those responses with reference to their matrices. The second task would ask them to speculate about the differences they have identified, necessitating use of the subjunctive. The resulting statement would use language generated by students, introduce subjunctive forms, but at the same time rely heavily on the language of the text. The example below (with subjunctive forms in italics) illustrates articulation of opinion anchored in the logic of the text in question:[7]

> Yo no creo que su demora *se pueda* leer como temor. Me parece que ella es una persona que quiere establecer un contacto espontáneo con otras personas. Es posible que su falta de tiempo *sea* causa de esta demora. Creo que le molesta que su entrevistadora la *trate* como mujer tímida cuyo mundo es el amor y la cocina. Por eso, es natural que *quiera* defender su vida social. Parece que tampoco le gusta que la entrevistadora la *trate* como persona especial por su éxito inmenso. Es indudable que el éxito ha cambiado su vida y su ritmo de trabajo. Pero a pesar de que su éxito lo *haya* alterado todo, ella quiere ser tratada como los otros.

> I don't think her delay [in publishing a second novel] should be read as timidity. It seems to me that she is someone who likes spontaneous contact with other people. It is possible that her lack of time is the reason for the delay. I think it bothers her that her interviewer treats her like a fearful woman whose world is love and

the kitchen. Therefore, it is only natural that she would defend her social life. It seems that she also doesn't want her interviewer to treat her in a special way because of her immense success. Doubtless, success has changed her life and her rhythm of work. But even though her success has altered everything, she wants to be treated like others.

A student who uses matrix information to write a statement like the one above has grasped that Esquivel resists the interviewer's attempts to essentialize her. Another such statement might refer to the way Esquivel counters with examples of her wider intellectual and social spheres: her great admiration for Thomas Mann's *Death in Venice*, her love of dancing, and the way she has dealt publicly with the challenges of success.

Such student insights lay the groundwork for looking at features like the typical obligatory moves of the celebrity interview. The central problems of Esquivel's cultural locus are addressed: mention of role models (Mann), her human side, her struggles with fame. Her readers wonder if she has sold out to the United States? Is she really still Mexican, familiar with the domestic scenes and like the "normal people" described in her books, or is she something else? In the course of the interview, Esquivel carefully erases such dichotomies, pointing out that *natural* does not need to mean "born domestic" and that *authentic* does not mean that a woman who writes cannot look outside her own culture for inspiration. Students looking for such differences will realize that this exchange is very loaded—but by implication only, since no overt rejection of interviewer questions or interrogation of the author's answers occurs.

REALIZING DIFFERENT CURRICULAR OBJECTIVES WITH THE PRÉCIS

We have illustrated how genre literacy and cultural literacy can be developed out of a student's language ability. We have also shown the degree to which the précis, a task sequence that leads a learner from identifying a particular perspective and logical system for information available in any genre into different forms of production, applies as a tool for flexible pedagogical and curricular design. As demonstrated in the examples above, the matrix section of a précis varies with the choice of instructor and reader goals. What the advanced foreign language learner reads to find out should, ultimately, be determined by pedagogical and curricular goals—by the focus and logic settings of the entire précis, which set up production holistically. In this sense, the précis functions merely as a template for fully developed exercises that serve particular instructional goals. It is a foundation on which to ease reading comprehension, to argue textual implications, to have classroom discussions, to make writing assignments, and to foster critical thinking.

The précis can also offer more; it can invite teachers and students to value multiperspectival approaches that allow one to approach texts at ever greater depths of understanding, interpreting them in acknowledged theoretical frameworks valued by scholars. Almost any area of cultural or literary theory can lead to discovery learning. Theoretical frameworks help direct students' attention to a pattern of information that can be put to strategic use in interpreting a text. Otherwise students form opinions based on loosely related or isolated language facts. The logic and implication of the précis are shaped by its interpretive goals, which in turn are set by the theoretical, cognitive, linguistic, and cultural ends of the instructor. When the cues for those logic and implication sections are provided, the précis connects this one specific act of cultural, cognitive, and linguistic learning to the larger goals of the class, as reflected in the initial and concluding phases of textual analysis.

Note that these overriding curricular goals do not restrict student creativity. Instead, they allow students to develop, in the framework of the précis matrix, their own chains of argument and evidence. Such chains lead them to the cultural stereotyping and magic realism used by Esquivel. The implications cued as the final stage should be set up adequately by the matrix's logic, in both its vertical and horizontal correlations, as textual evidence (including cultural specifics and exact language, which is telling in other ways) is presented for the more schematic logic proposed at the outset. The pattern of the interviewer's questions and Esquivel's responses enables readers to look at a text's macropropositions and their possible interpretations in a denser logical and critical context. Since students use their own examples, they evaluate the consistency of their logics instead of being graded by the teacher's norms. An exercise that is carefully targeted in a class syllabus can nonetheless allow much freedom of expression and preference. It is learner-centered without soliciting an inventory of purely subjective views; it produces substantiated response rather than free-wheeling opinion.

When instructors control the focus and logic of a textual reading, they have explicitly instrumentalized their students' readings toward the larger goals of a learning sequence. Such guided use of a précis format character-izes its implementation for novice readers. Beginners and intermediate stu-dents can gradually be encouraged to undertake unprompted précis as they become familiar with this key template in a developmental sequence—to provide all sections in the full précis themselves. By the time they qualify as advanced readers, they should be weaned from topic and logic statements that originate with their professor. They must provide such statements themselves, as standards against which to evolve their own arguments. Ad-vanced learners no longer require an external aide to develop strategies and facilitate cultural as well as textual analysis; they must get in the habit of setting guideposts for themselves. In other words, at some point the entire précis for advanced students should originate with the reader. Only when they can articulate the logic and goal of their reading are advanced learners prepared for fully independent reading and analysis, with content, linguis-tic, and cultural learning-to-learn strategies at least partially in place.

The précis helps join two horizons of expectation, that of the text and that of the reader, and so it is particularly important in uncovering patterns of cultural literacy and allowing cross-cultural comparisons. It helps readers create patterns out of data points. It is crucial that these patterns of textual convention be identified as genres. Familiarity with the concept of genre as an established, conventional form of cultural communication is integral to the development of independent reading and to a more holistic cultural lit-eracy. Awareness of who has written a text and for what audience remains the framework for any use of texts and textuality for both language acquisi-tion and cultural knowledge.

A prompted précis might point learners to the cultural uses of inter-views or reviews or how novelists transact and recast stereotypes to tell new stories. As a responsible template for tasks aiding learners in comprehend-ing a text and assessing its implications, joint consideration of reader goals and genre as a cultural convention of communication must go into the con-struction of each précis. The précis logic suggested by the genre itself in-volves the communication situation intimately. In the interview discussed above, there is internalization of the habit of viewing the interviewee as forced by the interviewer into a position that reflects the generic audience attitude for the publication. Distinguishing between what is asked and how questions are answered points to the stereotypes underlying the text and its "implied readership," to use Iser's phrase (*Implied Reader*). The semiotics of terms such as "force of nature" opposes Esquivel's language pointing to an independent authorial identity. This give and take is the essence and art of the interview as commonly practiced today. This public negotiation of distinct stereotypes defines the genre.

Genres with less generic audiences (generic audiences include the maximum number of users, regardless of age, cultural or class location, finances, and sometimes even gender) enable a wider range of reader options. They tend to be more "writerly" and less "readerly," as Roland Barthes explains in *The Pleasure of the Text*. Yet one can question assumptions about how culturally specific even these most formulaic or generic of genres become. One can point to how the gamut of theoretical approaches sets other instructional goals for further stages in that class. If the learning goal for Esquivel's novel is aesthetic (i.e., if the class is considering the novel as a form of art), the impact of realistic elements juxtaposed with magical ones might become a key reader strategy. To be sure, each novel has an implied reader, but the class would be looking at the text's storytelling logic, its language, and the like. When a student writes a précis on Esquivel's novel in this context, the implication stage that completes the exercise (after the reading, and after a class discussion of matrix details) might include references to the cultural significance implied by the patterns uncovered, but such references would not be the focus of the précis.

Quite the reverse might hold for a course in cultural history or women's studies. A précis constructed along the lines of a poststructuralist approach might lead readers to juxtapose the social constraints in any given situation with leading characters' responses to those constraints. Or readers might consider the breaking of rules and socially charged consequences or the ways in which such consequences are circumvented. A class may question whether the implied readership of the novel is male or female, rich or poor, depending on who in the text is represented as right or wrong over the course of the novel.

Acknowledging aspects of genre framing and the obligatory moves arising out of it can be deployed in précis strategies that lead students to identify aesthetic or cultural features. Such choices foster fulfillment of particular instructional objectives, which in turn can ease the reading task of the advanced learner. Applying the précis as an exercise template, crafting an approach to a chosen genre, enables teachers to develop exercises and exercise chains that designate the cultural literacies they want advanced students to achieve. At the same time, the exercise sequence encompassed in a précis allows those students to remain in charge of and responsible for their own work, as independent thinkers informing one another in a cohesive community of readers, sensitive to their own cultural contexts as well as to those of the texts they read.

NOTES

1. Note that typical reading questions are prejudicial, since they tell learners what the important information is, from the instructor's point of view, rather than help learners construct patterns of information so they can help make such decisions for themselves.
2. These approaches are sometimes referred to as text-immanent or formalist (see Richards; Marshall). Donald Marshall characterizes I. A. Richards's *Principles of Literary Criticism* as "the influential founding book for Anglo-American formalism" (46). In *The Verbal Icon*, William K. Wimsatt argues that the critic demonstrates a work's coherence in its verbal structures in order to reveal its unique aesthetic qualities. These two strands, humanist values and their aesthetic realizations, characterize interpretive work that today is often found in feminist, psychological, and new-historicist interpretations.
3. Kristine Ibsen views the novel as a post-Boom parody. Susan Dobrian assesses the work as a parody of popular myths about romance. Antonio Marquet turns to related reception issues in an article that looks at the basis for the novel's success. Maria Valdés looks for paradigms of social reality in the novel. Many studies consider the novel from the perspectives of gender and related cultural implications, exploring the identity of the Mexican woman (see Escaja; Whittingham and Silva). Touching on similar issues from a different vantage point, María Angélica Álvarez sees traditional norms interrogated by subversive discourses in the novel.
4. This is the approach found in texts like Michel Foucault's *Discipline and Punish*. In practice, poststructuralism, deconstructionism, and structuralism sometimes go together. See, for example, Berman; Fekete; Harland; Marshall. For purposes of this discussion, we focus on the historical dimension of poststructuralism, which is absent in both deconstructionism and structuralism. For work on how these power structures are administered through language use, see Bourdieu, *Language*.
5. Eagleton presents a similarly conceived Marxist analysis by arguing that "the primary terms on which Charlotte Brontë's fiction handles relationships are those of dominance and submission" (29).
6. For reasons of accessibility, we used the copy of this review ("Laura Esquivel") available on the Web through a link at home.t-online.de/home/Andreas.Huelsm/. This site offers pedagogical suggestions in conjunction with photographs, samples of music, transcriptions of selected scenes from the film, and links to information relating to the filming of the book and the novel's author.
7. This example is not an actual student essay. It was written for the authors by Laura Sager, based on the matrix of information she had selected from the interview, as noted in the text. We thank her for her help in translating and interpreting the Spanish-language segments in this chapter and an earlier version (Swaffar, "Template").

APPENDIX A: PROMOTIONAL REVIEW OF THE FILM
COMO AGUA PARA CHOCOLATE (Source: *Como agua*)

Sinopsis

Historia de amor y buena comida ubicada en el México fronterizo de principios de siglo XX. Tita y Pedro ven obstaculizado su amor cuando Mamá Elena decide que Tita, su hija menor, debe quedarse soltera para cuidar de ella en su vejez. Enmedio de los olores y sabores de la cocina tradicional mexicana, Tita sufrirá largos años por un amor que perdurará más allá del tiempo.

Comentario

Como agua para chocolate ha significado un fenómeno muy interesante dentro de la cultura mexicana contemporánea. La primera novela de Laura Esquivel obtuvo muy buenas críticas y un gran éxito de ventas, algo muy difícil de lograr en un país en el que la gente lee muy poco. Calificada como ejemplo del realismo mágico, la novela logró traspasar los límites de la mera curiosidad y colocarse como el libro de ficción más vendido en México en los últimos veinte años.

Su paso al cine fue producto de la buena suerte. Alfonso Arau—actor y director mexicano muy popular a principios de los setenta—se interesó inmediatamente en producir un filme basado en la novela de Esquivel. Al fin y al cabo ella no podía poner muchas objeciones, pues el interesado en filmar la historia de amor entre Tita y Pedro era su esposo. En los últimos años Arau no era muy popular en México, pues su carrera la había continuado en Hollywood, casualmente el lugar en donde hacer cine es algo de lo más común.

De esta manera llegó *Como agua para chocolate* el filme. Realizado con un presupuesto mucho mayor que el común para el cine mexicano, con técnicas cinematográficas hollywoodenses y con un gran sentido comercial. El resultado es un filme fiel a la novela original, excelentemente producido y, sobre todo, inteligentemente comercializado. Los diez Arieles otorgados a esta producción y el éxito internacional de la misma comprueban que Arau sabía muy bien lo que estaba haciendo.

¿Cuál fue la clave del éxito de *Como agua para chocolate*?

Indiscutiblemente el filme posee muchos valores estéticos, pero esto no valdría de nada si no tuviera nada qué contar. El cine es un arte que narra historias visualmente. Para que el público se interese por una película, ésta debe contar con personajes interesantes que vivan un conflicto que mantenga la atención del espectador. Una buena historia es la clave principal para un buen filme.

¿Se puede conjuntar un éxito económico con un éxito a nivel artístico?

Definitivamente la respuesta es sí. Desgraciadamente el cine mexicano se ha debatido en dos polos artificialmente opuestos: el cine comercial—barato y vulgar—y el cine de arte —pretencioso y aburrido. Los cineastas mexicanos de calidad han insistido en contarnos historias que no nos interesan, ya sea porque no se comprenden, o porque no tienen elementos que apelen a nuestra más elemental atención. *Como agua para chocolate* encontró el "hilo negro" del cine de éxito: una historia interesante, bien realizada y, no hay que olvidarlo, comercializada de manera inteligente.

APPENDIX B: INTERVIEW WITH LAURA ESQUIVEL,
by Cristina Pacheco (Source: "Laura Esquivel")

Laura Esquivel, al Rescate del Mundo Íntimo en el
"Siglo del Desequilibrio"

II y última

"El siglo XX será visto como el siglo del desequilibrio. El excesivo propósito de conseguir el progreso nos desequilibró; pero creo que la gente se está dando cuenta de que por eso mismo ha llegado el momento de recuperar su mundo íntimo, su mundo sagrado", dice Laura Esquivel. Consciente de la energía del universo, atesora recuerdos, sólo teme a los resentimientos y acaricia un sueño: "Ir a Venecia de luna de miel. Hace mucho tiempo que he querido ir allá, quizá porque la novela de Thomas Mann me fascinó tanto y luego también me encantó su versión cinematográfica".

Respetuosa y amante de las palabras, Laura Esquivel es apasionada del cine, "la manifestación artística de nuestro siglo", como espectadora y también como escritora: "porque es un medio que te brinda infinidad de posibilidades. Resulta apasionante la magia de poder narrar con imágenes". Laura Esquivel recurrió a las imágenes en partes de su segunda novela: *La ley del amor*.

La historia de una pasión

1. Entre tu primera novela y *La ley del amor* median seis años. Esta relativa demora podría leerse como cierto temor. Imposible que recuerdes cuántos ejemplares de *Como agua para chocolate* has autografiado, pero supongo que recordarás el momento en que lo hiciste por vez primera.

Claro que sí: estaba nerviosísima. Al principio, cuando alguien me pedía que le autografiara mi novela me costaba mucho trabajo pensar en lo que iba a poner en la dedicatoria, me sentía comprometida a escribir algo muy especial. Ahora es distinto. He eliminado ese tono de nerviosismo y sólo disfruto de la posibilidad de tener, aunque sea momentáneamente, una relación directa con el lector.

La invasión del tiempo

2. Ese cambio de actitud, ¿implica también un cambio en ti o crees ser la misma Laura Esquivel que hace años nos entregó *Como agua para chocolate*?

No soy la misma, por supuesto. Cuando escribí *Como agua . . .* no pude siquiera imaginar lo que pasaría con la novela. Su éxito inmenso cambió por completo mis circunstancias y automáticamente yo también cambié.

3. Madonna dice algo muy inteligente al respecto: "La gente siempre piensa la forma en que el éxito cambia a una persona, pero pocas veces toma en cuenta la manera en que las personas cambian frente a quien tiene el éxito".

Siempre existe un juego de interacción del mundo hacia ti y de ti hacia el mundo. En mi caso, lo que sucedió es que de pronto me sentí completamente invadida, atosigada casi, por algo que no había planeado ni esperaba y que me desconcertó muchísimo. Quizá todo hubiera sido distinto si yo hubiese tenido un periodo de preparación; es decir, si me hubiera llegado el éxito en la cuarta o quinta novela y no en la primera. Pero no fue así y el éxito removió y lo alteró todo.

4. ¿También tu relación con la literatura?

No. Tampoco variaron mis objetivos. Lo que cambió fue mi ritmo de trabajo. El éxito me dejó sin tiempo para mí o para trabajar con tranquilidad; me quitó la paz de que había disfrutado antes de que se publicara la novela. Entonces comencé una etapa muy difícil, donde tuve que seguir escribiendo enmedio de viajes, llamadas telefónicas, entrevistas, problemas personales. Me gusta hablar por teléfono, pero si respondiera a todas las llamadas que recibo al día ya no iba a quedarme tiempo para conversar con mi hija, para meterme a la cocina, para salir de mi casa o cocinar.

Laura, nada más

5. ¿Sigues cocinando?

Aquí ya no puedo hacerlo, por todos los compromisos que tengo. En cambio en Nueva York sí lo hago. Allá me pierdo. Puedo ir tranquilamente a los centros de abasto y comprar lo que necesito para hacer los platillos mexicanos que me gustan y de los que depende el sazón.

6. ¿Qué significa para ti el hecho de cocinar?

Es un acto amoroso en la medida que te brinda la posibilidad de producirle placer a otra persona.

7. También escribir es un acto amoroso.

Es cierto, y encuentro una relación muy estrecha entre uno y otro. Lo mismo pienso acerca del baile (entre paréntesis, te diré que me encanta bailar). La escritura tiene un ritmo, un movimiento, una especie de respiración a la que es necesario integrarse. Por eso procuro mantener cierta disciplina.

8. Háblame de ella.

Me levanto temprano, realizo una serie de prácticas de meditación que me permitan proteger mis silencios y escucharme. Después puedo ponerme a escribir.

9. Lo haces a la luz del día.

Sí, y no sabes hasta qué punto influye sobre mí, sobre mi trabajo, la luz del sol. Mirar el amanecer, la luz que avanza, me llena de ánimo y de energía, me entusiasma. Si me cuesta vivir en Nueva York es porque allá, en invierno, la noche llega a las cuatro de la tarde. Eso me deprime, entre otras cosas porque siento que perdí la mitad de un día.

10. En Nueva York, como en otras partes del mundo donde los inviernos son severos, pierdes parte del día, pero ganas algo: el anonimato. Eso ¿te desagrada o te libera?

Me encanta porque me permite establecer un contacto más espontáneo y natural con otras personas. Ninguna se me acerca porque escribí tal o cual cosa o porque piensa que soy importante debido a que mi obra fue traducida a tales o cuales idiomas. Las personas se acercan a mí sólo porque soy otro ser humano y ya. Allá lejos me vuelvo Laura, nada más. Luego, claro, hay que volver al medio y la vida que son míos. Eso también es muy hermoso, aunque tenga que compartir mis horas de trabajo o gastar mucho tiempo en responder llamadas telefónicas.

APPENDIX C: PRÉCIS FORMAT AND GRADING

Model for Précis (Weekly Analytic Assignments)

There is a difference between a text's facts and the strategy used to present those facts. A précis (*PRAY-see*) reflects this difference. It is designed to show the structure of a text's argument, not just be a set of notes on the text's contents. A précis is one typed page in length.

A Précis Has Four Parts

1. A statement about the text's FOCUS. This is the main issue that the text addresses. **You write* a concise statement (1–2 sentences) of that focus.
Likely alternatives:
issues or problems
representative concerns of a group or its interlocking set of beliefs
institutions/systems
events and their characteristics or repercussions
Examples:
"the structure of the mind and how it relates to behavior in the social world"
"roles available to professionals and the personality problems they cause"
What not to do: Do not include journalistic commentary, examples, or evalua-tions—just state what is there in the text.

2. A statement of the text's LOGIC and GOAL, which will introduce a CHART WITH HEADINGS, a MATRIX encompassing the text's data in two parallel columns of notes (usually with page references to the reading).
**You write* a sentence describing the logic pattern.
Examples:
"By examining the sources of _____, the author shows the consequences of _____."
"In order to _____, the text correlates the _____ and _____ of social behaviors"
Typical verbs marking such logic
compare
contrast
link causally
cause
follow

3. A MATRIX with two column headings creating classes of information that the author systematically correlates with each other. Under these headings, you typically add three or four examples that fit the content of the text into its form.
Typical categories of information:
characteristics of a model, role, event
stages in an event or process
sources, conditions, or restrictions on a context
participants or interest groups
effects, impact, consequences
goals, purposes to be realized

4. A paragraph indicating the IMPLICATIONS of the information pattern. This is *not* a description of the information pattern or focus, but rather an analysis of the covert statement made by the text through its information and pattern. That is, what is this text *good for*, especially as seen from the outside? In setting the text up this way, what is being hidden, asserted, or brushed aside? What is new or old-fashioned about the correlations made? Who would profit most by this arrangement?

From Reading to Reading Literature: A Language
Chapter 6 | Teaching Perspective

If the précis is a central tool for fostering access to more advanced forms of cultural and linguistic literacy in the context of a single-course sequence, then the study of genre, defined as a structured form of communication, serves a similar purpose for the FL curriculum whose goal is multiple cultural literacies. We are not simply pleading for a return to literature. Instead, we argue for changes in what is understood by literary studies to integrate advanced forms of literacy into the typical postsecondary curriculum. A central part of that fundamental reconsideration needs to be a renewed awareness of the language base of literary studies and of the links that exist between texts of various genres, including literature, and language acquisition.

Some brief historical framing may prove helpful in situating our concerns. In his history of the discipline, Gerald Graff has argued that the canon of what was considered literary studies in the nineteenth century encompassed a broad spectrum of text types, intended for mass as well as select audiences. More recently, however, from the 1950s into the 1970s, the teaching of literature became constructed as an exclusive enterprise, stressing its own body of knowledge: the period, genre, and formal features of written texts judged to be fine art or fine writing. The canon wars of the 1980s and 1990s challenged that educational approach, as questions about cultural authority, reader empowerment, and the ethics of hegemonic culture were raised. In consequence, students' experience in studying literature at high schools and colleges changed radically.

Earlier generations were trained in various forms of textual exegesis, in the kinds of systematic pedagogy associated with New Criticism (close readings, explications de texte), often formalist in inspiration. Literature classrooms in English and foreign languages today have moved away from such system-based training imperatives to classroom management strategies that stress student-centered approaches, critical writing, and critical thinking. Where poetics and linguistics once ruled as the tools to be taught to students, classrooms now privilege cultural studies and various reader-centered approaches (the most familiar of which appeared under the rubric of *Pedagogy of the Oppressed*, by Paolo Freire, but which can arguably encompass even much current work in composition theory).

We leave it to others to describe in detail the impact of this scholarly shift on the classroom dedicated to teaching literature in students' first or native language.[1] Our concern is instead with the consequences of that shift for those of us teaching literature in a student's first foreign language or L2.[2] Given that the rationale for including "great literature" in a secondary- or postsecondary-level curriculum has either faded or is at least seriously challenged, teaching FL literature seems to many teaching professionals daunting at best, undesirable or impossible at worst (see Kirkpatrick; Pratt; Sollors). The consequences are dire: FL curricula no longer have clear mandates for the teaching of literature (why, how, when, to whom?) or clear points of connection between FL classroom practices and those represented in the teaching of L1 literatures and cultures (see Scott and Tucker for a series of perspectives on these connections).

The bulk of this chapter suggests a new rapprochement between L1 and FL curricula and the study of literature, outlining how learning to read and learning to read literature and other genres can become concurrent goals for a holistic curriculum (see Byrnes and Kord; Swaffar, "Reading"; Burnett and Fonder-Solano). More specifically, we argue that the study of genre (literary and other) can offer a framework for inserting our scholarship into our pedagogies in new ways, principally in the FL classroom but also (at least) in the world-literature branch of the L1 curriculum. Genre can be redefined to accommodate both older and newer forms of cultural knowledge, foster cultural and multicultural literacies for our students, and close the gap between our roles as teachers and scholars.

PEDAGOGY IN LITERATURE TEACHING:
THE NEED TO REDEFINE GENRE

Among the reasons for arguing the place of literature in the undergraduate curriculum, the following is critical: while literary scholarship has over the last two decades called into question traditional assumptions about canonicity, few if any new approaches to teaching literature have resulted. This statement is bald but needs to be considered as at least an outsider's view of the collective enterprise of literature departments. Responding to Stanley Fish's question "Is there a text in this class?," FL departments originally answered, "No, only readings," an extreme response to a narrowly conceived "proper" study of literature.[3] In so doing, literature departments, L1 and FL alike, sacrificed a straightforward access to the specific content of literary studies without creating new approaches to teaching literature. What was left was reader-driven (customer-driven) readings of texts that encouraged students to react to literature instead of reading it as a specifically placed cultural artifact.

In practice, scholars of earlier days in literary studies defined their areas of specialization in terms of period; genre; and problems, themes, or approaches, taking the traditional high canon as their texts of choice. Each selection implied a specific content literacy that could be studied and taught; each suggested specific elements that could be incorporated into curricula designed to teach this literacy. Periodization referred to facts of literary history; a period was often defined through the stylistic preferences of an epoch or group. The study of themes tied literary texts to aesthetic or historical debates and could lead students most directly to today's ideology-driven approach to literary studies (e.g., the other in literature). Genres were arguably the most complicated framework for traditional literary studies, dealing with formal features of texts and with dialogues among the artists using them.

These earlier generations of scholars favored, as their classroom goals for learning, poetics and aesthetics, preferences that allied them with linguistics-based classroom pedagogies: each stressed the learning of patterns of formal features embedded in texts, making the literary work of art (Ingarden, *Cognition* and *Literary Work*) a well-wrought urn (Brooks) that exemplified artistic handling of the linguistic and symbolic systems of language. A student could therefore move from mastering the systems of syntax to other text systems, examining, for instance, mythopoetic spaces as described by Northrop Frye; the poetic patterns of alliteration, rhyme, meter, and symbols; or the narrator's point of view in prose (e.g., Hamburger). In textbooks and reference volumes, learners were directed to titles like *How to Read a Poem* (Raffel) and to anthologies containing individual interpretations of great works of art that showed how well wrought they were (e.g., Wimsatt; Staiger; Kayser).

Now, those kinds of formal analysis are either not taught at all in postsecondary L1 literature curricula or taught only sporadically. Some secondary-level curricula, particularly for AP English, may still teach in this fashion, but there is no guarantee that entering college students in general will have done more than write about their personal responses to the literature they have read. The traditional activity of close reading is largely lost. The FL professions also lost the anchor points around which the typical undergraduate literature curriculum until the 1980s had been organized: common modern Western definitions of literary periods or movements and of genres.

In their place we find courses (in both L1 and FL literatures), such as Francophone World Literature, that attempt to teach literature as one of the critical literacies of culture. Yet in these courses, serious differences emerge between L1 students' ability to assess an L1 author's position on the basis of a shared culture and FL students' approaches to cultural positions that are different, socially or historically, from their own.

Even multicultural impetuses from the L1 curriculum can become unreachable goals for FL programs that emphasize literature, because the discipline lacks clear pedagogical frameworks for creating sequences for FL literary studies. Teachers can provide missing cultural information, but doing so does not necessarily augment students' ability to read related texts on their own. In fact, lecture presentations may increase the distance between students and such readings, because listeners will be tempted to attribute an expert knowledge to the teacher that is beyond their reach.

In this situation, the stakes are high. Addressing it is crucial for the future of literary studies in either L1 or FL contexts. Without identifying specific forms of understanding unique to the study of literature, the field lacks a self-identity in relation to cultural history or the kind of cultural studies allied to ethnic studies or even mass communication studies. While the average literature curriculum has increased the variety of texts used in classrooms, scholars of literature have engaged in no larger discussions about what a redefinition of textuality might mean for their classrooms or for other purposes. Setting their field of inquiry apart from the other humanities rather than bringing the idea of teaching literature to new life, today's literary scholarship has in this respect betrayed its most cherished objects.

But textual studies and cultural studies can indeed be integrated in a systematic pedagogy in a curriculum aimed at multiple FL literacies. Specifically, teachers of literature can teach genre-based conventions in communication frameworks (rather than traditional close readings) as bridges between text structures and cultural meaning. By reconfiguring old models of textuality systematically, teachers redefine for students the structures of texts (well-wrought urns or not) as discourse genres (Todorov, *Genres*), as a specific culture's patterned uses of language in specific communication environments.

A compendium of such discourse genres, as forms familiar in particular cultural sites, would include not only written but also oral-aural and electronic media texts, each identified according to its purpose, sociology, form, and content. Every text would be situated in a specific cultural context—the romance novel in the United States, for example, is not the same as it is in Germany. In this redefinition, students who study genres learn to identify the social-semiotic means through which people gain agency in communication, acquire unique identity positions in a culture, or claim those positions that are legislated into specific social roles. These concerns would, in turn, be correlated with systematic elements of textuality, as discourse genres used in communication in various media.

REDEFINING GENRES AS TEXTS FOR COMMUNICATION

A return to the roots of Western genre theory can help clarify what is at stake in reappropriating genre as an approach to complex literacies. Since Aristotle, a huge superstructure for aesthetics has defined art texts as functioning in epic, lyric, or dramatic mode. The core identities of these modes in communication situations are conceived roughly in figure 6.1, no matter how a particular aesthetics program defines specific genres. These core distinctions were developed from the Renaissance on, as literature was cultivated in progressively more rarified high-culture forms from Homeric epic to Petrarchan sonnet to Shakespearean tragedy. Even then, Aristotles's poetics was the reference point for many discussions about the merits of these forms; it was the authority against which specific realizations of genre were discussed.

FIGURE 6.1. Traditional Genre Frameworks

Epic	Lyric	Dramatic
Historical Storytelling	Musical ("I sing") Expressive (praise, pain, scorn)	Dialogue, monologue Situations in progress
Third person Panoramic telling (*Iliad, Odyssey*)	*First person* Situated utterances (odes, lyric poetry, etc.)	*Second person* Scenes showing tragedy (Euripides) or comedy (Aristophanes)

While the historically attested social uses of such genre patterns are purportedly clear for European and European-derived high culture, it is less well known how many of today's text forms function socially and cognitively. This situation is not new: one of the longest-running aesthetic problems surrounding genre has been the justification of prose in a tripartite genre scheme that did not at first glance accommodate it. Prose had difficulty being accepted in early modern Europe, since it was epic in disposition but not in form. In many cases, prose genres became stepchildren, considered of mixed pedigree and lacking the provenance enjoyed by their more canonical siblings. When more middle-class readers appeared in the eighteenth century, the genre's popularity with them freed the novel from dependence on this model and started considerations of this form of cultural communication as valid in and of itself.

Such aesthetic debates about literary form may seem dated, but they cast long shadows in United States postsecondary education. Genres were used to organize parts of the literary studies curriculum well into the 1960s and 1970s: courses in the novel, lyric poetry, and tragedy remained mainstays of English and FL majors alike. To the extent that the notion of genre became entangled with debates about the canonical traditions of Western literature, the study of genre tended to be associated with the West's normative approach to fine literature. In consequence, noncanonical genres like Russian folk songs or story cycles like the *Arabian Nights* are still too easily marginalized, as other forms of texts associated with popular culture (despite their level of artistry), such as Japanese animated films (animé) or comics (manga). Marginalization of non-Western literary heritages is by no means new: early-twentieth-century scholars of Russian literature, for example, sought other markers of literariness, a major part of the poetic projects of Russian formalists since Boris M. Eikhenbaum and subsequent generations of Prague-school-derived poetics (see Garvin), through Roman Ingarden and Tzvetan Todorov (*Fantastic*). These critics were particularly interested in valorizing genres that had no western European precedents, many of which were at home in Slavic languages. Today's postcolonial theorists make that charge in other ways. No matter their extension beyond earlier understanding, poetics and the study of genre continue to appear as manifestations of upper-class taste and the imposed power of that taste.

Ironically, the heirs of this formalist legacy, especially Todorov, point to the way out of this dilemma. *Genre* in the more modern sense of a discourse genre is a "functional entity" in society without any necessary structural correlate (*Genres* 2). In other words, genres can more profitably be studied as conventional forms of expression in identifiable cultural communities than in isolation from that context. Each form will vary according to the time and spaces in which it is used; each serves in a specific framework of defined social purposes.

That is, genres are more than the formal structures designated by the Western classification of epic, lyric, and dramatic modes. Even when these traditional aesthetic discussions were at their height in the early nineteenth century, the relations between genres as specific forms and their modes were hotly debated, particularly because, as the nineteenth century proceeded, that undefined entity "prose" became for most audiences the dominant literary form, if not that always preferred in high culture. While prose narratives have existed in the West at least since Roman times, the modern sense of prose arose in conjunction with new forms of written text production and dissemination (see Watt) and not from the oral performance grounding the genres more familiar to Aristotle's time. Without a culture of scriptoria or print, poetry, especially metered and rhymed poetry, is the literary form par excellence of oral performance. As Albert Lord argued in *The Singer of Tales* (1960), metered, formulaic verse contributes to making the verse memorable. That longer verse was connected with oral performance reminds us of what this kind of verse meant as a discourse genre: a form of communication that functioned as a horizon of expectation between performer and listeners, a known social contract of the era.

Specific historical appearances of genres in the epic, lyric, and dramatic modes function in this same way. While each era's form of drama differs, for example, the specific contract between performers and audience that is a horizon of expectation in the dramatic mode will always involve certain patterns that do not appear in the storytelling that characterizes epic poems like the *Iliad* and that is taken up later by newly emerging prose forms. The mode is dramatic when dialogues are performed, whether the performance is a three-act play, a five-act tragedy, or a farce. The specific form assumed depends on a historical period and on the period's horizon of expectations and the stylistic features it particularly values.

When the traditional modes of epic, lyric, and dramatic become reified as genres in time and space, they become a specific pattern of communication. That generic pattern will then reflect issues like:

- the status of writer/speaker and reader/listener
- mechanisms of being public (publication, performance)
- community expectations (where, when, and how the communication is appropriate)
- the social roles of each genre (high culture, like tragedy; everyday culture, like ordinary conversations or bread-and-butter notes)
- narrative strategies (the story is told in the first or third person, performed in the present or told about in the past, represented as being real or as originating from one voice)
- the materiality of the written word and its distribution (is it memorized and recited, printed in expensive books or inexpensive broadsheets, included in lending libraries?)

The Western tradition of genre has created the illusion that the study of genre must be a study of high art—of the forms favored by the literate elite of a culture. Yet modern discourse analysis considers all formalized norms of communication as discourse genres that are grounded in the larger society. If there is to be a new genre theory focused on textuality in cultural context, then, it must include all formalized communication patterns, from the meeting and greeting rituals of everyday life all the way to the forms of literature proper cultivated by an elite. Each such pattern must be described as an act of communication in material space, not just as a grouping of words.

Over the last century, literature proper has been cultivated in the form of a limited number of genres, as part of elite, or high, culture. Accordingly, such literacy has identified communities through usages that needed to be mastered as part of high-status and high-register norms, part of the dominant culture. A specific literary scholarship emerged to describe the intricate forms of that literacy. From the perspective of literary studies before the canon wars, other spoken, written, or media genres were of markedly less interest. Only after the canon wars did films, folk ballads, rap music, and other popular forms of communication emerge as equivalent parts of a culture's horizon of expectation, though even now they tend to be marginalized in the academy.

This concept of equivalency provides the base for a new genre studies: nonhegemonic forms of communication (e.g., greetings, small talk), if they play a recognized role in a culture's horizon of expectation, need to be considered as discourse genres with particular social-cultural functions. Each genre, new or old, remains part of the materialities of communication in an era, is attached to specific groups in the larger community, and has specific obligatory moves that can become part of the genre's formal description that members of the community recognize and use in the performance of identity.

Genre can thus be redefined as a set of communication conventions, encompassing specific knowledge about who can speak, write, or communicate using that form; with what status, how, and where; and about what topics. To complete the redefinition of literary studies, we need to explain the culture's understanding of such acts of communication in contemporary terms, highlighting particular issues for its user group and the language-based conventions that are preferred to deal with them. Finally, the aesthetic movements so cherished by traditional literary scholarship can be defined as linguistic-stylistic or cultural-philosophical programs used to justify very specific speech acts in a given cultural context, privileging certain language or thematic references. Aesthetic ideologies shape elite gestures in the general culture of communication possibilities.

Teaching language, teaching culture, and teaching genres become three faces of what is essentially one activity: teaching patterns of communication in their material and cultural contexts, as marks of membership in a culture. Teaching genre therefore means teaching students how to learn language with specific reference to elements of the communication situation in which each genre is involved, as those elements become formalized into patterns, literary or otherwise. The cultural literacy that has now been identified as crucial for both language learning and the study of literature implicates students' ability to comprehend, create, maintain, or negotiate the specialized discourses that are being defined here as genres. Thus literature, alongside other complex genre formalizations of a culture, needs to form part of a language-learning curriculum. It provides examples of patterns of social communication that, although set apart from ordinary ones, actually represent extensions of the more familiar genres of everyday communication.

PREPARING TO TEACH NEW GENRES:
FROM DEFINITIONS TO PROGRAM BUILDING

Teaching literature by teaching genres necessarily involves multiple literacies, since genres are more than specific linguistic forms (e.g., twelve stresses per line, iambic pentameter, three acts) and the literacy of a certain mode of discourse; they are more than a function of high culture. All groups and subgroups, cultures and subcultures, operate with such typified forms of communication.

In the West, reading literature constitutes a particular kind of high-culture literacy. Yet other patterns of literacy can be cultivated by particular groups, oppositional or otherwise. Graphic novels appeal to one subgroup of readers, in a variant of mass-market printing. Films too often have mass-market appeal. Rap music, epic poetry, a sports report, a comedy-variety show on TV—each is a genre that is historically attested in a cultural era, one identifiable form of communication of that era. Readers, hearers, and consumers prove themselves members of a community by understanding how such narrative or language acts are structured, what status they have, what mechanisms and media occupy and disseminate them, and what the details are of debates about their role and value in the community. Some genres become identified with distinct user groups; others become associated with certain themes and social functions (e.g., in the late 1960s, folk music became identified with protest music).

The novel has had a fairly consistent range of forms for over a hundred years. The eighteenth-century novel throughout Europe often advocated social structures that acknowledged human rights and new definitions of human values in an era when new class formations were developing. The nineteenth-century novel specialized in human-interest and justice stories and focused on self-actualization, especially for women and the marginalized classes. Most twentieth-century novels in the Western canon have stressed psychology and perception. Yet all are novels, with roughly parallel economics, author status, and sociological values. Once one becomes a reader of novels, each century's details of form and ideology are accessible: one literary form takes on different thematics in a different cultural location and hence plays a somewhat different ideological role.

These shifts among a genre's forms, its specific cultural uses, and the themes that its communication community uses become key considerations for teaching cultural literacy through genres. Such teaching seems daunting if not impossible in the typical literature curriculum in an English department, let alone in a FL program. Yet a strong case can be made that FL cultural literacy can be acquired by adult readers through a study of genres anchored in a comprehensive curriculum. Students are, after all, already readers of novels about different cultural groups in the global community, watchers of soap operas set in different social milieus, and fluent communicators in conversations with people from different socioeconomic strata. Thus the actual problem for teaching is to identify the elements of such genre literacy—the building blocks for learning to recognize the formalized patterns of genres and how those patterns shift given the audience addressed and the function of a genre in a particular context.

The curricular goal set by an FL program might be expressed as follows: to help learners recognize and deal with genre formalizations, beyond the simple creation of the "correct sentence" or "correct paragraph" that has been the norm of earlier levels in the curriculum. Students can be guided to move from the who, what, where, and when of given texts to the discipline of genres: their forms, contents, social positions, and purposes. The tool to make that bridge is straightforward: each genre—high or popular—is understood and practiced as a stylized or extended pattern of communication in a particular medium and thus connected with certain linguistic and semiotic components, from simple to very complex. The dominant linguistic-semiotic markers for each genre almost always differ, not least because of the different communication media and social conventions involved, and each of these elements has a technical description (in linguistics, studies of film semiotics, poetics, or mass communication studies).

Thus to teach literature and other text genres means to teach advanced forms of literacy. If learners are to turn into competent readers of a genre, they must learn, in stages, to approach its language, culture, and purposes as well as the social psychology of the contexts in which it functions. They must enter into the horizon of expectation of a culture regarding that communication form. What needs to be learned to a high degree of sophistication are the linguistic, cultural, and pattern dominants of each genre.

All genres deal with narration on one level or another—as performed in the here and now (as a conversation or play), as a retrospective narrative (various prose forms), as a series of events and their hearer-readers' concomitant reactions (lyric poetry, song lyrics). In this sense, any genre has, as its cognitive foundation, some configuration of who, what, where, and when. Yet each also has a pattern that distinguishes it from the other genres available in its cultural context.

Basic patterns of cultural and linguistic knowledge defining the genres of high culture are summarized in figure 6.2 in terms of characteristic language markers and patterns, particular stylistic and formal patterns, and specific patterns of cultural reference and appeal.

Fictional prose traditionally communicates through setting and narrative points of view; it exploits degrees of realism, whether psychological or referential. Drama, in contrast, is structured principally around characters and their interactions; setting is less important (in a drama written for the proscenium stage, with its distinct limitations on scenery, setting functions simply as a logical connection). Poetry has many forms: an epic tells a story in meter, while lyric poetry expresses individuality. All poetry, however, deforms language poetically and thus manipulates standard expectations about usage (Mukarovsky). Film shares the narrative realism of many kinds of novels, but in addition it tells a story on several levels at once: not only through the verbal script but also through visuals and the sound track or Foley, all of which elements can be manipulated fairly independently of one another. What characters say can be contradicted by the visual settings in which utterances are made; the sound track may contradict both settings and utterances. Advertising, in contrast, must generally have visuals and verbals that support each other, or confusion may result.

Thinking of genre as a formalized pattern of communication or discourse opens up profoundly important teaching strategies. Learning genres becomes a matter not of high-culture preference but of a deeper kind of cultural literacy. Defining genre as a systematic discourse in a communicative framework also solves one of the most vexing problems of the undergraduate curriculum: the well-acknowledged disconnect between lower- and upper-division FL courses and between writing and content courses in English.

FIGURE 6.2. Information Patterns in the Horizon of Expectation
for High-Profile Cultural Genres

For (Fictional) Prose Setting: narrated details, purported reality behind the narrative Character: gender, status, communication norms Plots: problems, markers of language, time line Narrative point of view (POV): narrative as chronological logical or alogical   pattern (before, after, because, etc.)
For Drama Setting: time held constant, or at least linear or clearly marked Character: conversation, performatives, dialogues, behavioral norms Conflict-resolution structures (relations among scenes) Conversational norms for various sociological groups Conventional act structures (3- and 5-act forms, etc.) Acceptable plots (tragedy and fate, downfalls, moral censure)
For Poetry Epic: formal storytelling conventions, represented stereotypes and scene figures Lyric: grammar or mind links to POV of a speaking subject General: norm or deviance patterns of usage (semantics, syntax, figures,   dictionaries)
For Film Setting: who, what, where, when—visual and verbal Character: gender, status, communication norms Plots: problems, transition markers (cuts, dissolves), time line Visual logic and POV: camera focus, depth of field, framing, lighting, sound track Sound and spatial logics: foregrounding, backgrounding, cutting strategies and   effects
For Advertising Visual semantics as correlate to verbal semantics

FL programs have the mission of teaching language, often to incoming first-year students. But all too often those teaching activities stress learners' own literacy and cultural loci, the mechanics and ethics of self-expression in the learners' cognitive space, and not the loci of a particular FL culture. Focusing on the learners themselves (e.g., on what they wear, on their visit to a foreign locale), such language use is not part of any general cultural literacy or an instantiation of literacies associated with a genre, as outlined above. The divide between the learners' culture and the FL culture only gets worse when, for administrative reasons, FL teaching is removed from the purview of the language department proper, which often happens when FL centers are used. Such solutions can also remove FL teaching from the high-status content of the major.

All acts of communication in a community are texts documenting that culture's literacy. Each such act has a specific pattern of where and when it is appropriately used: who uses it, what is in it, and how it is to be marked. This definition of genre offers a way around the divide-and-conquer mentality of today's curriculum—the assumption that one level of a curriculum can be isolated from another. The study of basic language patterns should instead lead to a more detailed knowledge of sociocultural practices. The study of genre, therefore, like that of all other linguistic practices, must be developmental. Teaching and learning the elements of these acts of communication must be staged across levels in the classroom.

STAGES IN LEARNING GENRES

In order to establish an accountability hierarchy, a program must define the stages through which a student's learning is to progress. Those stages are determined by paying attention to the specific formalisms of genres in the various elements of communication.

Generally, students will have to negotiate three levels as they learn to read genres in the culturally literate sense: an initial stage, in which the

FIGURE 6.3. Three Stages for Teaching Literature as Genres

1. Learning Patterns in Context (in Lower-Division or Introductory Courses)

Texts: longer prose, film, drama, poetry
Preferred organizers: longer-arc structures (form); issues anchoring an era's
  concerns (content)
General-story or narrative markers: grammar; syntax; who, what, where, when
Cultural markers: facts, themes, concerns, institutions
First genre markers:
  grammar: normal versus literary uses as patterns of norm or deviance
  POV: conversations, verbal, visual, semantic, and syntax markers
  story grammars: action rhythms, behavior clues
Primary learning goal: learners' mastery of organizers around which single texts
  are built
Prototype tasks:
  Follow one or more patterns running through a discourse genre, to trace
    its system and see what the long arc does to the cultural and language
    material of individual parts.
  Enact one kind of communication in its correct register, with correct language
    and cultural markers.

Figure 6.3. Three Stages for Teaching Literature as Genres (*cont.*)

2. Reading Discourse Genres (in Upper-Division, Specialty, or Major Courses)
 	
Texts: pairs or longer series of texts in particular genres; read against materials on the historical setting of each
Preferred organizers:
  typologies of or standard strategies for storytelling
  specific formal patterns defining genres (e.g., 3- or 5-act plays, 14-line sonnets, "realist" narrators)
  institutional and material conditions through which these norms become familiar, and their effects (e.g., chapter length for serial novels)
Learning goals: building communities of genre readers who are familiar with the aesthetic and cultural factors that mark genres as part of cultural production, in various loci (high or popular culture, formal or informal conversations, business letters versus bread-and-butter notes)
Prototype tasks:
  Compare two versions of one genre, in the light of the prototype for the genre (e.g., *Don Quixote* as a picaresque novel, *The Bell Jar* as a feminist novel, playing master of ceremonies at a prize gathering or a roast).
  Perform an act of communication in more than one way (e.g., popular and formal).

3. Enabling Choice through Reflective Practice and Formal or Theoretical Descriptions of Genre (in a Capstone Seminar for Majors, in Graduate Courses)
 	
Texts: primary literature; secondary literature and reference materials
Preferred organizers: technical vocabulary describing systems, as key to organization of knowledge in the field (e.g., the vocabulary of bibliographies and reference books); obligatory moves of a given genre
Learning goals:
  to negotiate problems and ethics of cultural, literary, or genre studies, of social stratification
  to study the social uses of literature and patterns of exclusion using artificial distinctions as value structures
  to access technical discussions among experts and expert knowledge
Prototype tasks:
  Critique the poles in a professional debate.
  Bring a primary and a secondary text to bear on each other.
  Perform a genre's features as personal expression.

principal organizing elements of a genre are introduced; a stage that establishes the more extended patterns that define genres (the obligatory moves in communication); and a formal-operation stage, which confirms learners' ability to abstract rules and issues of genre and discuss them in professional terms, making choices about the appropriation of a genre and performing it orally or as a written text.

These levels, set for outcomes in a curriculum, may be summarized straightforwardly. Figure 6.3 offers an overview of possible goals for the three major stages in an undergraduate program designed to teach literature (after the first thousand words in a FL course or after general reading for gist in basic English courses) in terms of the cultural positions implied by individual works, where formal genres are read in a particular social-historical context.

The first element in the entry for each stage is the kinds of texts that need to be integrated into a FL program if the curriculum is to produce students who are culturally literate readers of text genres, comprehenders of films, audios, and the interactions common to social forms. In the first stage of learning, students must account for genres as discourse patterns that extend over longer sequences: scenes, not individual dialogues; books, not short stories; speeches, not responses.

In the second stage, texts are considered in sets: as tokens of known cultural discourse types that native speakers or comprehenders know how to associate with each other. Readers in their own cultures almost automatically reference soap operas against one another, as they do conversations, films, and speeches. Finally, in the third stage or capstone literacy—a literacy of high culture or of professional groups—metadiscourses about genres come into play: the stereotypes about how cultural forms are used, what the forms reveal about the status of their users, what cultural purposes they serve. Thus secondary literature, including popular or scholarly reviews, scholarly discourses, and the like, must be considered in relation to the genres they evaluate, qualify, or manage.

This metalinguistic perspective enables learners to make situated choices in a genre framework and lay a foundation for more theoretical engagement with issues. The goal of capstone tasks in reading literature is to poise students to use both the obligatory and optional moves of genre to communicate their own persona. For example, a job application letter requires some form of credentialing vis-à-vis the position. The writer who performs this credentialing chooses from a wide range of possibilities that are both culture-specific and personal. Awareness of that range seems best set in motion through reflective practice on the nature of the genre. At the undergraduate level, this practice remains quite closely tied to language use in a real-life situation. At an advanced or graduate level, that reflexiveness is expanded and yields more theoretical considerations, many of which are interdisciplinary in nature.

In each stage of figure 6.3, the second listing is a set of organizers to master: systems or patterns that lead readers, writers, and speakers to the kind of understanding necessary at that level. In the first stage, learners must see what elements of texts can be combined into patterns of meaning: aspects of grammar, narrative point of view, behaviors, themes, clothing or space descriptions, and the like. That is, the mass of largely unarticulated data must be sorted into categories and understood as patterns indicative of social expectations by the reader-hearer.

At the second stage, that general sense of pattern at work in individual texts (novels, films, conversations, letters) is given more contour, especially regarding how the texts are considered (as aesthetic objects, as examples of cultural norms and values, as examples of successful or unsuccessful social acts). Texts are compared with one another and with the performance norms that the culture imposes.

The organizers to master in the third stage are more complex: students need to consider not only the norms against which discourse genres are evaluated but also the social uses (professional, class-bound, regional) to which these norms are applied. As preparatory work for research and developing expertise in a discipline, this stage is appropriate for seniors (a capstone seminar) or graduate students.

Each stage has its own learning goals and its own set of tasks that can be used to assess competence. For the first stage, for example, learners must be able to generate a reading of a text; film; or successful performance of a conversation, speech, or act of letter writing. For the second, learners must have mastered, almost to the point of routine or automaticity, how to build meaning from various patterns of textual literacy, so that they can make generalizations about discourse genres. What distinguishes a successful speech from an unsuccessful one? an artistic novel from a popular one? a mass-market film from an art film? Which text will please a male audience more than a female one? a youthful audience more than an older one? an upper-class reader more than a working-class one? For the third stage, learners move from such simple comparisons to more complex arguments about cultural norms—about how specific text types, discourse genres, and communicative acts are managed, evaluated, and circulated as reflections of cultural values.

Figure 6.3 describes curricular benchmarks for a learning sequence specifically tailored to teaching literary works. In most FL programs today, literature is approached as cultural studies: related to social, political, and cultural concerns, not to aesthetic or formal ones, as we suggest here. The figure is not a template for any particular curriculum, because the learning levels depend on such institutional factors such as the hours required and the type of prior study. The genres to be studied also differ for various student bodies, institution types, and the resources and background literacy of the learners. The sequences given above simply summarize the ascending degrees of competency that must be acquired if learners are to reach a cultural literacy of genre by the end of four or more years of study. In all cases, the individual learner must move from being a competent reader of a single text, to taking each text type or discourse genre as a token in terms of the type it represents (comparing tokens against each other), then finally to analyzing both the tokens and their types as artifacts of cultures, in proper technical vocabularies. The learner moves from building blocks to patterns to evaluations of literacy patterns.

A LITERACY CURRICULUM FOR GENRE STUDY

We have argued that it is not only possible but necessary to put literary genres on a continuum with other kinds of genre knowledge, with genres defined as discourse genres—formalizations that function in a culture's horizon of expectation, guiding comprehension and production alike. Literary genres need to be accommodated at every stage of a curriculum, as part of the culture's fundamental literacies. Since they have more or less disappeared from the secondary school curriculum, this reconceptualization of genres is a key to integrating the teaching and learning of fundamental literacy.

The literacy of discourse genres will apply equally to FL frameworks and to those of the general humanities curriculum, because its acquisition relies on learners' adult cognition to stage their learning and to anchor their weaker language abilities. Learners need to see explicitly how to approach longer texts (prose, film) and stylized ones (drama, poetry) through the systems of meaning that operate in them. For long prose stories, students have to learn tactics to orient themselves in unfamiliar situations, historical eras, and narrative logics. They can learn to use advance organizers, previewing the who, what, where, and when that set the stage for a story and then working to build up patterns in the text. How are episodes marked? What results when shifts of tense or place occur? What explicit time markers are used ("two weeks later," "subsequently")? How are narrative elements like clothes, places, characters' actions, or events strung together in larger chains of meaning?

A curriculum cannot stop with prose (fictional or nonfictional) if one is teaching cultural literacy. For example, poetry—including rap and song lyrics—is familiar to expert readers as a genre that manipulates syntactic markers to establish points of view and to evoke states of mind and spirit. Because textuality has its own dynamic, texts need to be placed in their contexts: historical, aesthetic, social. To know genre, then, means to pay attention to different historical forms of each genre: how lyric poetry in the Romantic era differs from today's; how novelists from two eras told stories about women, using different narrative strategies and showing different ideologies about what women are and what their place in society was and ought to be. Comparing two texts is thus the core activity that must be built into an upper-division curriculum.

The specifically literary aspects of such comparison also need to be addressed in a language curriculum. In Western culture, certain texts are given privileged or canonical status as prototypes (*Don Quixote* is the prototype for the picaresque novel, *War and Peace* for the realist novel of history). Such texts set norms for the horizon of expectation of readers in their eras and create the obligatory moves that later authors react to or against. They also put into place stylistic, philosophical, and formal markers that others must follow.

These descriptions apply to every genre, literary and written, as well as those in other media. The film *Fatal Attraction* (1987) redefined the expectations of the mass audience: since its release, horror movies have two endings. The villain or monster must be killed twice before the film is over. Lincoln's Gettysburg Address and Churchill's war speeches set new standards for addressing political and social issues by reconfiguring public expectations about recent history. The materiality of these speech genres comes into play as well. The realist novel's form is influenced by the fact of its serialization or publication in multiple volumes. It makes a difference whether poetry was written as part of a society's notion of general cultivation (often in the form of individual poems, as in the eighteenth century) or to win poetry prizes (often as collections, in the twentieth century). The valuative discourses of elite culture set genres into plays of power as part of a particular historical moment's attention to specific groups, standards, or utterances (the oration versus the filibuster).

Not all FL students will move to the third stage of specifically aesthetic literacy. The standard language major who may become a high school teacher will be a competent reader who can introduce the facts of history, cultural and literary history, taste, and reception systematically (stage 2 literacy outcomes) but not necessarily engage in critical interpretations and professional discussions of the genres they take. FL students, however, are rarely challenged to reach these levels: many, if not most, undergraduate FL programs provide no systematic training in literature or other genres as formalized patterns of communication—and hence in the high-culture or high-status group literacies that would enhance students' critical thinking about cultures. The tasks of comparison suggested here set up production activities that require uses of language more sophisticated than the conversations and opinions that exhaust student production in most FL classes.[4]

But even the third stage of genre literacy is completely appropriate to undergraduate literature and culture curricula that have capstone courses. Such literacy is absolutely necessary for all graduate curricula. The materials to be treated in this level of instruction must now include more than primary literature, more than the texts themselves and the material facts of their contexts and circulation. Secondary literature and reference materials that contribute to professional understanding of the primary texts need to be drawn in; a technical vocabulary needs to be attached to the students' systems of understanding texts. Students must learn not only how to track the narrator's point of view and to compare that point of view in two different novels but also how and why scholars have differentiated between omniscient narrators and participant narrators in prose, between jump cuts and dissolves in film. Similarly, learners must practice tracking patterns of sound and rhythm in poems, must ascertain why Petrarchan sonnets are not Shakespearean sonnets. That is, they need to be introduced to perhaps the most technical context of genres: the work of scholars who generate their own practices, beyond what is inherent in a text's general social context.

In poststructuralist terms, advanced learners must be initiated into the discipline of language scholarship: the technical discussions; the organization of knowledge of the field (the forms in which it is produced, archived, distributed, and evaluated); and the practices of the field, from bibliographic and research norms through conference and professional organizations and the like. In literature, this process includes a critical reappropriation of literary history and scholarship, a reappropriation that allows a scholar to establish or question canonicity, to advance discussions, and to question ethics and uses of professional practice and expert knowledge. Narrowly, a graduate program addresses this task, but the study of professional norms also requires a historical dimension, because so many of the practices of a profession result from older settings and imperatives.

The proposals for curriculum building presented here are based on our conviction that the study of genres, a necessary key to cultural literacy, needs to be introduced at the advanced undergraduate level. By defining genres as dominant forms of literacy in cultural groups, one creates a bridge between the formal language learning of the lower division (in rhetoric and composition, in foreign languages) and more extended forms of comprehension and production in cultural contexts.

Such a bridge is not meant as a rearguard action to "save literary studies." Instead, it is an affirmation of the study of texts, textuality, and genre as part of cultural communication—as documents involved in various systems of cultural production and consumption and in the identity politics in cultures. Taking genre as we have outlined here, moreover, points to a productive way through (not around) today's still-fashionable questions of canonicity and cultural production, because any form of communication that is practiced in a group can be defined as a genre. A native speaker's horizon of expectation includes knowledge about the compulsory moves in a genre, the sociology of use as part of that horizon, and the various intertextual problems that tie into the materiality of culture.

Without taking seriously cultural literacy (a literacy of linguistic-semiotic form as well as of cultural content), the beginning and novice student learner, as comprehender or producer, will not be motivated to gain the kinds of insight necessary to move toward advanced levels of language use and of cross-cultural understanding.[5] Advanced undergraduate and graduate students will be cut off from two hundred years of professional discourse if they are not forced into dialogue with existing and prior scholarly communities about culturally accepted linguistic and semiotic interpretations of dominant and marginalized genres—either to espouse them or to refute them.

In such a reconceived genre study, the study of literature becomes that of cultural forms, what Julia Kristeva called a *sémanalyse*: a critical study of complex verbal forms of a culture; of their power relations; and of their ability to create, mediate, and re-create forms of subjectivity for people in the culture (Kristeva, *Language*; Kristeva and Coque). Just as important, teaching literature in this way brings undergraduate study closer to our mainstreams of scholarship, as a vital intellectual enterprise.[6]

1. Ample documentation for the discussion is found in the *PMLA* forum "Why Major in Literature—What Do We Tell Our Students?" See also Les Essif, who says the clock is ticking on the literature major: the teaching of literary periods might be passé, but the radical focus on the present that seems to be shifting departments' employment patterns will not be sufficient either.
2. David Bartholomae argues from the point of view of an English department that FL and English departments have many of the same problems, which emerge in both places because of cross-listing. He also notes that lower divisions have much in common. For details about the literacies involved, see Byrnes and Kord. For the description of a program that fostered "multicultural collaboration" (411) and changed the climate in something like a traditional French major, see Fallon.
3. This charge was made for other reasons by the National Association of Scholars, whose members broke with the MLA because of the alleged loss of interest in the literary qualities of texts from high culture.
4. Students could easily move to debates about which is the better novel; to book reviews of poetry collections; to character sketches of people in drama, poems, and song lyrics drawn from exemplars; to analyses of the relation of a text to its audience (a kind of market-research analysis, drawn from reception theory).
5. Nance makes the case that "very few students enter the literature classroom with the expectation of full participation" (31) and that we do not, in general, take pains to accommodate them. She suggests that one way to promote student participation is to change classroom management schemes.
6. This goal also has implications for the teaching of graduate students, an issue pursued in this volume's coda (see Bernhardt, "Research"). The case for altered graduate student training in teaching literature and culture is also made by Pfeiffer.

From Multiple Literacies to Cultural Studies: Constructing a Framework for

Chapter 7 | # Learning Culture

Chapter 6 addressed what the literacy of genres can add as a framework to the language and literature curriculum. Implementing that literacy into a curriculum, however, requires a broader sense of what it means to teach literature across learning levels. Texts, like all pedagogical materials (e.g., art, music, film), must be sequenced in a departmental curriculum, so that identifiable steps lead from setting learning goals and identifying learning styles to identifying the contents most appropriate to the context and learners.

Many traditional curricula are sequenced so that easier texts and topics lead to more difficult ones. Yet as we have demonstrated with the précis examples in earlier chapters, contents and language in texts are linked in systematic ways, reflecting complex cultural literacies. Other perspectives emerge when reading literature is not automatically equated with reading for personal purposes or reading for practical goals; conversely, reading non-literary texts need not be equated with reading for purely practical goals. There *is* a "text in this class" (contra the assertions in Fish). To find that text, the profession needs to align cultural studies and the study of literature in more complex ways. This chapter explores what the relations might be between reading literature and reading culture, especially across levels of a curriculum.

LEARNING LITERATURE, LEARNING CULTURE

Cultural studies theory has brought to the humanities a sociological or anthropological approach to teaching culture in our classrooms. As Heidi
Byrnes sees it, this shift has added to "familiar debates about which literary-
cultural content areas should be added, reduced or foregrounded in the re-
placement of canonical literature by previously marginalized materials and
authors" ("Cultural Turn" 114–15). As discussed in chapter 6, "previously
marginalized materials and authors" are often nonelite cultural forms: TV
instead of the auteur film; francophone writing, testimonials, or Holocaust
documents instead of the classics. Byrnes stresses that the kind of literacy
prioritized in cultural studies requires the "creation of an intellectual foundation that can truly accommodate all aspects of a department's work and
determination of a suitable goal" (115). Yet there has been little work on
how to build such a foundation, one that aligns itself with the cultural literacy expressed in competent use of genres.

Traditionally, the teaching of culture was represented as a difference between big *C* and little *c* culture, between high and popular culture, with
only high-culture learning taken as serious enough for upper-division work
and beyond. With the advent of poststructuralist and Marxist ideas of culture, especially theories like those of the Birmingham school (see Hall and
Jefferson), sociological and anthropological approaches to cultural critique
emerged as part of literary studies, but beyond their cultural imperatives
they offered few or no systematic approaches to curricula for culture teaching. So the question remains: What does it mean to teach culture, if that
culture lies outside the sociology of language or the bounds of anthropology and if it includes the explicit study of texts that has long been the
purview of literary studies?

Byrnes is not alone in critiquing FL curricula for failing to link cultural
studies to a solid notion of cultural literacy. Despite complex critical engagement with cultural forms, most cultural studies researchers have not
proposed ways to implement their theories as the basis for a curriculum
with clear developmental stages.[1] From the point of view of the theory and
language-teaching practice represented by the work of her department,
Byrnes suggests how a social literacy concept can be used as a responsible
and accountable goal for a department or program's students.

Like genre, culture cannot be defined in a single dimension. Even in the
context of traditional notions of high culture, many other groups claim co-

herence as a communication community and claim that their identity upholds the value of a discrete tradition. Additionally, there are many material forms of elite cultural expression (potential canonical texts of high culture), from books and art theory to music and rhetoric. Note that any in-group or community in a dominant culture can have its own elite texts and practices; both race-car addicts and opera buffs create a specialized language to communicate among themselves in a way inaccessible to nonparticipants.[2]

Given the many options for texts available today (proliferating media and the Internet enable specialized communication and create new forms), teaching culture implies an outcome that is even more complex cognitively than the cultural literacy about genres in their own right. Text genres drawn from literature, as we have described them, may be more elite—more linguistically or otherwise stylized—but when studied as communication systems, they emerge as simpler constructs than many other forms of social practice. A culturally literate reading of any text, elite or otherwise, requires an understanding of how it functions in cultural units.

The cultural literacy set as a goal for any program's curriculum is a set of multiple literacies, which refer not only to dominant genres like books and movies. They require competence in what can be called the "semiotic mechanisms of culture" (Lotman and Uspensky), the same sorts of systems of meaning that were explored by poststructuralists and semioticians (including Foucault, Barthes, Eco, and Kristeva). As the theory debates of the last quarter century have stressed, these systems of cultural meaning resemble linguistic systems. They are systems of signs, or representations, sustaining, and sustained in the materialities of, particular cultural formations—the various concretely available forms, acts, institutions, documents, and languages of cultures. These materialities can be viewed in historical perspective.

The language of computer use illustrates how systems of signs can create a new culture by acting as a group's new materiality. Their language sponsors a new consciousness and way of being—one that, as often happens, spread from a relatively small community to mainstream culture in the span of a few decades. Initially following a model signifying the elements of a real-world office, the labeling scheme for virtual "file cabinets" that was initiated in the early years of the PC (turning into Macintosh's more visual desktops) introduced users to *programs, menus, applications,* and *files* in a context other than concerts, restaurants, and office management.

As technology proliferated, new representations were added: the window option, for example, signaled the introduction of parallel processing (itself a specialized term) as an option for home computers. During this period the sign systems (the semiotic mechanisms) of the minority became mainstream. Today, a new materiality of culture has called a new state of being into existence. People unfamiliar with computers rapidly lose the thread of a conversation (or an instruction manual) unless they can comprehend and keep pace with these terms as related tokens that belong to the typology associated with computer use: sets and subsets that establish how to communicate in that culture. Teaching culture may therefore be constructed in parallel to teaching language and teaching literature, as a study of materialities as planes of communication occupied by communities with multiple literacies (knowing, for example, that the *files* on a computer are the same as but different from those in a cabinet). The communication framework involves both a set of forms and a content group from a particular cultural locus. To use computers, learners must be taught to comprehend a computer's language and literature (the conventions of its menus, the poetry of its intuitive layout, and the written forms in which it gives directions) and to use that language themselves.

Whether intending to teach the language (and worldview) of a computer or a foreign language, FL programs must again establish outcomes for learning about other cultures. Teaching culture requires an instructor or a departmental program to specify what sphere or spheres of culture will be the context in which a given textual (semiotic, artifactual, gestural) literacy is taught and whose words will be the signs at the base of its communication patterns. Each such culture possesses not only a historical tradition of representation but also various contemporary contents and contexts that can be invoked as part of learning outcomes: sociological, community, ideological, historical, or aesthetic and high-culture contents, for example. Thus to describe the learning outcomes of a course or sequence on a culture means to specify a system whose meanings must be taught—not as individual items but as patterns in an order of increasing complexity. Moreover, these patterns emerge in terms of interrelations with specific, in-group references.

To return to our computer example, consider the relations among the italicized terms—typical statements made by people talking about computers: "*Menus* change on a computer *desktop* when a *program* has been *activated*," "The *home directory icon* on the *Macintosh OS X system* enables multiple *users* of a single computer to each have their own separate *virtual machine*, an option not available with previous *operating systems* for the

Mac." If the reader fails to understand the computer context of these expressions, many of the italicized words are no more than dictionary entries. Their meaning derives from context—in specific materialities of culture and the communication patterns involved with them instead of in a cultural vacuum.

The necessity for understanding how such complexities form graduated patterns can be exemplified in the world of the humanities by looking at the *National Standards for History*, an initiative parallel to the *Standards for Foreign Language Learning*. Where the FL standards are a single list combining skills, social frames, and contexts, the history standards have two separate lists of learning goals: one is concepts central to a learner's understanding of an era, the other is distinctive cognitive strategies involved in historical analysis—one set of contents, one set of cognitive acts. These standards work toward the specific literacies required for knowing history, for being literate in historical thinking.

That these history standards can help define what it means to teach culture does not exhaust them. If they are statements characterizing learning goals for a course or curriculum, they also characterize a communication community—in this case, historians—and how historians transact and evaluate one another's understanding of historical facts. To teach culture in a language-literature department thus emerges as more than instruction in a set of concepts and cognitive acts. It refers to a particular communication community and provides a systematic accounting of that community's habits of context and evaluation. To take the knowledge and analytic skills specified in the *National Standards for History* and make of them a pattern enabling a more inclusive cultural studies, language-literature courses need to add conscious attention to the linguistic, anthropological, and sociological knowledge that is central to the notion of that field (Byrnes, "Cultural Turn"). The learning this project implies is very broad, anchored not only in history, literature, and language but also in other materialities of communication communities and their identity constructs, including such issues as:

media through which communication happens
identity markers for groups involved in communication
institutions conditioning culture
contents and preoccupations of particular cultures and their supporting
    communities (see Hall and Jefferson)
text types and functions in the culture
sociological and linguistic markers for authorized speaking

Thus teaching and understanding culture is more multifaceted than understanding history or language alone.

Once the decision is made to teach a particular domain or domains of culture, a course or program needs to select the distinctive contents and contexts of the literacies being taught as cultural materialities anchoring a communication community. To be credible, a program must establish a set of accountability criteria, evaluating as one of its levels competence in the culture learned. Teaching culture must include literature and other genres as part of its literacy, as argued in chapter 6, because the range of official, high, and popular literatures (and forms of textuality, from novels and poems to blogs) in most cultures today is an inventory of messages about the values and accepted or rejected behaviors in those cultures. To teach culture, then, an instructor must first define the kinds of culture taught: official, high, or popular.

Unless a program's students have the ability to read, view, hear, think about, and discuss at least some texts from various points of view or speaking positions from within those texts, a program cannot claim to teach cultural literacy. In the twentieth- and twenty-first-century cultures of the West, literature has a role. Often it has been aligned with a hegemonic or dominant culture, in complementary relation to the different groups in that larger community. Texts produced on the Internet, TV, radio, and film qualify as distaff literatures by virtue of their reflexes to written antecedents as well as their authority as documents of their time and place.

Teaching culture must range beyond teaching contents and systems of designation and communication as it sets goals for its learners. As in a literature-driven curriculum, articulation among levels and the inclusion of specific content and comprehension objectives become crucial. Language goals help bridge those levels of comprehension into levels of production. Basic constructivist learning must be set up, teaching students how to build systems of significant cultural markers, signs, practices, and facts—the learning-to-learn perspective in a cultural context.

In designing the levels for courses in a program of this type, high-status cultural learning (i.e., the best in any medium or genre, traditional literature or otherwise) must be distinguished from high culture (the genres preferred by dominant classes as reflected in most secondary and college curricula). Yet at the same time, curricula must accommodate individual institutions' students and their learning goals. If literary works are to complement and contribute to a cultural studies focus, such a program has to be configured as a professional or technical dialogue relating to canonical, professional, and cognitive norms for teaching and learning. That is, a curriculum that fosters study of texts as culture must encompass predictable and necessary stages of development in reading, extended to include not only the study of genre, as proposed here, but the study of multiple literacies—linguistic, cultural, historical, and literary alike—in a developmental hierarchy.

The section that follows introduces the question of teaching literature as part of today's interest in cultural studies, from the perspective of teaching the multiliteracies of culture. First, it expands on the notion of teaching literature in its various voices and genres; then it considers how the teaching of literature is a model for the teaching of culture in general—an expansion on the cultural theory imperatives that currently are as homeless as genre theory is in contemporary curricula.

TASK LEVELS FOR TEACHING CULTURAL STUDIES WITH LITERATURE

Deciding to teach literature as genre embedded in a cultural studies framework is only the first step in developing a curricular program for a typical FL department, one that takes students through a set of coherent learning levels and simultaneously fosters their linguistic and literary knowledge as part of the materiality of a cultural setting. As was argued in chapter 6, students of literature must grow through linguistic and formal practice if they are to acquire literacy about genres, in high culture or other contexts. Genres are not isolated from one another: when the historical evolution of the novel is mastered, for example, the patterns of drama become clearer, since there is overlap on how two genres represent dialogue. Yet each genre presents a set of sine qua nons that structure it as a recognizable cultural practice and circumscribe its meanings in the communication community and in the cultural locus.

The definition of genres as part of cultural literacy also means that in general education classes for the typical undergraduate curriculum outside the FL program, students can be taught the fundamental organizations of form and content that tell them how they speak, to whom, and for what reasons. Majors, graduate students, and scholars need a more specialized literacy about the relations between genres and culture, understanding genres in their precise historical and cultural contexts. Even when they engage in formalist literary scholarship, they must enter into some aspects of cultural studies.

Figure 7.1 shows the differentiation among genres, as specific forms of cultural literacy that may be targeted in a holistic learning framework. The figure can be read as a set of horizontal as well as vertical correlations expressing curricular goals. From top to bottom, it summarizes a pattern of incremental stages. Read from left to right, it proposes a parallel framework of genre types, differentiated less by formal complexity than by incremental demands imposed on learners.

To exemplify briefly: poetry and advertising appear in the table's first column as closely associated forms (one from elite culture, one from popular), because they generally constitute direct affective appeals to their readers, even when they seem to differ in their goal of telling stories or conveying information. In a lyric poem, that appeal is almost always couched in a single voice emanating from a single place and point in time. This specificity of origin simplifies the poem's message rather than valorizes the speaker-writer. While the language of a poem or ad often contrasts with standard usage, both address the reader directly, who is often a specific person or interest group targeted by the message. The origin is revealed in speaking, but the voice is allowed to preserve its idiosyncrasies (often for reasons of memorability).

Longer prose forms, including nonfiction and instructional matter, introduce a narrative point of view, which readers interrogate to uncover. Since these forms appear linguistically normal, it may be difficult for readers to see the strangeness in the point of view behind the surface prose, while a poem or ad will signal its difference more overtly. Consequently, learning tasks for prose must include organizing and reflecting on the sequence of materials and on the language modes used to convey information, no matter how natural they seem. Such interrogation is critical if a text is to be comprehended for more than its entertainment value or its representation of a point of view as universal. But the tendency of prose to universalize reveals the cultural values embedded in it.

The same kind of paired relation exists between film and drama. A film introduces not only verbal markers but also visual ones to create a multidimensional narrative that purports to be realistic; actually it naturalizes a particular point of view and reinforces the ideologies of the cultural group or

FIGURE 7.1. Suggested Task Stages for Specific Genres

Stage	Poetry (and Advertising)	Longer Prose (Fictional, Nonfictional)	Film	Drama
1. Generating competent readings, introducing systems of markers	Verbal markers	Verbal markers	Visual and verbal markers	Behavioral and verbal markers
Internal to text: who, what, where, when	Attention to norm and deviance patterns built on ordinary syntax and semantics	Attention to narrative point of view	Attention to narrative point of view in two channels (verbal-aural and visual) that might not coincide	Attention to sequence, presence and absence in storytelling, behavior interpolations, scene connections
External to text: cultural, historical, gestural, institutional, thematic	Special semantics: figures, tropes	Special organizing chains: episodes, settings, verbal figures, historical references	Identifying special point-of-view devices: camera angle, color, other sound and framing issues	Systematizing special stylization in drama (third wall, nonrealistic space, telescoped time)
2. Joining communities (comparing two readings, making types out of tokens)	Identifying conventional poetry types; using reference materials; style and aesthetic analysis	Taking genre prototype (e.g., Don Quixote) and comparing it with another member of the genre: by form, by epoch	Taking genre prototype (e.g., Gone with the Wind) and comparing it with another member of the genre: by form, by epoch	Taking genre prototype (e.g., Inherit the Wind) and comparing it with another member of the genre: by form, by epoch
Internal to text: conventional forms, prototypes (canons)	Content-media comparison: analysis vis-à-vis prototype			
External to text: history of the forms, sociology of the forms	Analysis of lyrical I and probable audience	Reception explanations (culture), modifications of genre	Reception, remakes	Restagings, reviews
3. Expert knowledge (generating genre and period knowledge)	Application of theory texts to genre; periodization	Application of theory texts to genre; periodization; cultural studies	Screenplay vs. film vs. technical systems—analyses of interrelations	Performance vs. textuality study; application of theory texts to genre; periodization

groups for which it is produced. Drama appears in the last column of the figure not only because it most frequently represents a high-culture genre but also because it is often a more consciously elite genre, lacking the additional descriptions and explanatory aids often associated with nonelite forms. Learners must be taught to read between the lines of a dialogue on the basis of what they know about the time, place, staging conventions, and presumed audience for a piece; drama gives them fewer clues than does the more realistic world of a film. But establishing cultural context is essential to read or view either genre as representative of a time, audience, place, and staging conventions. Because drama offers only dialogue that may or may not reflect cultural contexts, it often increases the cognitive burden for the reader or viewer more than is the case with poetry, longer prose works, and film.

Variants and hybrids of genres, such as opera, dance, or musical, are not dealt with in figure 7.1. Our objective here is merely to illustrate stages in cognitive complexity associated with the major genre categories found in most cultures today. The three stages reflect both learning levels and objectives for the cultural studies program we envision.

At the first stage of learning any genre—or, in fact, of learning any codified cultural practice, verbal, visual, or behavioral—students need to be alerted to the patterns of a text's elements. Students acquiring a foreign language are cognitively and linguistically overloaded, in most cases, and so should be directed toward building cognitive patterns that are central to the text's meaning. In-class discussions as well as assigned tasks must enable them to look for two or three factors that, when identified, give clues to the core messages of a text. In some lyric poems, for example, novice readers might profit from learning to trace shift of tense as an indicator of a step in the poem's logic. If they are led to collect word fields (colors, objects, place indicators), then patterns of the text's cultural context also begin to emerge. If readers try to approach prose as a representation of cultural meaning, then point of view and narrator become important, both of which are marked by tenses and adverbial expressions of place, time, or sequence ("early that morning," "shortly before noon"). Virtually all genres are also marked by specific patterns of cultural information (from the who, what, where, and when that members of the cultural community identify to dates and events from cultural history).

In all such cases, exercises for beginning-level students, both in class and as assignments or discussion projects, need to help them learn to learn the advanced organizers for genre types and for the cultural settings in which they achieve unique or more-nuanced meanings—to perform the kinds of mental bookkeeping that first-language members of a cultural community do as they read texts, engage in structured encounters, or read other cultural systems. The structures of meaning that learners practice must be those that help them make sense of the text's world through communication patterns from their own: patterns of knowledge, vocabulary, and syntax. That is, learning in stage 1 includes both cultural literacy and FL literacy and lies in the realm of everyday life. When students produce language about what they read, see, or hear, that production will be in the register of everyday speech and writing.

Stage 2 of the learning sequence modeled in figure 7.1 adds a greater degree of literacy about genre and cultural communication. Learners' tasks take them in two directions: they must read texts as concrete representations of the real world (a world not necessarily their own) and view those representations as abstract tokens. To illustrate, an interview is not only about a person's experiences in writing a book or making a movie (the concrete representation), it is also about the ideas that underlie the type and sequence of questions and answers—such as the premises about the status of the interviewer, interviewee, and audience. Such abstractions vary depending on when and where the interview occurred, on who distributed it, and on who viewed or read it. The general pattern of communication takes on more complex shades of cultural meaning as textuality reveals more of the communication community than its own genre norms. At this point, the who, what, where, and when acts of identification that learners engage in during stage 1 must move toward more sophisticated acts of analysis and synthesis, framed as abstract thought in the patterns recognized by the community. Negotiating those two levels of reading, the concrete and the abstract, increases both cognitive and linguistic demands on readers and brings the cultural context to the form as a necessary literacy.

At the second level of a program, therefore, the focus needs to be on building larger patterns in cultural-historical contents that specific genres treat. Two mystery stories—for example, by Edgar Allan Poe and Agatha Christie—share some characteristics in structure and execution and differ in others. What is shared defines their genre identities (a murder, an investigation); the differences emerge when readers abstract other cultural, sociological, or historical factors as systematic assumptions of the text—such as what social problems motivate the evil of the plot (espionage, smuggled art), what national conventions motivate style decisions (noir, police procedurals), or the shifts in time and audience.

The reading tasks must force learners into making comparisons, between texts and between contexts. After establishing the concrete and abstract patterns in one text, they must treat the patterns of difference between texts (the difference from the cultural norms grounding each text) and the similarities (the sameness that defines the genre type). This ability to work in different patterns goes further in establishing the formal schema of social and cultural literacy than does the simple logical work of the first level of instruction.

When learners are ready to join professional or elite communities through the highly formalized literacy of technical language, they can undertake stage 3, typically as seniors or when beginning their graduate education in the field of FL study. Whereas the abstract categories for tasks given students at stage 2 might be provided by the instructor in a précis format (the features of the murder, the implications of the historical period), at stage 3 students are encouraged to identify the relation between specific events and their tokens. Their use of technical language here should be appropriate to the professional registers involved—in terms of the professional community that sponsors its particular kind of cultural literacy. Thus the detective novels that are understood as members of genres such as noir or the police procedural in earlier stages of learning must now be described in more critical terms: as naturalist or possessing an omniscient narrator or representing different cultural norms and knowledge. The comprehension problem has grown more complex.

Speaking and writing the language of the genre's in-group becomes important for learners to cultivate as part of their increasing command of cultural literacies appropriate in the communication community of a foreign language. Only in such cognitively complex environments will they be obliged to use written and oral production with more sophisticated syntax and content, while still sounding natural. To develop the capacity to engage in more sophisticated speech acts, they must interact with both texts and cultural contexts. At this stage, instructors need to select high-status or elite texts, but not only high-culture ones from the dominant class, because such texts privilege norms of acceptability that can be used for exclusion as well. The elite status of such texts, whether dominant or marginalized, stems not from inherent qualities but from the fact that they privilege an artificial literacy, reflect a relatively restricted, in-group usage. Regardless of whether students at level 3 look at popular, elite, official, or high-culture works, culturally marked selections must be read to accustom them to interrogate how particular social, economic, or interest groups are addressed and placed by such acts of communication and understanding. Figuring out how to negotiate the highest levels of a culture's multiliteracy, they will juggle not only comparisons but also a culturally recognized pattern of substantiated evaluation, probably for the first time ("a good representation of police procedures, because . . . ," "a hostile interview, given that . . ."). They must take the step of joining the communication community, learning how to judge and evaluate as the community does. Such capabilities represent the full-discourse literacy that lifts the speaker or writer of a language into a position of authority on the materials spoken or written about.

Elite-status texts put the cognitive burden on the use of semiotics. Students need cognizance of the labeling schemes revealed in the linguistic or visual materials manipulated in texts. To be effective communicators, they must understand and use these materials as culturally elite production addressed to particular cultural groups.

In the section that follows, we argue a more detailed case for such claims about learning culture by illustrating the different stages in three variants of a course template. At the same time, we demonstrate how three courses can use the same cultural and literary subject matter but expand the textual offerings and the cognitive tasks posed for their respective audiences—first-year students, upper-division students, graduate students—as the texts and tasks stage their entry into the communication and culture communities in different ways.

LEVELS IN THE CULTURE CURRICULUM

Framed as possible levels in a curriculum, figure 7.2 includes a summary of what it might mean to learn culture. The first level's goals parallel those in teaching literature, albeit with broader attention to text types (cultural artifacts and monuments stand beside books and art) as the basis for learners' practice in building systems of information.

Higher levels of the curriculum require closer specification of learning outcomes. The study of literature becomes very technical above the

FIGURE 7.2. Curricular Levels for Teaching Culture

	Learning Goals	*Text Types*	*Content Issues*
LEVEL 1	Identification and assemblage of systems of culture (learning-to-learn perspective): linguistic, semiotic, behavioral, sociological; ability to correlate part to whole, transfer token to type, relate idea to practice	Media appropriate to learning goals; includes longer texts with reasonable content goals	Who, what, where, when: ability to locate systems in a basic network of culture-society-history, to identify basic patterns (genre, conversation, community), to identify productive rules in those patterns, to realize systems predictably
LEVEL 2	Comparisons and contrasts of systems from the point of view of people in them; ability to discern cause and effect between systems and personal behaviors, to shift among points of view, to argue of coherence of systems, to replicate canonicity in any of the three domains	Culture: literature, film, theater, opera Anthropology: popular writing, television, popular music, infotainment Sociology: essays, government documents, news Literature: as in previous level	Culture: aesthetics, including genre, norms of high culture; popular culture; media involved Anthropology: human behavior, interpersonal communication, community forms Sociology: power or distinction markers; praxis, correlated with economics, government, etc. Literature: as in previous level
LEVEL 3	Production and dissemination of professionally authorized sources of knowledge; power-knowledge links and channels (à la Foucault); analysis of canonicity; charting dynamics of marginalized and dominant groups; planning and organizing alternatives	Primary sources versus secondary literature; theory; official histories of the domain; canons; bibliographies, libraries (Chartier's "order of books" and other media)	Institutions, professional structures, laws that define culture, set a culture's practices into a values structure, and hold these practices in place

introductory level, with a significant body of elite patterns of knowledge and expression needing to be mastered. In contrast, the study of culture can take on very different disciplinary flavors, depending on what kinds of learning the curriculum specifies (or what outcomes the particular institution or student population favors). Consider in figure 7.2 the rough breakdown of differences among levels of learning culture. Each level has the potential to implement very different patterns of learning and hence of classroom practice.

The first level (introductory or lower-division courses) focuses on the concrete systems of culture learning: the who, what, where, and when facts of language, location, and social signification, with special emphasis on sociological-anthropological aspects. In the introductory course on the Enlightenment discussed below, starting with novels and films sets up the fundamental content issues whose systems of meaning frame more complicated understandings of culture. A novel like *La nouvelle Héloïse* (Rousseau) or a film like *Dangerous Liaisons* (1988), no matter how speculative or fictional, shows or tells stories of people in their environments; it works through typical concerns of the era, presenting modes of behavior sanctioned or decried by the era. The characters are significant aspects of the Enlightenment's dominant speaker types, which learners must be able to identify as part of that culture's representation of itself. The level's learning goals and necessary content focus rest on these systems of anthropological and sociological knowledge.

Cast in that framework, the question of text types to be represented becomes more complex. Culture learning requires input on more than the verbal level and in more than one form, because natives in a culture move freely between oral and visual representation; aural, visual, and symbolic comprehension; and the like. So it becomes crucial to note not only what Rousseau's Julie says but also what she might have worn (as documented in the art of the era or in a film that purports a degree of historical fidelity in its costuming), the tone of voice in which she speaks, and in what locations she moves—as a rule, location is more comprehensively presented by a film than by prose fiction.

A decision about genre must be made: certain forms of expression, behavior, and writing are favored in the Enlightenment (e.g., travel writing, open letters), which do not necessarily have the same cultural weight today. So the learning of content must be sensitive to what kinds of cultural literacy are sought as the outcome. It is one thing to be able to understand the concepts in Rousseau's novel (concepts also of the philosophy that was such an integral part of high culture in the era) and quite another to see the social nuances implied in his use of the epistolary novel form (an aesthetic problem) or the significance of location and character names as cultural references (generally a popular-culture issue). Which kind of learning is defined as the appropriate outcome will determine which text types are chosen.

Attention to text types might profitably be seen as an attention to building appropriate contexts—as answers to the problem of what specific knowledge about habits of the Enlightenment is required in order for a learner to have access to more complex forms of social expression, anthropological knowledge, and cultural understanding. For example, what were the signs that Enlightenment people used to determine and reinforce class boundaries? Where did they learn those markers of in-groups—did they read newspapers, visit the theater, hear popular songs? The genres through which particular communities learned to identity themselves in the greater culture should therefore be presented as the texts chosen to stage learners' engagement with such systems. Those texts may be institutions, pictures, social practices, or any system of expression that bears investigation as seminal to cultural identity. Their cultural meaning and expression will ground students' learning and be the basis for assessing that learning.

When the second level of the curriculum is constructed (including upper-division courses in the foreign languages or critical writing and critical thinking classes), the learning situation requires analytic reasoning to set up understanding and expression.

The text types that are represented must work toward typologies of cultural systems, communities, institutions, or discourses in a particular cultural setting (including consideration of the markers that differentiate among subcultures, institutions, high and popular culture). Those texts must be longer and more nuanced, as were literature curricula based on genre literacy, and they must be in more than one medium. They also must be studied in the culture's contexts, that is, in its chosen patterns of social and anthropological meaning.

Given the range of possibilities, it is difficult to specify the content of the learning for the course's or level's outcomes. Are teachers interested in having learners master the anthropological facts of a culture (the way

Rousseau's Julie would behave, the values she would gain) or master socio-logical facts about status, power, and distinction (the question of birth class versus ability that distinguishes people in *Dangerous Liaisons*)? Should course planning target facts about high culture (manners, mores, dress, law) or about official structures of society (a poststructural analysis of institutions)? Sociological questions specifying content force learners to practice compar-isons and contrasts between points of view (e.g., which men and women would deal with a situation and how). Aesthetic or political questions require knowledge of how high culture is made, put into circulation, and supported by institutions. Each domain of content has its own discourse. Its preferred genres; loci of communication; and patterns of information, behavior, and signs need to be represented as texts if cultural learning is to take place. Readers cannot learn the nuances of clothing and status simply from a novel; they must see the clothing in context, possibly in paintings or another visual medium.

At the level of senior seminars or basic graduate teaching and learning, the staging for cultural teaching and learning adds yet another dimension of complexity: synthetic reasoning. It must respect not only the contexts of the culture but also content and context issues from the point of view of the learners. Learners must comprehend the culture on its own terms, in a way dependent on a specific field, but they must also move toward a field-independent understanding, reflecting on how the cultural systems at play in a context represent conscious strategies of knowledge—production, power, and self-assertion on the part of individuals and groups. These tasks are more synthetic, complex, and reflective than the analytic tasks of un-derstanding at intermediate levels.

Ultimately the solution to the difficulty of teaching culture revolves around building sequences of courses. It is easy to conceive of level 2 and level 3 courses; constructing a sequence is another matter. Because the focus of such a sequence is culture, literature and film would have to be included. If courses are unconnected and have no curricular framework, they will pose hardships for students. They require background. They require some content knowledge, some familiarity with text types, and extensive practice in building semiotic systems that represent the complex symbolizing acts of culture and practice in comparing artifacts on the first two levels. In our ex-perience these requirements hold as much for humanities or interdiscipli-nary programs as they do for program development in a foreign language.

THE PAST IS A FOREIGN COUNTRY:
INTRODUCING EARLY MODERN STUDIES

Among early casualties of budget cuts are often studies of premodern literatures and cultures, since students are less familiar with the materials and
hence less likely to choose such courses as an elective. Even graduate students tend to shy away from premodern studies, often because such studies
require additional language abilities (specialists in European culture might
need Latin, Middle or Old English, Provençal, Old Church Slavonic; those
studying Mediterranean trade routes as cultural nexes might need Turkish,
Swahili, or Arabic). Some professional organizations, such as the American
Society for Eighteenth-Century Studies, have been exemplary in further-
ing the development of teaching materials and in recommending that
eighteenth-century studies take an interdisciplinary approach to cultural
studies, integrating art, history, and literature

Such courses expand the scope of traditional curricular offerings by focusing on single authors or on political history. At the same time, they pose
the need for faculty members to rethink how to develop courses for a holistic, interlocked program: what it means to study older cultures or what
interdisciplinarity might mean for their students, cognitively or culturally.
The kind of courses proposed here must engage the undergraduate curriculum in conversations about what humanist disciplines mean as intellectual
enterprises, across the disciplinary and national lines that currently characterize institutions.

This problem is highlighted by the historian Margaret C. Jacob in her
letter to the newsletter of the American Society for Eighteenth-Century
Studies. She speaks of New York's state-mandated global studies curriculum
and "the ASECS model of interdisciplinarity," then calls on ASECS to work
to specify what such an institutional framework means and to consider becoming more interdisciplinary in order to increase enrollments. Jacob
stresses the need to recognize that textual comparisons involve "different
languages, even periods." Consequently "the lettrists have everything to
teach us" (1). She concludes that interdisciplinary course work on particular
historical eras remains rare in the undergraduate curriculum.

This rarity stems in part from the economics of undergraduate courses.
To introduce such a course, faculty members must establish, for example,
whether or not it can span two or more departments (e.g., Science in the

Age of Revolution) or substitute for a more conventional, core course. Departments must agree about which of them gets enrollment credits. Unfortunately, it is often easier to reject such a course than it is to negotiate the answers, particularly in large state schools.

What is at stake in teaching the past as a foreign country, as part of general education rather than as the study of a museum curiosity? One first-year or first-level introduction to eighteenth-century studies designed to serve the general learning needs for the humanities at the University of Texas, Austin, was selected as an illustration of how an interdisciplinary course might show students what it means to think, speak, and write in terms recognized in humanities courses—as well as promote the cause of several different national cultures and their presence in the undergraduate curriculum. While this example stems from one particular institutional environment, the course's design logic responds to a specific learning level, content, and context and opens a different vision of what thinking interdisciplinarily might mean for a course that combines history and literature.

The design process was begun with the question of how first-year students could learn to read texts from at least two disciplines and in historical context. The aims that ultimately became the backbone of the course were two: to foster learning to learn at the early levels of the undergraduate curriculum and to sensitize students to the riches of the eighteenth century, especially the literary, sociopolitical, and historical problems with which that century grappled. In the larger institutional context of program building, such a course could also provide a baseline from which to develop variants appropriate for an upper-division undergraduate course or for a course appropriate at a senior seminar or a graduate-student offering.

One course that resulted, Romance, Revolution, and Reason: Europe and the American Revolution, was designed to occupy a very particular niche on the campus: a course for first-year students that could be cross-listed from a German department into American studies (a popular area studies choice for students filling a social sciences or history distribution requirement) and one that would satisfy the university's writing requirement.[3] In this way, students could more easily find the course and receive a preliminary orientation in context and content: the known (the American Revolution, Benjamin Franklin) could be used to lead them to the unknown (German and French authors, Enlightenment philosophy).

The assignments were designed and sequenced to train students in interdisciplinary reading and writing as well as in the historical imperatives of the eighteenth century. Just as if they were being introduced to a foreign culture, students needed to be led into the vocabulary and mental world of the Enlightenment. The strategy that guided the organization of readings was a consideration of how everyday life in Europe and America could lead average people to support a revolution. The answer sought was in personal identities and motivations, not in the field of national politics, of the economic and material advantages for crowns and parliaments. It is a long leap from "no taxation without representation" to a full-fledged act of treason.

The texts ultimately chosen for this course still favored the dominant culture of the age—a cosmopolitan high culture. The course compared terms, concepts, and individual types across national lines as it studied the revolution's progress and the rise and fall of Napoleon. Official culture was posited as a community that reached across national lines yet was also distinctly part of the eighteenth century. The strategy was to start with those individuals who were identified as heroes and villains and see how their personal motivations converged with the ideas of the time.

The approach changes if the course is designed for upper-division students or a graduate seminar. An upper-division undergraduate course presupposes a better grasp of history than that expected of first-year students. After several years of college courses in the humanities and social sciences, a student is more likely to understand that eighteenth-century people were not like people today, and such a student tends to bring more spirit of inquiry about the differences. The upper-division undergraduate still needs to be introduced to the specifics of the eighteenth-century norm of personhood, but whereas beginners learn that alien texts are nevertheless intelligible, intermediate learners move to more precise comparison and contrast of patterns of behavior and knowledge. They consider values, behaviors, and concepts from texts more as abstract categories of eighteenth-century assumptions than as simple facts of human behavior. More advanced learners have these learning-to-learn skills already at hand, even if they do not yet know much about eighteenth-century culture. Their goal, in a cultural studies approach to the same kinds of texts, is to discover the themes of the age and the relation of complex philosophical assumption to observed facts of politics, behavior, art, and sociology.

The first-year course described here began with the classic definition of *enlightenment* by Immanuel Kant—an act of primary naming, introducing perhaps the master signifier for understanding the era. This first reading assignment was set up with a précis worksheet that compared two translations of the brief essay. Note that in both figures 7.3 and 7.4, the worksheet is formatted to allow students space for writing.

This assignment introduces students to what historical comprehension means in practical terms. The differences in translation result from the fact that the two translations were made a half century apart. Comparison highlights how artificially familiar a translation makes a text and that different translations in language or time represent different kinds of foreignness. Ideas that are still alive in our lived United States experience today didn't necessarily mean the same thing more than two hundred years ago. Setting

---

FIGURE 7.3. Précis Worksheet for "What Is Enlightenment?"

Focus: Two translations of Kant's famous essay "What Is Enlightenment?" interpret the purpose and content of the essay differently.

Logic: A comparison of key passages reveals the translators' different images about what a human being should be, showing that today's scholars do not agree about what the values of the Enlightenment were.

Pair of Texts (= Issue)	*What the Differences Imply*
1. "Enlightenment is man's release from his self-incurred tutelage." ("What Is Enlightenment?" 1)	man vs. mankind = ?
"Enlightenment is mankind's exit from its self-incurred immaturity." ("Answer" 58)	release vs. exit = ?
2.	
3.	

Implication: (Address which translation speaks more to you today, and why, or which one seems more plausible.)

the problem in this way opened an opportunity for brief lectures explaining the chronology and impact on governments of the Enlightenment revolutions, reminding students that the age of revolution was dated differently in each country: 1776, 1789, the Terror, Napoleon's rise and fall. A first step was thus established in how historians and literary historians work with texts that correlate political sea changes and (if popular or very public) represent dominant ideas of the era.

This exercise is also profitable in a graduate course, but with a different goal. That translations differ should be no surprise to advanced students, but this exercise might sensitize them to scholarly bias behind choices of terminology.

Two novels were the follow-up and true introduction to the course; each was a best seller of the Enlightenment: Rousseau's *La nouvelle Héloïse* and Goethe's *Sorrows of Young Werther*. Again, for each text a page-length précis worksheet was provided. Figure 7.4 gives the worksheet for *La nouvelle Héloïse*.

This exercise replicates one's approach to a contemporary text that deals with unrequited love, but for a novel over two hundred years old it has the additional advantage of forcing learners to identify as problems what the text identified as problems. This shift in focus makes learners

FIGURE 7.4. Précis Worksheet for *La nouvelle Héloïse*

Focus: Rousseau's novel tells the story of a pair of lovers who are fated to be separated because they do not fit together socially—a kind of Romeo and Juliet story based on the stereotypes of the day.

Logic: The problems that the lovers encounter lead them to try solutions that ultimately drive them apart. By tracing these problems and the resulting actions, we can see how the old order (Julie's family) and the new (Saint-Preux) are in conflict.

Problems They Had	Resulting Actions
(Give 3–5 examples)	

Implication: (What is modern / not modern about their dilemma? What are the strengths and weaknesses of society that Rousseau wants to expose?)

acknowledge items that are culturally strange, if not linguistically so, and begin to reconstruct class-bound behaviors characteristic of the period.

Like *Werther*, *La nouvelle Héloïse* goes to the heart of the era's class structure in virtually every scene. Although Rousseau's Saint-Preux, a tutor, is ultimately valorized by the upper classes (a lord offers him support), he loses the girl. But the lovers each contribute to a new vision of what the world should be as they maintain a lifelong bond of sympathy. The worksheet helped structure for students what was important to read out of a complex novel: elements that focused on how people lived then and what spurred them to question prevailing standards about social justice and equality, about the head and the heart, and about what makes a proper world. Because of its length, only part of Rousseau's novel was assigned in the freshman class, but intermediate learners had to read the bulk of the novel and advanced or graduate students its entirety, preferably in the original French.

Other choices of text in the class catered specifically to the needs of the first-year students, who are likely to have less systematic cultural knowledge or access to such knowledge. To reinforce for them the sense of how everyday life was lived in the Enlightenment, a film was also assigned, *Jefferson in Paris*, which was made in period locations and acts almost as a digest of the era's problematic themes (sexism, racism, reason, revolution). The film has flaws, but its images give a sense of what the houses looked like, what kinds of conversations were conducted, and which careers and talents were valued. As a bonus, the film also uses a frame narrative that highlights the gap in expectations between the early twentieth century and Jefferson's era.

For advanced students, such a film provides a springboard for discussing period issues but from a different perspective. Students are told from the outset that the film is a reconstruction that may or may not represent the eighteenth century (the final project for the first-year class). Juniors or seniors are expected to compare episodes from the film with the texts they are reading, because they have more practice in building patterns than do the freshmen in the course presented here and so can be expected to engage in comparisons, contrasts, and evaluations.

The various materials used in this course are canonical texts from the era, but in excerpt. The beginning texts happened to be unfamiliar to the class, but many of the subsequent ones were not. First-year students who had had AP history or government (most of the class) had already read many American political texts and often the American fiction read at the end of the course. Moving from the language of the enlightened community (Kant's essay) to incidents from the lives lived according to this language (Saint-Preux's loss, Jefferson's lapses in democratic thinking, Werther's weakness) made students work from the concrete to the abstract, to remember incidents from the novels or film, and to associate later essays and readings with the actors in those scenes. If Werther were to be judged by the standards of "What Is Enlightenment?," for example, what would his contemporaries think of him? Was Saint-Preux like Jefferson or not? To reinforce these points, students read excerpts from other autobiographies of the era (by Franklin, by Equiano, by Bishop), which showed how people of different classes, genders, and races described themselves and discussed others in many of the same terms.

More advanced students must negotiate national types as well. Some differences between Saint-Preux and Jefferson reflect their status as Swiss or American, not just their class positions, and the plots definitely highlight specific national situations (e.g., the distinction between high aristocracy and the middle class in France, regional differences in what would become the United States). Honors majors or graduate students dealing with this material must factor in the distance between an author and the intended audience, a question of the cultural politics of representation that brings under closer scrutiny the author's negotiation with the contemporaneous environment.

No matter what the learning stage, the first section of the class builds the context of the Enlightenment: its communities and their ideas about how reason, the mind, and the group were defined. Lower-division learners need to see or read graphic moments where those ideals were not always put into practice; more advanced students need to work on identifying contrasts and comparisons; graduate students need to contrast texts but also to explain and evaluate their weight as documents in a cultural context.

The second section builds on such tasks as it introduces excerpts from major texts in Enlightenment philosophy, especially from the French and American Revolutions. The goal in reading is to insert ideas into concrete contexts. The philosophical language must be put back into the mouths of characters the students have met: who in which novel (or the film) would these texts be written for, and how would the characters react to the sentiments in the essays? This act of resituation not only builds a historical horizon of expectation for the text but also explores the question of readership and a text's sociopolitical impact (Benedict Anderson's "imagined community").

The third section of the first-year class moves beyond the revolutions and into the generation born during them, to ask what happened to the ideals of the Enlightenment after the political climates changed on the Continent and in the United States, as anti-Enlightenment and post-Enlightenment sentiments arose. *The Scarlet Letter* and "The Legend of Sleepy Hollow," like *Jefferson in Paris*, both have frames that explicitly tie the prerevolutionary era to the new United States, contrasting the founders with the present day, usually twenty to thirty years after the revolution. Here again the problem of time and values is highlighted, allowing students more practice in reading values out of literature and correlating philosophical ideals with class and gender positions. By this time in the class, learners are creating their own précis instead of using teacher-guided worksheets. They engage in systematic analysis, building arguments for evaluation, at all levels of the course.

Longer writing assignments echo the logic of the class structure, stressing period-correct communication norms and issues analysis. By following the logic of analysis that the class sequence taught them, beginning students gain the cognitive and linguistic tools to make their own way into a particular historical space. They learn to identify an era's general issues, key terms, and sociopolitical practices (through the novels) and then work toward ever more sophisticated expressions of how those issues played out in that time and in comparison to ours. The final paper for the freshman class was a developed piece of issues analysis: to critique the film *Jefferson in Paris* as a good or poor representation of the era.

To this point in the class, students had worked toward a communication goal, assessing how particular texts fit in the dominant representation of a historical era. By starting with people and not abstract ideas, which are more easily misread, the class learned to monitor themselves: they could hold one another responsible for the details of the novels they had read and could debate one another's readings of an essay by reference to a real or fictional character's behavior. The teacher did not need to monitor a debate, when facts from Saint-Preux's or Benjamin Franklin's life spoke eloquently to the issues. The differences between disciplinary discourses were also reduced, since in a historical framing *Héloïse* was just as much about the Enlightenment as Kant's essay.

Intermediate and advanced students (stage 2) can be held to the same standards of evidence and argumentation, but they must also be responsible for more complex acts of explanation and analysis. They must do more than argue that a text belonged or did not belong to the Enlightenment. They must also offer systematic readings of the relations among texts in the era, or between text and context. At stage 3, honors majors and graduate students must apply scholarly concepts to such analyses.

Regardless of its place in a curricular sequence, the interdisciplinary course Romance, Revolution, and Reason is accountable to the general curriculum in ways not ordinarily seen: as a course that meets writing or other general education requirements, as practice in reading fictional and philosophical works in historical context, as practice in argumentation in period- and group-correct language, as practice in referring to texts in several fields. The course promotes several kinds of cultural literacy and in more than one discipline, but it remains in the cultural context of a period, as preparation for future, more technical analyses of novels, philosophy, government documents, and historical assessments. Designed to approach interdisciplinary work through literacy and analysis, it introduces students with little background in the humanities to a new range of analytic constructs.

A course designed in this way can conceivably function as a core offering for more than one major sequence—in history, literature, philosophy. Its framework is broadly based in historical thinking, and it includes both excerpts and longer texts from a wide range of material in several disciplines. This broad selection allows students many paths to enter the eighteenth century.

Instructors of undergraduates who wish to redefine a learning sequence in the fashion outlined here will clearly have to assemble tasks in terms of their complexity (linguistic, cognitive, cultural, social). Moreover, when that curriculum extends over several courses, it will ideally recycle texts used in earlier courses, requiring students to revisit and analyze them in greater depth, to move from the general humanistic concerns expressed in the course we have presented here toward discipline-specific concerns in the upper-division and graduate sequences.

By offering students, early in their college careers, the opportunity to read capstone texts, by training them how to read analytically, and by introducing them to the essay-writing styles of the humanities, courses in general humanities can be more than introductions. By presenting a sequence of learning rather than a sequence of materials, instructors can help students evolve cross-cultural perspectives and the consciousness of historical difference. Students will learn to join new groups, groups that have different cultural norms, different patterns of self-expression, and different concerns. At the same time, courses of this type can put otherwise less accessible realms of humanist thinking (e.g., eighteenth-century studies) at the heart of the undergraduate curriculum, by capitalizing on their inherent interdisciplinarity and cultural studies perspective. Both cultural studies and FL studies require strict attention to historical data, because the past is indeed a kind of foreign country.

LEARNING STAGES AS BENCHMARKS FOR ACCOUNTABILITY IN CULTURAL STUDIES

Learning culture requires a curriculum to identify structures not only for linguistic arguments and text genres appropriate to certain levels and their goals but also for content knowledge. Such learning necessarily involves literature, at the very least for those outcomes that concern the identities of dominant groups in a culture. Whether in opposition or in concert, all groups in a culture define themselves vis-à-vis this dominance. The literature taught in a culture course often needs more varied forms than the literature taught in a literature-as-culture course, which, to address the discrepancies between dominant and nondominant voices, necessarily includes popular and high-end media not tailored for the general public and showing more semiotic innovation.

Cultural studies, however, needs to deal with more canons than those associated with high culture or literature classes: popular culture, government documents, and mass media, along with the critical reading and analysis skills necessary to deal with them. Teaching culture is a content-based activity, and it must also help learners orient themselves in coherent structures of context and intertextuality. But an understanding of abstracts should be grounded on concrete categories of cultural information, because of the possible diffusiveness of the contents and contexts involved. The accountability of the culture classroom comes from setting clear benchmarks for what is learnable.

We stand at a crossroads. Cultural studies as preset analyses—of marginalization, of particular resistant groups without reference to the larger context of dominant groups, and of popular culture isolated from high or resistant culture—can become as vacuous as *l'art pour l'art* studies of literature. This chapter has argued for a curriculum design that builds literacy systematically. The sample course we presented had students learn to negotiate systems as authorized and self-authorizing subjects—subjects considered in their larger cultural context rather than as propagators of opinion in isolation.

TES

1. For a study that suggests that students who learned about the Ivory Coast from a poem showed richer, less stereotyped understanding than those who learned it from a fact sheet, see Scott and Huntington (622). The necessity of using more-nuanced approaches to teaching culture as part of the study of language is also supported by Wright. The classic study on this subject is Steffensen, Joag-Dev, and Anderson. See also Borst.
2. This phenomenon is the point of Pierre Bourdieu's *Distinction: A Social Critique of the Judgment of Taste* (1984). Bourdieu traces the role of class affiliation in the knowledgeable consumption of and transactions with elite-status texts.
3. The complete course materials are posted at www.utexas.edu/courses/arens/.

Professional Responsibility and the Identity of Foreign Languages in Higher Education

Coda

We have addressed the goals for and approaches to an undergraduate curriculum, elaborating on these in terms of curriculum building and pedagogy in line with an orientation to multiple literacies. We have stressed the need to rethink the learning sequences of current programs with regard to the cognitive and linguistic abilities of students, from beginners to the most advanced foreign language learners. In addition, we have proposed that language, literature, and culture can be foundational for such a sequence, and we suggested materials and tasks for it.

We have illustrated how language programs can move through reading-, viewing-, and listening-comprehension stages to sophisticated production in courses designed for students studying a foreign language, for courses in writing across the curriculum, or for general education. Texts, their print and other media genres, have been discussed as central to this effort, because the obligatory and optional moves of genres that structure communication provide students with both conceptual and linguistic frameworks on which they can build their own discourse capacities in reflective, substantive fashion.

Such rethinking of curricula cannot happen in a vacuum. One must start with an inventory of a program's existing resources in its institution. What is currently being taught or can be taught? What supplemental resources are available on the campus? What faculty and student populations exist or are likely to develop? And what kinds of professional engagement are valued and represented by faculty members? Such an inventory indicates a campus's features that can be capitalized on for professional preparation, teaching areas, and institutional opportunities. A list of campus offerings also often suggests an appropriate rhythm of offerings, showing how a two- or three-year cycle of courses can be structured to fill student expectations, while satisfying the faculty's needs to innovate and also to commit to teaching in general education offerings.

The questions provide a baseline from which to start.

How many courses can a program offer over a one- to two-year cycle?
How are the strengths of existing faculty members represented in the proposed offerings?
How are the resources across the institution utilized? Is their utilization optimal? For example, do they complement courses in the FL department?
What course contents are needed? Which are offered in-house and which in neighboring departments?
Which approaches and contents need to be staggered across a successful degree program? (Does a German department, for example, need a course on the history of the German language if a strong history of English exists?)

Answers to these questions lay out the larger institutional and programmatic context in which a second set of questions must be posed, about how a program fulfills its responsibilities to the students it serves. Those responsibilities include not only disciplinary concerns but also forms of communication, research and documentation, text choices appropriate to future professional environments, and what kinds of evaluation (certifications, portfolios, or theses, aside from normal class work) may be appropriate. Most faculty members cannot claim to be experts in a project of such scope. But they can act as expert resources, people who can illustrate such transactions and enable the learners in their charge to identify and employ the language and message patterns of authentic materials as the basis for personal speech acts and extended discourse.

After resources are inventoried, a program must define which multiple literacies it wishes to privilege and which stages of acquisition will be implemented and rewarded. In working through those stages, students become empowered as readers, listeners, or viewers who are able to identify how cultural production in a foreign language is negotiated and how foreign language speakers contact and influence one another in cultural and multicultural frameworks.

After a general program framework is settled in this way, individual courses must be planned. Every course must be planned with respect to the learners' position, the materials that need to be introduced and revisited during the curriculum, and the stages for classroom tasks that move from comprehension to production. Those tasks must refer to the program's consensus about goals, especially those regarding the relation of the pedagogy taught to the subject matter and approaches used by faculty members.

We have, then, recommended a learner-based pedagogy that provides students with opportunities to develop multiple literacies. Initially, the materials and challenges of cultural communication can overwhelm learners who are unguided and unpracticed in assuming such responsibility—a problem that novice course designers often overlook. Our solution is the adoption of the précis format, an exercise that integrates language and content and helps forestall learner confusion by structuring what should be looked for and where. The précis helps create organizers for what can appear to be a flood of unrelated information. In such assignments, language and content are covalent at all levels.

Remapping the Foreign Language Curriculum advocates programs that have their coherence based on a consistent teaching philosophy, reflected in a pedagogy that privileges multiple literacies and structures learners' encounters with many different kinds of cultural texts, including literature and film. Most programs, whether graduate or undergraduate, have courses linked by the material covered and not by what learning levels or program aims have been set by the faculty as a whole. Today's literary studies illustrate what happens when curricula change and departments fail to see the broader classroom implications of those changes: scholars add new topics courses to a program without considering the pattern of total course offerings. In the past twenty years, the once relatively narrow spectrum of positivism, intellectual history, and text-immanent criticism has expanded into a multitude of competing critical theories, each claiming its own literacy. The current generation's expansion into cultural studies, a rich and interesting area, also brings with it questions about the language to be used in the classroom and the particular contribution that foreign language teachers can make. We see such problems as closely linked to the proposals in this book.

In the absence of a coherent pedagogy about how to teach students to learn and apply theories and with expanding demands for students to become literate about historical, sociological, psychological, and anthropological content, the burden placed on learners can lead to confusion about standards for competence. Often students in a FL department remain unclear about their aims as learners. They see their goal as fragmented, with competing demands for them to learn about literature, culture, or a critical mode, as they try to master a particular culture or language. Without a teaching philosophy that can accommodate a broadened scope of foreign language study, the holistic possibility of acquiring multiple literacies remains in doubt, not integral to learning.

We have argued that programs must apply the organizational principles of these theories in the undergraduate curriculum, thus bringing research and the classroom closer than they have been. Yet the curricular reforms discussed in this volume have not been factored into the training of teachers. To a degree, multiple literacies have been integrated into today's graduate programs, in concentrations like cultural geography, dialect studies, (post)colonial literary studies, women's studies, and minority studies. Yet these new theories have not been particularly successful in generating, for example, new frameworks for textual interpretation. Even when graduate students work intensively with literary analysis, "training in the teaching of literature is a glaring omission in graduate programs and in secondary certification programs" (Bretz 336).

For the high school or undergraduate teaching that today's MA and PhD students will engage in after they finish their theses and dissertations and become faculty members in more traditional programs, the theories of literature and linguistics (reader response, translation as reception, semiotics, poststructuralism, deconstruction, structuralism, formalism, phenomenology, feminist criticism) remain largely unconnected to their work in the classroom. Dissertation titles alone betray the exclusionary focus of graduate schools on academic treatments of language and literary topics. Gilbert Jarvis reports that among the forty-five dissertations listed in foreign language education in 1988, only four "clearly relate directly to teaching and learning behavior" (297). Small wonder that programs for undergraduate majors emphasize language or literature instead of taking an integrated cultural studies approach.

In view of this lack of common objectives among FL departments nationwide (see Devens and Bennett for an early statement of that assertion), most articles that address curricular problems do so from the standpoint of a single feature of the departmental enterprise—issues such as teaching literature in the original or in translation (Lindenberger) or the role of specific grammatical features or, in rare cases, linguistics (Fleischman). Studies make suggestions about language for special purposes (Feustle; Elling) or issues surrounding proficiency (Richardson), but rarely do they treat upper-division or graduate programs as an integral part of the larger educational community.

Some graduate schools are exploring ways to help their students from all disciplines in a Research University I[1] find and articulate their fields to faculty members and students in other types of institutions and other fields, to help students across disciplines write dissertations and articles for publication, present at conferences and other professional forums, intern at neighboring schools and colleges, converse with a peer group of disciplinary outsiders, edit and evaluate one another's work, or learn about issues in education that affect different types of courses and ways to develop teaching portfolios. These initiatives have caught the attention of national funding agencies and *The Chronicle of Higher Education*, among others, as filling a void in current departmental training that will determine undergraduate teaching in the next generation.[2] Here, we content ourselves with noting that preparation in professional roles and pedagogies fosters the future effectiveness of graduate students as scholars and teachers, which will strengthen undergraduate programs. Departmental initiatives to stage educational conversations in their own disciplines about who they are and what they do that contributes to higher education in the United States are a productive step toward full agency in the future of foreign languages as a discipline.

This volume proposes that departments of foreign languages can ill afford indifference to their own needs and ultimately to their future role in higher education. To have learners in undergraduate (and graduate) programs in these departments become able to comprehend messages and exert agency when literacies converge is now a preeminent concern of policy makers at home and abroad.

If English is indeed the lingua franca of global communication, then let our nation remember that such status can be exclusionary as well as inclusive. Failure to understand the multiliteracies of foreign languages can preclude successful negotiation of meaning, even when all the words of a text are understood and its genre presumed familiar.

Foreign language studies must teach how factors such as point of view or use of grammar norm and deviance influence the patterns of messages in texts, for such patterns reveal how language means and creates meaning. Instructing students to comprehend and effectively interact with the meanings in text genres from cultures that are often unlike those of North Americans remains the field's raison d'être. Departments must be responsible for coherent teaching practices that inform their program as a whole. They must join the support systems available in their institutions to develop graduate and undergraduate curricula founded in a meld of language and content that shapes teaching and learning at all levels.

NOTES

1. The current term is a "research-extensive university." See the Carnegie Foundation Classifications, posted at www.carnegiefoundation.org/Classification/.
2. For an example of ongoing institutional commitment to this kind of professional development of graduate students, see the Graduate School's Intellectual Entrepreneurship Program at the University of Texas, Austin, and the various commendations posted at www.utexas.edu/ogs/development.html. Some work in this vein is represented in a course developed by us for graduate students on pedagogy. See the materials posted at www.utexas.edu/courses/arens/GRS_f390J/.

WORKS CITED

Adams, Hazard, and Leroy Searle, eds. *Critical Theory since 1965*. Tallahassee: Florida State UP, 1986.

Allende, Isabel. *The House of the Spirits*. Trans. Magda Bogin. New York: Knopf, 1985.

Álvarez, Mariá Angélica. "El discurso / los discursos: Tradicion/subversion en la escritura de Laura Esquivel." *Celehis: Revista del Centro de Letras Hispanoamericanas* 5.6–8 (1996): 5–11.

Anderson, Benedict R. *Imagined Communities: Reflections on the Origin and Spread of Nationalism*. London: Verso, 1983.

Anderson Imbert, Enrique. "La muerte." *Cuento en miniatura: Antología*. Caracas, Ven.: Equinoccio, U Simon Bolivar, 1976. 47–48.

Arens, Katherine. "Teaching and the *MLA International Bibliography*." *Profession 2002*. New York: MLA, 2002. 158–63.

Austen, Jane. *Emma*. Penguin Complete Novels of Jane Austen. Harmondsworth: Penguin, 1983.

———. *Pride and Prejudice*. New York: Heritage, 1940.

Baker, Steven J. "The Monterey Model: Integrating International Policy Studies with Language Education." Krueger and Ryan 120–29.

Bakhtin, Mikhail. "The Problem of Speech Genres." Bakhtin, *"Speech Genres"* 60–102.

———. *"Speech Genres" and Other Late Essays*. Trans. Vern W. McGee. Ed. Michael Holquist. Austin: U of Texas P, 1986.

Barthes, Roland. *The Fashion System*. Trans. Richard Howard. New York: Hill, 1983.

———. *The Pleasure of the Text*. Trans. Richard I. Miller. New York: Hill, 1973.

Bartholomae, David. "Literacy and Departments of Language and Literature." *PMLA* 117 (2002): 1272–78.

Berman, Art. *From the New Criticism to Deconstruction: The Reception of Structuralism and Post-structuralism.* Urbana: U of Illinois P, 1988.

Bernhardt, Elizabeth B. "A Model of L2 Text Reconstruction: The Recall of Literary Text by Learners of German." *Issues in L2: Theory as Practice / Practice as Theory.* Ed. Leslie M. Bailey. Norwood: Ablex, 1990. 21–43.

———. "Research into the Teaching of Literature in a Second Language: What It Says and How to Communicate It to Graduate Students." Scott and Tucker 195–210.

Birdsong, David, and Michelle Molis. "On the Evidence for Maturational Constraints in Second-Language Acquisition." *Journal of Memory and Language* 44 (2001): 235–49.

Borst, Stefanie Christine. "Context and Comprehension: A Cross-Cultural Comparison of Germans and Americans Reading Authentic Texts." Diss. U of Texas, 2004.

Bourdieu, Pierre. *Distinction: A Social Critique of the Judgment of Taste.* Trans. Richard Nice. Cambridge: Harvard UP, 1984.

———. *The Field of Cultural Production: Essays on Art and Literature.* Ed. Randal Johnson. New York: Columbia UP, 1993.

———. *Language and Symbolic Power.* Trans. Matthew Adamson. Ed. John B. Thompson. Cambridge: Harvard UP, 1991.

Bretz, Mary Lee. "Reaction to 'Literature and Communicative Competence: A Springboard for the Development of Critical Thinking and Aesthetic Appreciation.'" *Foreign Language Annals* 23 (1990): 335–38.

Brooks, Cleanth. *The Well Wrought Urn: Studies in the Structure of Poetry.* New York: Reunal, 1947.

Burnett, Joanne, and Leah Fonder-Solano. "Crossing the Boundaries between Literature and Pedagogy." Scott and Tucker 195–210.

Byrnes, Heidi. "The Cultural Turn in Foreign Language Departments: Challenge and Opportunity." *Profession 2002.* New York: MLA, 2002. 114–29.

———, ed. *Learning Foreign and Second Languages.* New York: MLA, 1998.

———. "The Role of Listening Comprehension: A Theoretical Base." *Foreign Language Annals* 17 (1984): 317–29.

Byrnes, Heidi, and Susanne Kord. "Developing Literacy and Literary Competence: Challenges for Foreign Language Departments." Scott and Tucker 35–73.

Chartier, Roger. *The Order of Books: Readers, Authors and Libraries in Europe between the Fourteenth and Eighteenth Centuries.* Trans. Lydia G. Cochrane. Cambridge: Polity, 1994.

Como agua para chocolate (1992). Películas del cine mexicano: El cine mexicano de los noventa (1989–1996). Más de cien años de cine mexicano. Ed. Maximiliano Maza. 1996. 7 Sept. 2004 <http://cinemexicano.mty.itesm.mx/peliculas/chocolate.html>.

Davis, James N. "The Act of Reading in the Foreign Language: Pedagogical Implications of Iser's Reader-Response Theory." *Modern Language Journal* 73 (1989): 420–28.

Derrida, Jacques. "Différance." *"Speech and Phenomena" and Other Essays on Husserl's Theory of Signs.* Evanston: Northwestern UP, 1973. 129–60.

———. "Structure, Sign, and Play in the Discourse of the Human Sciences." Trans. Alan Bass. *Writing and Difference.* Chicago: U of Chicago P, 1987. 278–93.

Devens, Monica S., and Nancy J. Bennett. "The MLA Surveys of Foreign Language Graduate Programs, 1984–85." *ADFL Bulletin* 17.3 (1986): 19–27.

Dobrian, Susan. "Romancing the Cook: Parodic Consumption of Popular Romance Myths in *Como agua para chocolate.*" *Latin American Literary Review* 48 (1996): 55–66.

Doughty, Catherine, and Jessica Williams, eds. *Focus on Form in Classroom Second Language Acquisition.* New York: Cambridge UP, 1998.

Eagleton, Terry. "Jane Eyre." *Myths of Power: A Marxist Study of the Brontës.* London: Macmillan, 1975. 15–32.

Eco, Umberto. *A Theory of Semiotics.* Bloomington: Indiana UP, 1976.

Elling, Barbara. "The German Business Diploma: A Model for Testing and Evaluation." *ADFL Bulletin* 18.1 (1986): 46–49.

Escaja, Tina. "Reinscribiendo a Penelope: Mujer e identidad mejicana en *Como agua para chocolate.*" *Revista Iberoamericana* 66 (2000): 571–86.

Esquivel, Laura. *Como agua para chocolate: Novelas de entregas mensuales con recetas, amores y remedios caseros.* México: Planeta, 1989. Trans. as *Like Water for Chocolate: A Novel in Monthly Installments with Recipes, Romances, and Home Remedies.* Trans. John Christensen. New York: Anchor-Doubleday, 1992.

Essif, Les. "The Literature of Foreign Language Programs: The Road to Cultural Studies Is Not Paved with Literary History . . . Tick Tock . . . Tick Tock . . ." *ADFL Bulletin* 34.1 (2002): 15–20.

Fallon, Jean M. "On Foreign Ground: One Attempt at Attracting Non-French Majors to a French Studies Course." *Foreign Language Annals* 35 (2002): 405–13.

Fanon, Frantz. *Black Skin, White Masks.* Trans. Charles Lam Markmann. New York: Grove, 1967.

Fekete, John, ed. *The Structural Allegory: Reconstructive Encounters with the New French Thought.* Minneapolis: U of Minnesota P, 1984.

Feustle, Joseph A., Jr. "Spanish and Legal Assisting: A Collaborative Venture." *ADFL Bulletin* 17.2 (1986): 50–52.

Fish, Stanley. *Is There a Text in This Class? The Authority of Interpretive Communities.* Cambridge: Harvard UP, 1980.

Fleischman, Suzanne. "Getting Calliope through Graduate School? Can Chomsky Help? or, The Role of Linguistics in Graduate Education in Foreign Languages." *ADFL Bulletin* 17.3 (1986): 9–13.

Foucault, Michel. *The Archaeology of Knowledge.* Trans. A. M. Sheridan Smith. New York: Pantheon, 1972.

———. *Discipline and Punish: The Birth of the Prison.* Trans. Alan Sheridan. New York: Pantheon, 1978.

———. "What Is an Author?" *Language, Counter-memory, Practice: Selected Essays and Interviews.* Ithaca: Cornell UP, 1977. 113–38.

Freire, Paolo. *Pedagogy of the Oppressed.* Trans. Myra Bergman Ramos. Rev. ed. New York: Continuum, 2000.

Frye, Northrop. *The Anatomy of Criticism.* Princeton: Princeton UP, 1957.

Garrett, Nina. "Technology in the Service of Language Learning: Trends and Issues." *Modern Language Journal* 75 (1991): 74–97.

Garvin, Paul L., ed. *A Prague School Reader on Esthetics, Literary Structure, and Style.* Washington: Georgetown UP, 1964.

Geertz, Clifford. *The Interpretation of Cultures.* New York: Basic, 1973.

Graff, Gerald. *Professing Literature: An Institutional History.* Chicago: U of Chicago P, 1987.

Greene, Graham. *The Quiet American.* New York: Viking, 1956.

Hall, Stuart, and Tony Jefferson, eds. *Resistance through Rituals: Youth Subcultures in Post-war Britain.* London: Routledge, 1993.

Hamburger, Käte. *The Logic of Literature.* Trans. Marilynn J. Rose. 2nd ed. Bloomington: Indiana UP, 1973.

Hammett, Dashiell. *The Maltese Falcon.* New York: Knopf, 1930.

Hanley, Julia E. B., Carol A. Herron, and Steven P. Cole. "Using Video as an Advance Organizer to a Written Passage in the FLES Classroom." *Modern Language Journal* 79 (1995): 57–66.

Harland, Richard. *Superstructuralism: The Philosophy of Structuralism and Post-structuralism.* London: Routledge, 1988.

Hjelmslev, Louis. *Principes de grammaire générale.* Copenhagen: Bianca Lunos, 1928.

Hosenfeld, Carol. "A Preliminary Investigation of the Strategies of Successful and Non-successful Readers." *System* 5 (1977): 110–23.

Hulstijn, Jan H. "Retention of Inferred and Given Word Meanings: Experiments in Incidental Vocabulary Learning." *Vocabulary and Applied Linguistics.* Ed. Henri Béjoint. London: Macmillan, 1992. 113–25.

Husserl, Edmund. "Phenomenology." Adams and Searle 658–64.

Ibsen, Kristine L. "On Recipes, Reading, and Revolution: Postboom Parody in *Como agua para chocolate.*" *Concerns: Women's Caucus for the Modern Languages* 25.2 (1995): 7–20.

Ingarden, Roman. *The Cognition of the Literary Work of Art.* Trans. Ruth Ann Crowley and Kenneth R. Olsen. Evanston: Northwestern UP, 1973.

———. *The Literary Work of Art: An Investigation on the Borderlines of Ontology, Logic, and the Theory of Literature.* Trans. George G. Grabowicz. Evanston: Northwestern UP, 1973.

Irving, Washington. "The Legend of Sleepy Hollow." 1819. *"The Legend of Sleepy Hollow" and Other Tales; or, The Sketchbook of Geoffrey Crayon, Gent.* New York: Modern Lib., 2001. 293–320.

Iser, Wolfgang. *The Act of Reading: A Theory of Aesthetic Response.* Baltimore: Johns Hopkins UP, 1981.

———. *The Implied Reader: Patterns of Communication in Prose Fiction from Bunyan to Beckett.* Baltimore: Johns Hopkins UP, 1974.

Jacob, Margaret C. "From the President." *American Society for Eighteenth-Century Studies Circular* 106 (1997): 1–3.

James, Dorothy. "Bypassing the Traditional Leadership: Who's Minding the Store?" *ADFL Bulletin* 28.3 (1997): 5–11.

Jarvis, Gilbert A. "Research on Teaching Methodology: Its Evolution and Prospects." *Foreign Language Acquisition Research and the Classroom.* Ed. Barbara F. Freed. Lexington: Heath, 1991. 295–306.

Jauss, Hans Robert. "Literary History as a Challenge to Literary Theory." Trans. Timothy Bahti. *Toward an Aesthetic of Reception.* Minneapolis: U of Minnesota P, 1982. 3–45.

"Jeder fünfte Baum geschädigt." *Frankfurter Allgemeine Zeitung* 25 Nov. 2000: 4.

Jefferson in Paris. Dir. James Ivory. 1995. DVD. Buena Vista Home Video, 2004.

Kafka, Franz. "Die Verwandlung." 1915. *Sämtliche Erzählungen.* Ed. Paul Raabe. Frankfurt am Main: Fischer, 1970. 56–99.

Kant, Immanuel. "An Answer to the Question: What Is Enlightenment?" Trans. James Schmidt. *What Is Enlightenment? Eighteenth-Century Answers and Twentieth-Century Questions.* Ed. Schmidt. Berkeley: U of California P, 1996. 58–65.

———. "What Is Enlightenment?" *The Portable Enlightenment Reader.* Ed. Isaac Kramnick. New York: Penguin, 1995. 1–7.

Kayser, Wolfgang. *Das sprachliche Kunstwerk: Eine Einführung in die Literaturwissenschaft.* Bern: Franke, 1948.

Kecht, Maria Regina, and Katharina von Hammerstein, eds. *Languages across the Curriculum: Interdisciplinary Structures and Internationalized Education.* Columbus: Ohio State UP, 2000.

Kern, Richard G. *Literacy and Language Teaching.* Oxford: Oxford UP, 2000.

———. "Reconciling the Language-Literature Split through Literacy." *ADFL Bulletin* 33.2 (2002): 20–24.

———. "The Role of Mental Translation in Second Language Reading." *Studies in Second Language Acquisition* 16 (1994): 441–61.

Kintsch, Walter. *Comprehension: A Paradigm for Cognition.* New York: Cambridge UP, 1998.

Kintsch, Walter, and Teun A. van Dijk. "Toward a Model of Text Comprehension and Production." *Psychological Review* 85 (1978): 363–94.

Kirkpatrick, Susan. "E Pluribus Unum." *PMLA* 117 (2002): 1279–83.

Kord, Susanne. "Contribution to Question-and-Answer Session." Curriculum consultation, Dept. of Germanic Studies, U of Texas, Austin. 25 Apr. 2004.

Kristeva, Julia. *Language, the Unknown: An Initiation into Linguistics.* Trans. Anne M. Menke. New York: Columbia UP, 1989.

——. "Stabat Mater." Trans. Leon S. Roudiez. *Tales of Love.* New York: Columbia UP, 1987. 234–63.

Kristeva, Julia, and J.-Cl. Coque. "Sémanalyse: Conditions d'une sémiotique scientifique (Enretien)." *Semiotica* 5 (1972): 324–49.

Krueger, Merle, and Frank Ryan, eds. *Language and Content: Discipline- and Content-Based Approaches to Language Study.* Lexington: Heath, 1993.

Kuhn, Thomas S. *The Structure of Scientific Revolutions.* 2nd ed. Chicago: U of Chicago P, 1970.

Lacan, Jacques. "The Mirror Stage as Formative of the Function of the I." Trans. Alan Sheridan. *Écrits: A Selection.* New York: Norton, 1977. 1–7.

Lariviere, Richard W. "Language Curricula in Universities: What and How." *Modern Language Journal* 86 (2002): 244–46.

"Laura Esquivel, al rescate del mundo íntimo en el 'siglo del desequilibrio.'" *Como agua para chocolate: Sugerencias y materiales para el trabajo en la sala de clase.* Ed. Andreas Hülsmann. 13 Sept. 2000. 7 Sept. 2004 <http://home.t-online.de/home/Andreas.Huelsm/esqui.htm>.

Lindenberger, Herbert. "Teaching Literature in the Original or in Translation: An Intellectual or a Political Problem?" *ADFL Bulletin* 17.2 (1986): 35–39.

Lord, Albert. *The Singer of Tales.* Cambridge: Harvard UP, 1960.

Lotman, Yurij, and B. A. Uspensky. "On the Semiotic Mechanism of Culture." Adams and Searle 410–22.

Marquet, Antonio. "¿Cómo escribir un best-seller? La receta de Laura Esquivel." *Plural: Revista Cultural de Excelsior* 237 (1991): 58–67.

Marshall, Donald G. *Contemporary Critical Theory: A Selective Bibliography.* New York: MLA, 1993.

Marshall, James D., Peter Smagorinsky, and Michael W. Smith. *The Language of Interpretation: Patterns of Discourse in Discussions of Literature.* Urbana: NCTE, 1995.

Morewedge, Rosemarie Thee. "Entering the House of General Education: Foreign Language Instruction in a General Education Framework at SUNY Binghamton." *ADFL Bulletin* 33.2 (2002): 72–77.

Morgan, Martha. "The Achievement of First-Year College German Students at the University of Texas at Austin: A Comparison of a Comprehension-Based Reading Curriculum and a Speaking-Based Four Skills Curriculum." MA thesis. U of Texas, Austin, 1980.

Mukarovsky, Jan. "Standard Language and Poetic Language." Trans. Paul L. Garvin. Garvin 17–30.

Mulvey, Laura. "Visual Pleasure and Narrative Cinema." *Visual and Other Pleasures.* Bloomington: Indiana UP, 1989. 14–26.

Nance, Kimberly. "'Authentic and Surprising News of Themselves': Engaging Students' Preexisting Competencies in the Introductory Literature Course." *ADFL Bulletin* 34.1 (2002): 30–34.

National Standards for History. Los Angeles: Natl. Center for History in the Schools, U of California, Los Angeles, 1996.

Nichols, Geraldine Cleary. "Spanish and the Multilingual Department: Ways to Use the Rising Tide." *Profession 2000.* New York: MLA, 2000. 115–23.

Norris, John M., and Lourdes Ortega. "Effectiveness of L2 Instruction: A Research Synthesis and Quantitative Meta-Analysis." *Language Learning* 50 (2000): 417–528.

Parry, Kate. "Too Many Words: Learning the Vocabulary of an Academic Subject." *Second Language Reading and Vocabulary Learning.* Ed. Thomas Huckin, Margot Haynes, and James Coady. Norwood: Ablex, 1993. 109–29.

Pfeiffer, Peter C. "Preparing Graduate Students to Teach Literature and Language in a Foreign Language Department." *ADFL Bulletin* 34.1 (2002): 11–14.

Porter, Catherine, and Walter Sanders. "Merging English and Foreign Language Departments: The Mansfield Example." *ADFL Bulletin* 33.3 (2002): 56–60.

Pratt, Mary Louise. "What's Foreign and What's Familiar?" *PMLA* 117 (2002): 1283–87.

Radway, Janice. *Reading the Romance: Women, Patriarchy, and Popular Literature.* Chapel Hill: U of North Carolina P, 1991.

Raffel, Burton. *How to Read a Poem.* New York: NAL, 1984.

"Response to Dorothy James, 'Bypassing the Traditional Leadership: Who's Minding the Store?'" *ADFL Bulletin* 29.2 (1998): 39–76; 29.3 (1998): 46–68.

Richards, I. A. *Principles of Literary Criticism.* London: Kegan, 1924.

Richardson, Peter N. "Proficiency-Based Curricula: The View from the Hill." *ADFL Bulletin* 18.1 (1986): 38–42.

Robb, Thomas, Steven Ross, and Ian Shortreed. "Salience of Feedback on Error and Its Effect on EFL Writing Quality." *TESOL Quarterly* 20 (1986): 83–95.

Rosenblatt, Louise M. *Literature as Exploration.* 1938. 5th ed. New York: MLA, 1995.

Scott, Virginia M., and Julia A. Huntington. "Reading Culture: Using Literature to Develop C2 Competence." *Foreign Language Annals* 35 (2002): 622–31.

Scott, Virginia M., and Holly Tucker, eds. *SLA and the Literature Classroom: Fostering Dialogues.* Boston: Heinle, 2002.

Sollors, Werner. "Cooperation between English and Foreign Languages in the Area of Multilinguial Literature." *PMLA* 117 (2002): 1287–94.

Staiger, Emil. *Die Kunst der Interpretation: Studien zur deutschen Literaturgeschichte.* Zurich: Atlantis, 1955.

Standards for Foreign Language Learning in the Twenty-First Century. Ed. Natl. Standards in Foreign Language Educ. Project. Lawrence: Allen, 1999.

Stauffer, Russell G. *Directing the Reading-Thinking Process.* New York: Harper, 1975.

Steffensen, Margaret S., Chritra Joag-Dev, and Richard C. Anderson. "A Cross-Cultural Perspective on Reading Comprehension." *Reading Research Quarterly* 15 (1979): 1–29.

Stenhouse, Lawrence. *An Introduction to Curriculum Research and Development.* London: Heinemann, 1975.

Sternfeld, Steven. "The University of Utah's Immersion/Multiliteracy Program: An Example of an Area Studies Approach to the Design of First-Year College Foreign Language Instruction." *Foreign Language Annals* 22 (1989): 341–54.

Swaffar, Janet. "German Studies as Studies of Cultural Discourse." *Teaching German in Twentieth-Century America*. Ed. David P. Benseler, Craig W. Nickisch, and Cora Lee Nollendorfs. Madison: U of Wisconsin P, 2001. 230–46.

———. "Reading the Patterns of Literary Works: Strategies and Teaching Techniques." Scott and Tucker 131–54.

———. "A Template for Advanced Learner Tasks: Staging Genre Reading and Cultural Literacy through the Précis." *Advanced Foreign Language Learning: A Challenge to College Programs*. Ed. Heidi Byrnes and Hiram Maxim. Boston: Thompson, 2004. 19–45.

Swaffar, Janet, Katherine Arens, and Heidi Byrnes. *Reading for Meaning: An Integrated Approach to Language Learning*. Englewood Cliffs: Prentice, 1991.

Todorov, Tzvetan. *The Fantastic: A Structural Approach to a Literary Genre*. Trans. Richard Howard. Ithaca: Cornell UP, 1975.

———. *Genres in Discourse*. Trans. Catherine Porter. Cambridge: Cambridge UP, 1990.

———. *The Poetics of Prose*. Trans. Richard Howard. Ithaca: Cornell UP, 1977.

Valdés, Maria Elena de. "Questioning Paradigms of Social Reality through Postmodern Intertextuality." *Poligrafías: Revista de literatura comparada* 1 (1996): 227–39.

Watt, Ian P. *The Rise of the Novel: Studies in Defoe, Richardson, and Fielding*. London: Chatto, 1957.

Whittingham, Georgina J., and Lourdes Silva. "¿El erotismo? ¿Fruto prohibido para la mujer? en *Como agua para chocolate* de Laura Esquivel y *Del amor y otros demonios* de Gabriel García Márquez." *Texto Crítico* 4.7 (1998): 57–67.

"Why Major in Literature—What Do We Tell Our Students?" *PMLA* 117 (2002): 487–521.

Wimsatt, William K. *The Verbal Icon: Studies in the Meaning of Poetry*. Lexington: UP of Kentucky, 1954.

Wright, David A. "Culture as Information and Culture as Affective Process: A Comparative Study." *Foreign Language Annals* 33 (2000): 330–41.

NAME INDEX

Allende, Isabel, 108, 122, 124
Álvarez, Maria Angelica, 134n3
Anderson, Benedict R., 185
Anderson, Richard C., 41, 48, 188n1
Anderson Imbert, Enrique, 81, 86, 94, 96, 97, 115
Arau, Alfonso, 135
Arens, Katherine, 12, 79
Aristophanes, 144
Aristotle, 143, 145
Austen, Jane, 44, 47, 52–54

Baker, Steven J., 39
Bakhtin, Mikhail, 3, 101
Barthes, Roland, 49, 133, 163
Bartholomae, David, 160n2
Beckinsale, Kate, 56
Bennett, Nancy J., 192
Berman, Art, 134n4
Bernhardt, Elizabeth B., 41, 160n6
Birdsong, David, 16
Bishop, Elizabeth, 184
Bonaparte, Napoleon, 180, 182
Borst, Stephanie Christine, 188n1
Bourdieu, Pierre, 4, 49, 50, 134n4, 188n2
Bretz, Mary Lee, 192
Brontë, Charlotte, 134n5
Brooks, Cleanth, 141
Burnett, Joanne, 140

Byrnes, Heidi, 12, 20, 29, 79, 140, 160n2, 162, 165

Chartier, Roger, 174
Christie, Agatha, 171
Churchill, Winston, 157
Close, Glenn, 122
Cole, Steven P., 19
Coque, J.-Cl., 160

Davis, James N., 40
Derrida, Jacques, 3, 49, 50
Devens, Monica, 192
Disraeli, Benjamin, 46
Dobrian, Susan, 134n3
Doughty, Catherine, 39

Eagleton, Terry, 134n5
Eco, Umberto, 49, 163
Eikhbaum, Boris M., 145
Elling, Barbara, 193
Equiano, Olaudah, 184
Escaja, Tina, 134n3
Esquivel, Laura, 98, 99, 111, 112, 116, 120, 121, 123, 127–31, 133–37
Essif, Les, 160n1
Euripides, 144

Fallon, Jean M., 160n2
Fanon, Frantz, 49

Fekete, John, 134n4
Feustle, Joseph A., Jr., 193
Fish, Stanley, 141, 161
Fleischman, Suzanne, 193
Fonder-Solano, Leah, 140
Foucault, Michel, 2, 49, 134n4, 163, 174
Franklin, Benjamin, 179, 184, 185
Freire, Paolo, 140
Freud, Sigmund, 51
Frye, Northrop, 142
Fuentes, Carlos, 108

García Márquez, Gabriel, 108
Garrett, Nina, 27n1
Garvin, Paul, 145
Geertz, Clifford, 44
Glenister, John, 56
Goethe, Johann Wolfgang von, 182
Graff, Gerald, 139
Greene, Graham, 107

Hall, Stuart, 162, 165
Hamburger, Käte, 142
Hammerstein, Katarina von, 25
Hammett, Dashiell, 107
Hanley, Julia E. B., 19
Harland, Richard, 134n4
Heckerling, Amy, 56
Herron, Carol A., 19
Hjelmslev, Louis, 49
Homer, 143
Hosenfeld, Carol, 84
Hulstijn, Jan H., 84
Huntington, Julia A., 188n1
Husserl, Edmund, 48

Ibsen, Kristine L., 134n3
Ingarden, Roman, 141
Iser, Wolfgang, 18, 47, 54, 83, 133

Jacob, Margaret C., 178
James, Dorothy, 12
Jarvis, Gilbert A., 192
Jauss, Hans Robert, 99
Jefferson, Thomas, 183–84
Jefferson, Tony, 162, 165
Joag-Dev, Chritra, 41, 48, 188n1

Kafka, Franz, 52, 54, 108
Kant, Immanuel, 181, 184, 185
Kayser, Wolfgang, 142

Kecht, Maria Regina, 25
Kern, Richard G., 20, 74, 97n1
Kintsch, Walter, 36, 87, 88
Kirkpatrick, Susan, 140
Kord, Susanne, 20, 30, 140, 160n2
Kristeva, Julia, 49, 159, 160, 163
Krueger, Merle, 39
Kuhn, Thomas S., 4

Lacan, Jacques, 49
Lariviere, Richard W., 23
le Carré, John, 46
Lincoln, Abraham, 157
Lindenberger, Herbert, 192
Lord, Albert, 145
Lotman, Yurij, 163

Malkovich, John, 122
Mann, Thomas, 130, 136
Marquet, Antonio, 134n3
Marshall, Donald G., 134n2, 134n4
Marshall, James D., 80
McGrath, Douglas, 56
Molis, Michelle, 16
Morewedge, Rosemarie Thee, 25
Morgan, Martha, 17
Mukarovsky, Jan, 49, 116, 150
Müller-Stahl, Arnim, 122
Mulvey, Laura, 122

Nance, Kimberly, 160n5
Nichols, Geraldine Cleary, 25
Norris, John M., xiii, 16

Ortega, Lourdes, xiii, 16

Pacheco, Cristina, 136
Paltrow, Gwyneth, 56
Parry, Kate, 88
Petrarch, 143, 158
Pfeiffer, Peter C., 160n6
Poe, Edgar Allan, 171
Porter, Catherine, 25
Pratt, Mary Louise, 140

Radway, Janice, 107
Raffel, Burton, 142
Richards, I. A., 134n2
Richardson, Peter N., 193
Robb, Thomas, 35
Rosenblatt, Louise M., 85

Ross, Steven, 35
Rousseau, Jean-Jacques, 175–77, 182, 183
Ryan, Frank, 39

Sager, Laura, 134n7
Sanders, Walter, 25
Schlöndorff, Volker, 122
Scott, Virginia M., 140, 188n1
Shakespeare, William, 143, 158
Shortreed, Ian, 35
Silva, Lourdes, 134n3
Smagorinsky, Peter, 80
Smith, Michael W., 80
Sollors, Werner, 140
Staiger, Emil, 142
Stauffer, Russell G., 82
Steffensen, Margaret S., 41, 48, 188n1
Stenhouse, Lawrence, 29

Sternfeld, Steven, 39
Streep, Meryl, 108, 122
Swaffar, Janet, 50, 79, 97n2, 134n7, 140

Todorov, Tzvetan, 101, 143, 145
Tucker, Holly, 140

Uspensky, B. A., 163

Valdés, Maria Elena de, 134n3
van Dijk, Teun A., 36, 87

Watt, Ian P., 145
Whittingham, Georgina J., 134n3
Wilde, Oscar, 46
Williams, Jessica, 39
Wimsatt, William K., 134n2, 142
Wright, David A., 188n1

SUBJECT INDEX

abstractness versus concreteness, 58–60,
72, 171, 172, 187
academic discipline, 1–3, 11, 12, 20, 22,
26, 29, 50, 79, 139, 142, 158, 193
acquisition of language, xi, xiii, 15–21,
26, 29, 32, 50, 66, 132, 139, 190
See also learning
activity
in class, 110, 112
outside class, 32
comprehension, 120
decoding, 43, 67
encoding, 20, 62, 109
reading, 71, 74, 82
Act of Reading (Iser), 47, 54, 83
American Associations of Teachers of
French, German, Spanish, and
others, 12
analysis
aesthetic, 169
issues, 185
literary, 156, 192
anthropology, 2, 44, 47, 52–54, 80, 94,
162, 165, 174, 175, 176, 191
art history, 2
articulation, 39, 166
audience
appeal, 126
expectations of, 107, 108, 125, 155,
157

intended, 50, 58, 60
popular, 122
as social factor, 34
specialist, 60
as stereotype, 132
target, 5, 106, 122
See also horizon of expectation
authentic materials, 18, 21, 33, 36, 39,
40, 42, 65, 70, 111, 190
authority, 6, 17, 106, 113, 120, 166,
173

budgetary pressure, 6, 25, 178

canon, 3, 4, 122, 139, 141, 144, 147,
148, 157, 159, 162, 163, 167, 169,
174, 183, 187
Carnegie Foundation, 194n1
Clueless (film), 54–56
cognates, 37, 60, 65, 69
cognition
burden of, 170, 173
complexity of, 37, 93
framework of, 72
overload of, 72, 80, 101
coherency and cohesion, 12, 44, 57, 59,
163, 174, 191
communication
act of, 8, 31, 44, 65, 79, 146, 147, 152,
153, 173

communication (*cont.*)
  community, 9, 149, 163, 165–67,
    171–73
  context of, 41, 110, 121, 143
  convention, 132, 147
  cultural, 111, 132, 144, 159, 171, 191
  element, 152
  as exercise, 69, 100
  formal and informal, 69
  forms of, xii, 139, 145, 147, 148, 150,
    159, 189, 190
  framework for, 3, 16, 29, 72, 143, 150,
    164
  gesture, 5, 24, 147
  global, 193
  goal of, 185
  interactive, 40
  loci of, 177
  materiality of, 147
  natural, 30
  norm, 80, 116, 146, 151, 185
  pattern, 62, 105, 113, 146–50, 157,
    164, 165, 171
  situation, 102, 108, 109, 111, 121,
    132, 143, 147
  spoken, 48
  system of, 48, 162
  visual, 48
communicative act, 155
communicative approach, 31
Como agua para chocolate. See *Like Water
  for Chocolate*
comparison, 52, 55, 66, 120, 125, 156,
  157, 169, 173, 174, 180, 181,
  183–85
complexity, 37, 58, 61, 76, 89, 92, 93,
  125, 164, 168, 177, 186
comprehension, 74, 76, 87, 88
compulsory move. See genre markers,
  obligatory move
concreteness. See abstractness versus
  concreteness
contrast, 88, 91
correctness
  of content, 36, 37, 69
  of form, 17–19, 31, 49, 88, 149,
    152–54
  of grammar, 35, 68–69
  linguistic, 4
  of meaning, 20
  misreading, 42, 89, 115
  reading, 44

  right answer, 80, 95, 97, 115
course material
  art, 161
  diary, 68, 75
  drama, 152
  everyday speech, 68
  extended narrative form, 51
  film, 3, 40, 44, 51, 66, 68, 96, 152,
    161, 177, 183–85
  film review, 75
  high-culture text, 40
  literature, 3, 40, 51, 78, 177
  longer prose, 152
  music, 161
  newspaper, 40
  novel, 44, 66, 184–86
  personal letter, 75
  poetry, 152
  popular culture text, 40
  popular writing, 3
  short book, 75
  short interview, 66
  story, 44, 66, 68
  on World Wide Web, 3
  See also genre
course planning, 177, 191
courses
  advanced, 8, 29, 100
  advanced grammar, 2
  beginning language, xi, 8, 13, 21, 26, 29
  capstone, 153, 155, 158
  college-level, 17, 180
  composition, 14
  content, 12, 150
  conversation, 21
  conversation and composition, 40, 92
  culture, 30, 187
  first-semester, 61
  first-year, 179, 180, 183, 185
  foreign-language, 150, 159
  graduate, 21, 22, 26, 153, 177, 180, 182
  humanities, 55
  interdisciplinary, 179, 186
  intermediate, 8
  introductory, 152, 175
  language, 13, 30, 40, 165
  language and literature, 165
  literature, 80, 165, 187
  lower-division, 29, 150, 152, 159,
    160n2, 175
  major, 153
  performance-based, 21

remedial, 14
rhetoric and composition, 159
second-semester, 61
seminar, 153, 155, 177, 179, 180
sequence of, 22, 177, 185, 186
specialty, 153
stylistics, 40
topic, 100
upper-division, 12, 13, 21, 22, 40, 43,
    44, 100, 150, 153, 176, 179, 180
writing, 150, 186
    See also curriculum
cultural attitude, 96
cultural community, 170, 171
cultural context, 5, 38, 92
cultural literacy
    achievement of, 133–34
    advanced forms of, 139
    advanced learner, 110
    of audience, 108
    defined, 6, 159
    development of, 130
    at elementary level, 61
    elements of, 121, 157, 163, 166
    entry point into, 32
    fostering of, 46, 125
    genre as part of, 156, 159, 167, 168, 172
    and holistic learning, 98, 132
    kinds of, 172, 175, 186
    language teaching, as, 26
    learning of, 26, 76–77, 81, 88, 121,
        154
    one of multiple literacies, 167
    patterns of, 48, 88, 132, 152, 172
    reading as key to, 78, 81
    relation to cultural studies, 162
    stage of, 171
    in upper division, 50, 52, 154
cultural politics, 11, 184
cultural stereotype, 42, 43, 93
culture
    assumptions about, 81
    dominant, 2, 5, 9, 26, 118, 147,
        162, 166, 172, 180, 182, 185,
        187–88
    elite, 40, 47, 146, 157, 162, 163, 168,
        170, 172, 173
    familiar, 9, 26
    formal, 37, 153
    hegemonic, 5, 166
    high, 2, 3, 8, 26, 60, 78, 122, 143–46,
        148–50, 153, 154, 160n3, 162–64,

166, 167, 170, 173, 174, 176, 177,
    180, 187. *See also* culture, elite
    marginalized, 9
    mass-market, 122, 148
    nonelite, 162
    official, 7, 166, 173, 177, 180
    political, 2, 95, 155, 184
    popular, 7, 46, 60, 144, 149, 153, 162,
        166, 168, 173, 174, 176, 182, 187
    public versus private, 20, 75, 99, 182,
        187
    resistant, 187–88
    social, 95, 155
    theories of, 118
    unfamiliar, 9
    white-collar, 43
    women's, 157
    working-class, 43
curriculum
    accountability of, 9, 152, 166, 186, 187
    building, 28, 80, 159, 189
    change, 79, 191
    culture of, 158, 162, 173, 177, 187
    design, 26, 29, 82, 130, 141, 186, 188
    development, 7, 28, 76, 167
    FL, 8, 97, 143, 162
    goals, 16, 17, 26, 44, 65, 70, 76, 100,
        131, 139, 149, 154, 162, 163, 165,
        168
    graduate, 158, 159, 194
    holistic, 8, 29–32, 40, 48, 56, 57–77,
        78, 97, 140, 178
    humanities, 1, 2, 4, 5, 12, 25, 26, 56,
        143, 156, 162, 165, 177–80, 186
    interdisciplinary, 7, 9, 25, 177–80,
        186, 187
    L1, 140, 142
    language, 157, 161
    language and literature, 161
    language-driven, 74
    and language learning, 148
    levels, 9, 66, 166, 173, 174, 176, 177
    literacy-oriented, 26, 156
    literature, 142, 149, 158, 161, 166,
        176
    literature and culture, 158
    literature in translation, 4
    lower-division, 19
    performance-based, 6, 23, 39
    postsecondary, 12, 13, 139, 140
    practices, 26, 40
    problems, 192

curriculum (*cont.*)
  remedial, 19
  secondary, 140, 156, 166
  social sciences, 180
  track, 21
  traditional, 161, 178
  undergraduate, xi, 6, 21, 56, 141, 142,
    150, 158, 166, 167, 178, 179, 187,
    189, 192, 194
  upper-division, 100, 157
  user-centered, 19, 26, 29
  See also courses

Dangerous Liaisons (film), 175, 177
dehydrated sentence, 15
dictionary use, 86, 88
discourse analysis, 15, 22, 146, 154
discourse and content, 50
discourse genre, 99, 102, 143, 145, 147,
  153, 155, 156
Don Quixote (Cervantes), 153, 157, 169

Emma (Austen), 52–56
episteme, 117
error correction, 31
evaluation forms, 190

film adaptations, 52, 54, 108, 110, 112,
  121–25
FL department, xi, xii, 3–7, 11–14, 17,
  21–26, 28, 29, 33, 38, 61, 64, 78,
  100, 141, 151–52, 160n2, 162, 165,
  167, 190–94
fluency, 15
form and content, 12, 16, 18, 19, 21, 22,
  34, 37, 55, 100, 143, 152, 159, 167
form and context, 12, 14, 16, 19, 21, 22,
  28, 32
form and meaning, 7, 12, 13, 16, 19, 35

genre, 8, 72, 99, 139, 147, 150
  academic handbook, 106
  actor interview, 126
  advertisement, 38, 101, 126, 150, 151,
    168, 169
  animé, 144
  author interview, 110, 126–30
  autobiography, 125, 184
  bibliography, 153, 174
  biography, 101, 125
  blog, 104, 166

book report, 75
book review, 99, 160n4
business letter, 102, 153
comedy, 144
conversation, 49, 100, 150, 153–55
dance, 170
debate, 75, 153
detective novel, 107, 172
dialogue, 30, 86
diary, 67, 74–75, 101, 121
diary written for publication, 101, 104
documentary film, 55
drama, 150, 151, 156, 160n4, 167–70
dramatic mode, 143–46
encyclopedia, 67, 105, 121
epic mode, 143–46, 151
epic poetry, 143, 148, 150
essay, 50, 125, 174, 181, 184
fairy tale, 94, 101
fantastic story, 81, 82, 95
farce, 146
feminist novel, 153
filibuster, 157
film, 51, 55, 99, 110, 121–30, 147,
  148, 150, 151, 154–58, 168–70, 174,
  175, 183, 184
film review, 67, 100, 110, 125
film synopsis, 99
folk music, 144, 147, 148
folk tale, 94
government document, 174, 186, 187
graphic novel, 148
Harlequin romance, 107
horror film, 157
horror story, 107
instructional material, 168
interview, 50, 99, 125, 130, 132–33,
  171, 173
job application letter, 154
Latin romance, 123
letter, 38, 74–75, 100, 101, 155
letter written for publication, 2, 3, 101
literature, 106, 155, 174
lyric mode, 49, 143–46, 151
lyric poetry, 49, 144, 150, 157, 168, 170
magazine article, 101
mail-order catalog, 67
manga, 144
monologue, 49, 86
musical, 170
mystery, 73, 107, 171

narrative, 150
newspaper article, 96, 100, 101
nonfiction, 107, 168, 169
note, 153
novel, 51, 54, 99, 110–14, 117, 118,
    121–30, 133, 144, 148, 149, 155,
    157, 158, 160n4, 166, 167, 175–77,
    182–84
nursery rhyme, 101
ode, 144
open letter, 175
opera, 170, 174
oration, 157
personal letter, 75, 102
petition, 38
picaresque novel, 153, 157
play, 73, 74, 146, 150, 153
poetry, 150, 151, 156–58, 160n4, 166,
    168–70
political text, 184
popular fiction, 107, 174
popular song, 174, 176
postcard, 38, 42, 74
primary literature, 153
prose fiction, 107, 150, 151, 156, 169,
    170, 184
protest music, 148
rap, 147, 148, 157
reference material, 153, 158, 169
review, 75, 125, 126, 132, 169
roast, 153
romance, 47, 73, 107, 111, 118, 143
scholarly review, 154
screenplay, 110, 169
secondary literature, 153, 154, 158,
    174
sermon, 49
short literature, 100
short story, 68, 86, 97, 122
soap opera, 101, 149, 154
song, 49, 101, 150, 157, 160
sonnet, 143, 153, 158
speech, 49, 75, 154, 155, 157
sports report, 149
spy novel, 107
story cycle, 144
tragedy, 143, 144, 146
travel writing, 121, 175
TV variety show, 148
    See also course material

genre markers
    aesthetic, 153
    per audience, 20, 50, 52, 101, 105,
        132–33, 149, 169–72, 184
    behavioral, 169
    cultural, 152, 153, 166, 176
    discourse, 38, 44
    and identity, 165
    and in-groups, 176
    and language, 150, 151, 153
    for a limited audience, 106
    linguistic, 149, 165
    and literariness, 145
    obligatory moves as, 98, 100, 104–07,
        109–10, 112–14, 121, 125–27, 130,
        133, 147, 153–54, 157, 189
    optional moves as, 100, 121, 154,
        189
    philosophical, 157
    register as, 50, 105, 125
    rhetorical, 73
    semantic, 151–52
    semiotic, 149
    sociological, 165
    stylistic, 157
    syntactic, 113, 151–53, 157, 169
    time as, 151, 156, 170, 172
    transition as, 104, 151
    verbal, 152, 168, 169
    visual, 152, 168, 169
Genres in Discourse (Todorov), 143, 145
gloss, 63
grading, normative, 19, 26, 39
grammar, 15, 19, 21, 28–31, 35–37, 44,
    49, 64, 68–70, 82, 85, 86, 90–92,
    95, 111, 113, 151–52, 155, 193

holistic learning, 1, 8, 29, 32, 35, 40, 51,
    76, 89, 91, 95, 97, 98, 109, 115,
    131, 132, 168, 192
horizon of expectation, 72, 106–08, 110,
    120, 122, 132, 145–47, 150, 156,
    157, 159, 184–85
House of the Spirits, The (film), 108, 122,
    124

identity politics, 2, 4, 11, 159
ideology, 118, 127, 149, 157, 164, 168
Iliad, The (Homer), 144, 146
Implied Reader, The (Iser), 18, 133

informational pattern, 131, 151, 170
information matrix, 109
intellectual history, 191
intent, 30, 31, 35, 49, 55, 60, 90, 92,
    104, 115, 126
    See also point of view
interdisciplinarity. *See* courses,
    interdisciplinary; curriculum,
    interdisciplinary; learning,
    interdisciplinary; studies,
    interdisciplinary
interpretation, 5, 12, 21, 22, 44, 79–81,
    84, 86, 89, 91–97, 100, 116, 117,
    120, 121, 129, 131, 158, 181, 182
intertextuality, 96, 108, 187

Jefferson in Paris (film), 183, 185

knowledge
    adult, 35
    aesthetic, 177
    anthropological, 165, 175, 176
    background, 26, 68, 79, 80, 106, 177
    content, 34, 95, 177, 187
    cultural, 25, 37, 43, 46–48, 53, 55, 66,
        68, 85, 99, 112, 132, 140, 150, 172,
        183
    expert, 142, 153, 159, 169
    of genre, 156, 169
    of language, 8, 35, 62–63, 84, 86
    linguistic, 150, 165, 167
    literary, 167
    pattern of, 175
    of period, 169
    political, 177
    prior, 33, 57, 72, 73, 80, 99
    professional, 106
    schematic, 55
    shared, xiii
    social, 40, 46, 53
    sociological, 165, 175
    See also literacy

L1 department, 141
language
    acquisition of. *See* acquisition of
        language
    center, 23, 24, 151–52
    competency, 60
    and language meaning, 21
    practice, 89, 91, 92

production, 83
    register, 34, 50, 51, 53, 67–69, 101,
        104, 107, 152, 171
    visual, 62
language across the curriculum (LAC),
    25
Language and Symbolic Power (Bourdieu),
    49, 50, 134n4
language for special purposes (LSP), 55,
    193
language instruction
    early, 71
    intermediate, 71
    lower-division, 23, 28
Law of Love, The (Esquivel), 127, 136
learner
    adult, xi, 16, 17, 19, 21, 26, 31, 32, 34,
        56, 70, 97, 156
    advanced, 14, 40, 49, 51, 98, 100, 101,
        104, 108, 110, 133, 158, 180
    beginner, 14, 19, 36, 49, 61, 79, 83,
        94, 159
    child, 16
    demographics, 60, 61
    graduate, 172, 177
    intermediate, 49, 79, 91, 98, 180,
        183
    lower-division, 52, 184
    novice, 105, 108, 159
    older versus younger, 60
    upper-division, 52, 172
    See also native speaker; reader;
        student
learning
    experience of, 18, 35, 39, 49, 63, 73,
        80, 94
    feedback role of, 30, 35, 86, 88
    goals of, 96, 133, 153, 155, 166, 174,
        175
    holistic. *See* holistic learning
    individuated, 17–19
    integrative, 15, 24, 31, 46
    interdisciplinary, 154
    level, 167, 175
    pattern, 152
    recursive, 33, 34
    redundancy in, 19, 34, 91, 92
    by role-playing, 75
    simulation in, 31
    stage of, 8, 57, 89, 92, 93, 95, 111,
        115, 130–32, 152–55, 158, 170–73,

176, 184–88
strategy of, 55
support environment for, 12, 18, 51, 63, 79, 88
task of, 8, 18, 30, 33, 34, 36, 42, 50, 51, 53, 61, 68, 73, 78, 89, 91, 129, 132, 168, 171–73
learning to learn, 72, 90, 166, 170, 174, 180
level
advanced, 76, 154
advanced undergraduate, 159
graduate, 154
intermediate, 76
lower-division, 92
undergraduate, 154
upper-division, 82, 92, 99
ley del amor, La. See *Law of Love, The*
Like Water for Chocolate (Esquivel), 98, 111–16, 118–21, 123–30, 135, 136
linguistic framework, 5, 189
linguistic innovation, 49, 92, 110
listener, 5, 33, 142, 145, 146, 190
literacy
artificial, 173
critical, xii, 191
cross-cultural, 5, 123
cultural. See cultural literacy
defined, 2
discourse, 173
FL, 74, 99, 171
genre, 9, 110, 130, 149, 158, 167, 171, 176
historical, 5, 167
language, 78, 82
linguistic, 139, 167
literary, 167
multicultural, xii, 140
social, 31, 48, 162, 172
textual, 155
See also multiple literacies
literature. *See* analysis, literary; course material, literature; genre markers, and literariness; knowledge, literary; literacy, literary; meaning, literary; "Reading the Patterns of Literary Works"; studies, colonial literary; studies, literary; studies, postcolonial literary; theory, literary
lower division. *See* courses, lower-

division; curriculum, lower-division; language instruction, lower-division; learner, lower-division; level, lower-division; matrix, in lower division; pedagogy, lower-division; studies, lower-division; teaching, lower-division

magic realism, 89, 93–95, 108, 116, 121, 124, 131
markers. *See* genre markers
mass media, 7, 187
film, 148, 166
infotainment, 174
magazine, 59
music, 148, 174
newspaper, 59, 93, 176
radio, 166
TV, 93, 106, 122, 148, 162, 166, 174
World Wide Web, 17, 35, 101, 126, 166
materiality, 157, 159, 163–67
matrix
for beginners, 90, 92
categories, 90
format of, 89
information, 8, 90
in intermediate learning phases, 92
in lower division, 92
partial, 87
student interpretation, basis for, 95
task of, 46, 86, 88, 89, 97
meaning
anthropological, 176
cultural, 24, 47, 94, 108, 143, 163, 170, 171, 176
and genre structure, 101
indices of, 65, 66
literary, 94
multiple layers of, 120
negotiation, 193
pattern, 53, 54, 97, 155
production, 48, 51
reception of, 48, 51
reconstruction of, 81
recovery of, 51, 52
representation of, 48, 51
social, 42, 54, 176
system, 18, 51, 62, 80, 86, 163, 164, 171, 175
systems of, 52, 122, 156

meaning (*cont.*)
  typology, 91
meaning and language, 13, 28, 90
media. *See* mass media
memory
  form of, 20
  long-term, 34–36
  macro versus micro, 33
  passive, 89
  short-term, 34, 35
  working, 62
"Metamorphosis" (Kafka), 52, 54, 108
minimal pair, 71
mission
  departmental, 7, 23
  intellectual, 13
  refocused, 7, 11, 78
  teaching, 1, 7, 11, 12, 151
  traditional, 78
Modern Language Association, 11, 12,
  160n3
morphosyntax, 15, 17, 92
"muerte, La," 81, 83, 85, 89, 93, 96
multicultural framework, 5, 55, 96, 142,
  190
multiple literacies
  acquisition of, 36, 191
  in course design, 50, 82, 85, 110
  in cultures, 47
  in curriculum design, 76, 130, 139,
    163, 167, 189–91
  defined, 40
  encode, help students to, 20
  in FL, 143
  genre literacy leads to, 110
  as goals, 36
  in graduate programs, 192
  language teaching as, 26
  multiple communities, due to, 114
  multiple cultures, due to, 148
  reading as key to, 97
  stages leading to, 8
  teaching of, xii, 18
  teaching tasks, built into, 16
  theory as path to, 79
  as tools for readers, 77
  in undergraduate programs, 31
  in upper division, 40, 43

narrative
  act, 148
  aesthetic, 96–97

continuity of, 59
development of, 111
focus, 113
frame, 183
master, 5
point of view, 44, 142, 150, 151, 155,
  158, 168–70
strategy, 89, 113, 114, 146, 157
voice, 122, 123
native speaker, 1, 16, 18, 21, 33, 34, 55,
  66, 108, 123, 140, 154, 159
nouvelle Héloïse, La (Rousseau), 175, 182,
  183, 185

obligatory move. *See* genre markers,
  obligatory moves in

parallel text, 63
pattern
  textual, 80
  typological, 91
pedagogy
  coherent, 191
  learner-centered, 191
  lower-division, 14
  model, 21, 191
  strategy, 18, 79, 191
perception
  of audience, 122
  cultural, 2, 25, 42, 81, 108, 149
  everyday, 81
  human, 2
  organized, 80
  student, 44, 47, 113, 125
performer, 145
periodization, 169
philology, 3
philosophy, 2, 23, 50, 176, 179, 184,
  186, 191, 192
phonology, xii, 28
point of view, 30, 35, 62, 63, 67, 69,
  90–92, 110, 121–23, 157, 170, 174,
  177, 193
  See also intent; narrative, point of
  view
précis
  at advanced level, 113
  in course design, 99, 110–11, 139
  defined, 109, 130, 137, 138, 191
  example of, 114, 116, 181, 182
  format of, 137, 138
  formatted to reflect genre features,

121–30
in four parts, 110, 138
guided, 8, 114, 115, 185. *See also*
    précis, prompted
as in-class activity, 112
as interpretation, 131
learner-created, 110, 120, 185
and matrix, 113–21
multiple uses of, 120
the novel, applied to, 111–13
pedagogy of, 111–13, 116, 117, 121, 125
poststructuralist approach to, 119, 133
prompted, 132. *See also* précis, guided
task, 98, 124, 172
as template, 98, 99, 111, 131, 132
type and token of, 45
précis sections
    focus, 111, 138, 181, 182
    implication, 110, 117, 119, 129–30,
        133, 138, 181, 182
    logic, 110, 138, 181, 182
    matrix, 110, 111, 115, 117, 119, 130,
        133, 138, 181, 182
Pride and Prejudice (Austen), 44–46
processing
    bottom-up, 33, 79, 81
    top-down, 79–81, 111
production
    framework, 92
    practice, 70, 91–92
pronunciation, 15, 65, 71
proposition
    macro, 87–89, 93, 112, 114–15, 131
    micro, 87, 89, 93
psychology, 2, 80, 124, 149, 150, 191

readability, 8, 57–64, 76, 104, 106
reader
    adult, 149
    competent, 149
    demographics of, 58
    first-language, 79, 171
    independent, 82
    literate, 3, 154
    novice, 50, 83, 170
    upper-division, 55
    See also learner
reading
    model, 79
    process, 80
reading strategy

close reading, 46, 116, 140, 142, 143
directed, 82, 83, 95
initial reading, 71–73, 80, 82, 84–86
prereading, 39, 71–72, 80, 82
reading aloud, 82
reading word for word, 87
rereading, 61, 71, 74–75
sequence, 94
skimming and scanning, 72
"Reading the Patterns of Literary Works"
    (Swaffar), 97, 140
recall, 100, 113
recognition, 74, 82
research
    linguistic, 41
    on reading, 15
    on retention, 83
rhetoric, xii, 14, 22, 50, 55, 59, 73, 76,
    94, 99, 106, 110, 111, 163

self-correction, 19, 33
sémanalyse, 159–60
semantics, 22, 28, 90, 108, 109, 151, 169
semiotics, 121, 133, 159, 163, 164, 173,
    174, 177, 187, 192
sign, 163, 166, 177
sign system, 5, 48, 163
skills, 15, 16
    analytic, 165, 187
    cognitive, 70
    critical reading, 187
    four, 32
    isolated, 14
    language, 19, 70, 91
    literacy, 33
    negotiation, 39
    oral, 15
    productive, 33
    receptive, 33
    separate, 15, 32
    social, 70
    speaking, 33
skills, four
    listening, 15, 19, 31, 33, 34, 39, 40,
        53, 70, 189. *See also* listener
    reading. *See* reader; reading; reading
        strategy
    speaking, 14, 15, 19, 22, 31, 33, 34,
        39, 49, 53, 66, 68, 92, 93, 100, 113,
        151, 166, 168, 172. *See also* speaker
    writing, xii, 2, 3, 13, 15, 17, 19, 22,

writing (*cont.*)
  31, 33–35, 39, 54, 68, 69, 74–76,
  85, 90, 92, 100, 101, 105, 115, 128,
  131, 139, 140, 150, 155, 171, 172,
  175, 176, 185, 189. *See also* writer
social anthropology, 47, 53, 65
social psychology, 2, 149
social science, 7
sociolect, 69
sociolinguistics, 2
sociology, 2, 44, 50, 80, 96, 143, 149, 159,
  162, 169, 174, 175, 177, 180, 191
Sorrows of Young Werther (Goethe), 182,
  183
speaker, 20, 33, 35, 49, 53, 67, 73, 92,
  146, 168, 173, 175
Standards for Foreign Language Learning,
  165
stereotype. *See* audience, as stereotype;
  cultural stereotype
"Structure, Sign and Play in the
  Discourse of the Human Sciences"
  (Derrida), 49, 50
student
  advanced, 159, 182–86, 189
  beginner, 14, 24, 39, 90, 170, 185, 189
  first-year, 28, 151, 173, 179, 183
  graduate, xi, 28, 155, 159, 160n6, 167,
    173, 178, 179, 183, 184, 186, 192
  honors major, 184, 186
  intermediate, 14, 183, 186
  junior, 183
  major, 167
  senior, 28, 155, 183
  undergraduate, 159
  upper-division, 173
  See also learner
studies
  American, 179
  area, 179
  colonial literary, 192
  cultural, xiii, 3, 22, 50, 51, 79, 80, 96,
    140, 142, 143, 153, 155, 161, 162,
    165, 167–70, 175, 178, 180, 187–88,
    191, 192
  dialect, 192
  early modern, 178
  eighteenth-century, 178–80, 187
  ethnic, 142
  film, 4, 149
  foreign-language, 11, 142, 187, 192,

  193
  French, 4
  genre, 140, 144, 147, 149, 153, 156,
    159, 167
  global, 178
  humanist, 26
  interdisciplinary, 178
  Italian, 4
  language, 13, 51
  linguistic, 22, 149
  literary, 22, 51, 139–42, 144, 147,
    153, 159, 161, 162, 173, 178, 188,
    191
  lower-division, 100
  mass communication, 142, 149
  minority, 192
  poetics, 149
  postcolonial literary, 192
  premodern, 178
  rhetoric and composition, 2
  semiotics, 149
  textual, 143, 159
  theory, 51
  urban, 51
  women's, 133, 192
syllabus, 30, 31, 131
syntax, 28, 59, 69, 87, 88, 93, 108, 141,
  151–52, 169, 171, 172

teaching
  culture, 147, 149, 160n6, 164, 174
  genre, 147–49
  language, 147, 151
  language learning, 147
  literacy, 149
  literature, 148, 149, 152, 160n6
  lower-division, 23
  method of, 14, 18
  pattern of communication, 147
  stage, 152, 153
  tasks in, 8, 16, 61, 64, 89, 159
template, 42, 43, 98, 99, 110, 111,
  131–33, 173
text
  choice, 39, 47, 61, 64, 176, 190
  extrinsic, 3, 95
  status of, 40, 108, 116, 157, 172
  suitability of, 111
  type of, 59, 64, 108, 155, 156, 173,
    175–77
textuality, 101, 143, 159, 171

theater, 174, 176
theory
 aesthetic, 96
 anti-Enlightenment, 185
 art, 163
 Birmingham school, 167
 cultural, 50, 51, 162
 deconstructionist, 192
 Enlightenment, 175, 176, 179–86
 feminist, 53, 153, 192
 formalist, 192
 genre, 167
 humanist, 7, 9, 26, 51, 178, 187
 literary, 2, 8, 47, 48, 79, 81
 Marxist, 53, 162
 New Critical, 116, 117, 140
 new-historicist, 50
 phenomenological, 192
 positivist, 7, 191
 postcolonial, 145
 post-Enlightenment, 185
 postmodernist, 3
 poststructuralist, 11, 118, 119, 158,
  162, 163, 177, 192
 Prague school, 145
 reader-response, 3, 50, 54, 85, 192
 realist, 19, 21, 153, 157
 reception, 3, 50, 158, 160n4, 169
 Russian formalist, 145
 sender-receiver, 102, 104, 109

sociological. *See* sociology
structuralist, 192
text-immanent criticism, 191
translation as reception, 192
topic and comment, 34, 88
translation, 32, 88, 92, 109, 112, 181,
  182, 192
typology, 88, 92, 93, 164, 176

upper division. *See* courses, upper-
 division; cultural literacy, in upper
 division; curriculum, upper-
 division; learner, upper-division;
 level, upper-division; multiple
 literacies, in upper division; reader,
 upper-division; student, upper-
 division

vocabulary, 14–16, 19, 21, 32, 34,
  37–39, 42, 44, 54, 65, 68, 69, 71,
  72, 91–93, 96, 100, 105, 107, 110,
  111, 117, 125, 153, 158, 171, 180

"What is Enlightenment?" (Kant), 181,
  184
words, 71, 88
 See also vocabulary
worksheet, 87
writer, 20, 33, 35, 92, 102, 105, 146,
  154, 168, 173